D1536997

FINANCIAL MARKET HISTORY

REFLECTIONS ON THE PAST FOR INVESTORS TODAY

Edited by David Chambers and Elroy Dimson

CFA Institute
Research
Foundation

UNIVERSITY OF
CAMBRIDGE
Judge Business School

Statement of Purpose

The CFA Institute Research Foundation is a not-for-profit organization established to promote the development and dissemination of relevant research for investment practitioners worldwide.

Cover Image Photo Credit: bunhill/Getty Images

ISBN 978-1-944960-13-1

June 2017

Editorial Staff

Abby Farson Pratt
Assistant Editor

Julia Mackesson, PMP
Manager, Publishing,
Standards and Advocacy

Anh Pham
Publishing Technology Specialist

Biographies

Olivier Accominotti is associate professor of economic history at the London School of Economics and Political Science and an affiliate at the Centre for Economic Policy Research. He is a specialist in international financial history and has published extensively in this area. Professor Accominotti is also a member of the editorial board of *Financial History Review*, and his current projects focus on currency markets and the international propagation of financial crises. He holds a PhD in economics from Sciences Po Paris and has held postdoctoral or visiting positions at Princeton University; the University of California, Berkeley; the European University Institute; and the Bank of France.

Jan Annaert is professor of finance at the University of Antwerp and at the Antwerp Management School. He is chairman of the Study Centre on Stock Exchanges and Enterprises (SCOB), the university's research center for financial history. Professor Annaert also serves as independent director on the board of mutual funds and is an external member of the Pricing and Valuation Committee of KBC Asset Management. His teaching and research interests include portfolio theory, asset pricing, financial risk management, and financial history. Professor Annaert has published his research in a variety of publications, including *Cliometrica, Explorations in Economic History, Financial History Review*, the *Journal of Banking and Finance*, and the *Journal of International Money and Finance*.

Stephen J. Brown joined Monash Business School as professor of finance in January 2016, transitioning to emeritus status at New York University (NYU) Stern School of Business. Before joining NYU in 1986, Professor Brown worked at Bell Telephone Laboratories, where he spent time as district manager at AT&T Pension Fund, as well as at Yale University. He has published widely in a range of high-quality journals and is the author of five books. Professor Brown has recently been appointed executive editor of the *Financial Analysts Journal®*. He graduated from Monash University in 1971 and earned an MBA and a PhD from the University of Chicago in 1976.

Frans Buelens is senior researcher at the Study Centre on Stock Exchanges and Enterprises (SCOB) at the University of Antwerp. He is responsible for supervising the work on the digitization of the Brussels and Antwerp Stock Exchanges. Dr. Buelens is the author (and coauthor) of several books, including *Congo 1885–1960* and *Beurzen van België: een geschiedenis van het beurswezen, 1801–1867* (*Stock Exchanges of Belgium: A History of Stock Exchange Life*). He has published in *Economic History Review, Explorations in*

Economic History, the *Journal of European Economic History*, *Financial History Review*, *Cliometrics*, and other journals.

Carsten Burhop is professor of economic and social history at the University of Vienna and a research affiliate at the Max Planck Institute for Research on Collective Goods in Bonn, Germany. His research focuses on many aspects of economic and business history, including the history of stock markets, financial institutions, corporate governance, and the management of innovation. Professor Burhop has published in the *Journal of Economic History*, *Business History Review*, *European Review of Economic History*, *German Economic Review*, and *Schmalenbach Business Review*.

David Chambers is a reader in finance, a Keynes Fellow, and academic director of the Centre for Endowment Asset Management at Cambridge Judge Business School. His research interests span asset management and financial history, and he has published in the *Journal of Finance*, the *Journal of Financial and Quantitative Analysis*, the *Journal of Economic Perspectives*, the *Journal of Economic History*, *Economic History Review*, *Explorations in Economic History*, the *Financial Analysts Journal*, and the *Journal of Portfolio Management*. Prior to returning to full-time education in 2001, Dr. Chambers worked for 20 years in investment banking and asset management at Barings, Hotchkis & Wiley, and Merrill Lynch. He sits on the editorial board of the *Financial Analysts Journal*.

Elroy Dimson is chairman of the Centre for Endowment Asset Management at Cambridge Judge Business School, emeritus professor of finance at London Business School, and adviser to the board of FTSE International. He previously served London Business School in a variety of senior positions and the Norwegian Government Pension Fund Global as chairman of the Strategy Council. Dr. Dimson is coauthor of *Triumph of the Optimists* and has published in a number of journals, including the *Journal of Finance*, the *Journal of Financial Economics*, the *Review of Financial Studies*, the *Journal of Business*, the *Journal of Portfolio Management*, and the *Financial Analysts Journal*, where he serves as a member of the Advisory Council.

Barry Eichengreen is George C. Pardee and Helen N. Pardee Professor of Economics at the University of California, Berkeley, a research associate of the National Bureau of Economic Research, and a research fellow of the Centre for Economic Policy Research. He is a fellow of the American Academy of Arts and Sciences and a member of the Council on Foreign Relations.

Caroline Fohlin is a professor of economics at Emory University. She has published extensively on the history of financial markets, institutions, and systems, including two monographs: *Finance Capitalism and Germany's Rise* *to Industrial Power* and *Mobilizing Money: How the World's Richest Nations Financed Industrial Growth*. Professor Fohlin has recently completed the first comprehensive high-frequency transaction and quote database for the NYSE for the period 1900–1925. She holds the position of Distinguished Visiting Professor, Economics, at Emory University. Professor Fohlin holds a BS in mathematics and quantitative economics from Tufts University and a PhD in economics from the University of California, Berkeley.

William N. Goetzmann is the Edwin J. Beinecke Professor of Finance and Management Studies at Yale School of Management. His research topics include asset pricing, the equity risk premium, arbitrage strategies, selecting investment managers, global investing, and financial history. Professor Goetzmann's work has been featured in most of the major financial news publications and his academic research has been published in all of the major academic finance journals. His current work focuses on endowments, financial history, operational risk, securitization, credit risk, and behavioral finance. Professor Goetzmann is the director of the International Center for Finance at the Yale School of Management, where he has been since 1994. Previously, he taught investments and real estate at Columbia Business School.

Charles Goodhart, CBE, FBA, is emeritus professor of banking and finance with the Financial Markets Group at the London School of Economics (LSE), having previously been its deputy director. Until his retirement in 2002, he had served as the Norman Sosnow Professor of Banking and Finance at LSE since 1985. Dr. Goodhart also worked at the Bank of England for 17 years as a monetary adviser, becoming a chief adviser in 1980. In 1997, he was appointed one of the outside independent members of the Bank of England's new Monetary Policy Committee. Dr. Goodhart also taught at Cambridge University.

Leslie Hannah is visiting professor of economic history at the London School of Economics. He lives in Tokyo and specializes in global corporate and financial history of the 20th century. Professor Hannah also is a visiting professor at Cardiff Business School and formerly served as pro-director of the London School of Economics.

Antti Ilmanen is a principal at AQR Capital Management, where he heads the Portfolio Solutions Group. Before AQR, he spent seven years at Brevan Howard, a macro hedge fund, and a decade at Salomon Brothers/Citigroup. Dr. Ilmanen has advised many institutional investors, including Norway's Government Pension Fund Global. He has published a book, *Expected Returns*, as well as numerous articles in finance/investment journals and has received the Graham and Dodd Award from the *Financial*

Analysts Journal and the Bernstein Fabozzi/Jacobs Levy awards. Dr. Ilmanen holds two MSc degrees from the University of Helsinki and a PhD in finance from the University of Chicago.

Paul Marsh is emeritus professor of finance at London Business School, where he previously served as chair of the finance department, deputy principal, faculty dean, and elected governor and dean of the finance programs. He has advised on several public enquiries, was chairman of Aberforth Smaller Companies Trust and a nonexecutive director of M&G Group and Majedie Investments, and has acted as a consultant to a wide range of financial institutions and companies. Dr. Marsh is coauthor of *Triumph of the Optimists* and has published articles in the *Journal of Business*, the *Journal of Finance*, the *Journal of Financial Economics*, the *Journal of Portfolio Management, Harvard Business Review*, and other journals. With Elroy Dimson, he co-designed the FTSE 100-Share Index and the Numis Smaller Companies Index, produced since 1987 at London Business School.

Larry Neal is emeritus professor of economics at the University of Illinois at Urbana–Champaign, a research associate at the National Bureau of Economic Research, and a fellow of the Cliometric Society. He is co-editor of the two-volume *Cambridge History of Capitalism* and *The History of Financial Crises*. Professor Neal's books include *The Rise of Financial Capitalism: International Capital Markets in the Age of Reason*, *"I Am Not Master of Events": The Speculations of John Law and Lord Londonderry in the Mississippi and South Sea Bubbles*, and *A Concise History of International Finance: From Babylon to Bernanke*.

Tom Nicholas is the William J. Abernathy Professor of Business Administration in the Entrepreneurial Management Group at Harvard Business School. His research focuses on the history of the venture capital industry, entrepreneurship and wealth accumulation, intellectual property rights, and the foundations of new technology formation, especially in relation to the financing of innovation. Professor Nicholas holds a doctorate in economic history from Oxford University.

Angelo Riva teaches finance at the European Business School, where he is dean of research and director of the finance research department. He is also an affiliate researcher at the Paris School of Economics. Dr. Riva is the scientific manager of the "Data for Financial History" project and the principal investigator of the projects "Systemic Risk in the 1930s" and "Parisian Financiers' Belle Epoque (1871–1913): Space, Organizations and Social Structure." His research focuses on European monetary and financial history. Dr. Riva has published in the *Journal of Monetary Economics*, the *Economic History Review*, and *Explorations in Economic History*, among others.

K. Geert Rouwenhorst is the Robert B. and Candice J. Haas Professor of Corporate Finance at the Yale School of Management. He has held visiting positions at MIT and the International Monetary Fund. Professor Rouwenhorst's research interests include the empirical trade-off between risk and return in financial markets, hedge fund strategies, commodity markets, and the history of finance. His articles have been published in academic as well as in applied journals. His book *The Origins of Value: The Financial Innovations That Created Modern Capital Markets* surveys key historical innovations in the field of finance. Professor Rouwenhorst holds a PhD from the University of Rochester.

Janette Rutterford is a professor of financial management and research professor of the True Potential Centre for the Public Understanding of Finance at the Open University Business School. Professor Rutterford also worked at Credit Lyonnais as a gilts analyst, taught finance at the London School of Economics, and worked in corporate finance at N.M. Rothschild & Sons Limited.

Christophe Spaenjers is an associate professor at HEC Paris. His research interests include alternative investments, investor behavior, household finance, and financial history. Professor Spaenjers has published in a number of journals, including the *Journal of Financial Economics*, *American Economic Review* (*Papers and Proceedings*), *Management Science*, and the *Financial Analysts Journal*. He teaches in the MBA program at HEC Paris. Professor Spaenjers holds a PhD from Tilburg University.

Mike Staunton is director of the London Share Price Database, a research resource of London Business School, where he produces the London Business School Risk Measurement Service. He has taught at universities in the United Kingdom, Hong Kong, and Switzerland. Dr. Staunton is coauthor of *Advanced Modelling in Finance Using Excel and VBA* and writes a regular column for *Wilmott* magazine. He is coauthor of *Triumph of the Optimists* and has published in the *Journal of Banking & Finance*, the *Financial Analysts Journal*, the *Journal of the Operations Research Society*, and *Quantitative Finance*.

Eugene N. White is distinguished professor of economics at Rutgers University and a research associate at the National Bureau of Economic Research. His current research focuses on bank supervision, the 1920s housing market boom, stock market booms and crashes, and the management of financial crises in Great Britain, France, and the United States. Professor White has written more than 50 scholarly articles. He was recently a member of the advisory council for the Federal Reserve Centennial, the Houblon-Norman fellow at the Bank of England, and a visiting professor at the École des hautes études en sciences sociales.

Contents

CE Qualified Activity ⚜ **CFA Institute** This publication qualifies for 6 CE credits under the guidelines of the CFA Institute Continuing Education Program.

Preface

Since the 2008 financial crisis, there has been a resurgence of interest in economic and financial history among investment professionals. Some practitioners have long understood the benefit of learning from our financial past. For example, Russell Napier in his book *The Anatomy of the Bear* and Andrew Smithers and Stephen Wright in their book *Valuing Wall Street* use financial history to inform and guide their investment strategy. Many other excellent publications would repay any practitioner who wishes to gain a deeper understanding of why financial markets have developed in the way they have over the last several hundred years. Examples include Niall Ferguson's *The Ascent of Money*, William Goetzmann and Geert Rouwenhorst's *The Origins of Value*, Raghuran Rajan and Luigi Zingales's *Saving Capitalism from the Capitalists*, and William Goetzmann's recently published *Money Changes Everything*.

In July 2015, we hosted a workshop at University of Cambridge Judge Business School to bring together many of the world's leading academics in the area of financial market history, as well as some 30 senior investment professionals, to discuss what practitioners need to know about financial history. This monograph, edited by us with support from the Newton Centre for Endowment Asset Management at Cambridge Judge Business School, consists of a series of chapters first presented at this workshop, together with several other important contributions.

Comprising contributions by 22 leading financial historians, the monograph is organized into four main sections. The first section discusses the current state of academic research on the risk and return of such traditional assets as stocks, bonds, bills, and currencies, as well as such alternative assets as real estate, collectibles, precious metals, and diamonds. Practitioners can benefit from the great care that financial historians bring to the collection and construction of historical datasets such as these. The more reliable the quantitative information about long-term returns that investors possess, the more informed their investment decisions will be.

The second section focuses on the historical development of stock markets. There are chapters on the growth and development of the London Stock Exchange, the world's most important market until 1913; the evolution of trading on the New York Stock Exchange in the early 20th century; and the development of IPO markets around the world over the last 100 years or so.

Bubbles are usually mentioned in the same breath as stock markets. Hence, the third section discusses what we can learn from studying previous stock market bubbles. Equally, stock market and real estate bubbles are very often followed by the onset of financial crises and a variety of policy responses that have been used to reduce the probability of their happening again. History again provides academics with plenty of material from which to draw lessons for the benefit of practitioners.

The last section considers the role of innovation in financial markets and surprises us with just how long ago some innovations first occurred. We think of structured finance as a latter-day invention. However, these securities in their elemental form first appeared over two centuries ago. The first collective investment vehicles—namely, mutual funds—also made their appearance around the same time. More recently, 20th century financial markets have witnessed two major innovations: venture capital and the institutionalization of investment activity.

The final essay of this volume looks to the future and guides the reader through the likely avenues of future academic research on financial history in the wake of the Global Financial Crisis.

The CFA Institute Research Foundation has recorded a series of informative interviews with some contributors to this collection. We encourage readers to access the videos, which will be disseminated over the months following the publication of this monograph.

We thank Walter (Bud) Haslett, CFA, and Laurence B. Siegel, respectively executive director and research director of the CFA Institute Research Foundation, and Barbara Petitt, CFA, managing editor of the *Financial Analysts Journal*, for encouraging us to pursue this project and for providing us with their very substantial support, guidance, and encouragement throughout. We are grateful to the Research Foundation, the lead supporter of the July 2015 Financial History Workshop, and to the Cambridge Judge Business School, Carn Macro Advisors, the CFA Society of the UK, the Credit Suisse Research Institute, Fidelity International, J.P. Morgan Asset Management, Newton Investment Management, and Sandaire Investment Office for their support of the workshop, which was the starting point for this monograph.

In addition, we thank Professor Joost Jonker (University of Utrecht), Dr. Duncan Needham (Cambridge University), and Rasheed Saleuddin (PhD candidate, Cambridge University) for acting as discussants, and Professor Harold James (Princeton University) and Charley Ellis for their keynote speeches at the workshop. Special appreciation goes to Sarah Carter, Executive Director of the Newton Centre for Endowment Asset Management, for organizing the workshop, and to Ellen Quigley (PhD candidate, Cambridge University) for proofreading the manuscript.

Our sincere wish is that this volume will provide investment professionals, especially CFA charterholders and students, with some of the necessary background knowledge on the history of financial markets. We hope that our monograph helps them make more informed investment decisions for the future.

David Chambers and Elroy Dimson
Cambridge Judge Business School
University of Cambridge
November 2016

Introduction

Stephen J. Brown

Executive Editor, Financial Analysts Journal
Professor of Finance, Monash Business School
Emeritus Professor, NYU Stern School of Business

Thirty-three years ago, I started my teaching career at Yale. Burton Malkiel, Yale School of Management dean at the time, explained to me that master's students there were articulate and trained in literature and history. If he had any advice to give, it would be to weave into my lectures as much historical detail and as many references to literary associations as I possibly could. As things turned out, these details and references were not particularly well received. There was, however, one student in the class who appreciated my efforts. He became my teaching assistant the following year, and I persuaded him to enter the doctoral program. That student was William Goetzmann.

Over the years, I have spent a lot of time developing historical antecedents in teaching introductory finance, from a conviction that the only way to fully understand modern financial contracts is to understand the problems for which they represent the answer. In his most recent book, *Money Changes Everything: How Finance Made Civilization Possible*, William Goetzmann argues that far from merely representing the ephemera of Wall Street, financial innovations are in fact an important factor responsible for the growth of human civilization.

In July 2015, the editors of this volume, Dr. David Chambers and Professor Elroy Dimson, convened a gathering of many of the world's leading academics and thought leaders from the investment profession who share a deep interest in financial history. They debated a series of papers by financial market historians to discuss what investment practitioners need to know about financial history. This monograph continues the discussion and shows that financial history does indeed have significant practical importance.

The first section of this monograph examines what we can learn about the trade-off of risk for return from an extensive analysis of historical returns on equities, bonds, and other assets. Elroy Dimson, Paul Marsh, and Mike Staunton examine the long-term returns of stocks, bonds and bills, and exchange rates, all adjusted for inflation, for 23 countries over the 116 years since 1900. They find that the long-run history of returns provides the broadest possible range of historical market conditions necessary for practitioners to fully understand the range of possible investment outcomes. The markets have undergone substantial changes over that period: At the beginning, the UK market was the largest, but by the early 20th century, the United States had surpassed it. There were also significant sectoral and industry realignments within each of the markets during that time. Despite setbacks, over the 116 years equities have outperformed fixed income in all countries studied; for the world as a whole, equities outperformed bills by 4.2% per year and bonds by 3.2% per year. Antti Ilmanen makes the important point that these numbers provide our best estimate of future returns assuming constant expected real returns. He documents the important shift in academic and practitioner thinking that recognizes that expected returns are not constant but are, in fact, time-varying returns. Still, he shows that exploiting this time variation has historically been difficult. Jan Annaert, Frans Buelens, and Angelo Riva address the practical difficulties that arise when analyzing historical data and how they may be resolved.

The first section concludes with an extension to other financial markets. Olivier Accominotti examines the history of foreign exchange markets and currency speculation from the Middle Ages to the current epoch. He shows that the history of high returns to trading is frequently offset by the incidence of large losses, which suggests that the returns to speculation compensate for risk taking. Christophe Spaenjers examines the history of returns to durable assets and real estate, often the most significant component of investor portfolios. Since the start of the 20th century, he finds that durable assets have had modest capital gains with substantial price fluctuations offset by rental income in the case of real estate. Collectibles have experienced higher returns, offset by high transaction costs. The lack of an income stream for gold, silver, and diamonds explains why these are poor long-term investments, although these assets may be useful for diversification purposes.

The second section of this monograph explores the historical evolution of how financial claims are traded. Although the technology of trading has changed dramatically since the emergence of global financial markets in 1871, the essential conflicts between bankers and investment management firms on the one hand and stock traders on the other have not changed. Larry Neal illustrates this point with his history of the growth and development of the London Stock Exchange. He argues that the current trend of corporate governance of stock exchanges, with banks taking major ownership stakes, reflects the conflicts between owners and operators at the time the exchange was established in 1801. Caroline Fohlin describes the evolution of trading in these markets—from the small-scale call auction markets to continuous markets enhanced by improvements in technology—that has allowed for dramatic improvements in informational and cost efficiency. This history allows us to better understand the conflicts that arise in the trading structures and informational flows and their impact on market quality. Of particular concern is the uneven distribution of information and the role this plays in the propagation of panics and liquidity crises. Carsten Burhop and David Chambers argue that this concern is also a particular issue in the market for initial public offerings. IPO markets have existed as long as the stock markets themselves, and history has shown that these markets are cyclical in nature. However, evidence of IPO underpricing at issue and poor long-run IPO performance may be more of a feature of the way in which capital markets have developed over the 20th century.

The third section of this monograph addresses the perception that financial markets are inherently prone to irrational exuberance and bubbles. William Goetzmann explains that financial bubbles are actually extremely rare events. Precisely because they are so rare, we have to be careful when drawing inferences from historical experience. A careful examination of stock market data going back to 1900 shows that although the limited number of market crashes follow substantial run-ups in market prices, not every boom results in a market crash. The bubbles that do not burst are important to know about because avoiding them unnecessarily will lead to poor investment outcomes. Eugene White agrees with this conclusion. Although bubbles are infrequent, history shows that they are initiated by changes in fundamentals that may be inflated by irrational market exuberance. However, avoiding assets with strongly rising prices may result in missed opportunities that arise from strong fundamentals. Nevertheless, even if the role of irrational exuberance is understood, it is still difficult to determine with any precision how much asset prices may rise or when they may collapse. This uncertainty has important investment management implications. It also suggests that central banks should not actively intervene because it is difficult to get the timing of the intervention correct; moreover, any intervention may undermine goals of price stability and full employment. This point is taken up by Charles Goodhart, who observes that although the economic history of the past 300 years has shown many instances of financial crises and bank failures, their effects on asset values and on the real economy have been quite varied. Much depends on how the authorities react to these events. He argues that although we understand from history the factors that lead to and exacerbate crises, attempts to make such crises less frequent and less virulent have been largely misguided. As a result, he believes that the achievement of a financial-crisis-free economy is "chimerical."

The fourth and last section of this monograph addresses the history of financial innovation. Structured finance is often thought of as a relatively recent development, often closely associated with the excesses that preceded the recent financial crisis. Geert Rouwenhorst shows that the idea of bankers marketing securities that were comprised of repackaged claims to existing financial instruments was a common feature of innovations that emerged in 18th-century Netherlands. The first mutual funds arose from tontines established in that period as well as from plantation loans designed to securitize mortgages in the West Indies, and they shared certain lottery characteristics. It is important to understand that few equities were available to investors during that period, and these structured finance products were a better gauge of what was available to investors at that time. Tom Nicholas examines the history of high-tech investment finance in the United States, which is intertwined with the development of venture capital finance. He notes that the United States has been characterized by an auspicious link between finance and innovation, and he recounts the history of the American Development Corporation (ADC) as a pioneer in this area. ADC's strategy of screening multiple investments and governing the best ones with the expectation of a liquidity event is something all venture capital firms today try to emulate, although the organizational model has evolved. Janette Rutterford and Les Hannah document the rise of institutional investors through the 20th century to the point of market dominance in the 1990s in both the United States and the United Kingdom. The insurance industry was initially responsible for this growth—followed by pension funds after World War II—growth that was largely the result of active government encouragement. Mutual funds also grew dramatically in the immediate post-World War II period.

This monograph concludes with a contribution from Barry Eichengreen, who argues that the research frontier in financial history will be driven by current concerns motivated by the 2008–09 financial crisis. He points to a number of studies that reexamine the historical record on the basis of what we now understand about the role of banks and systemic risk. This research is now possible through low-cost and easily accessible historical data. There is the danger that access to these data may inappropriately frame research questions being asked. He concludes that looking to the past may not of itself allow us to predict what might happen in the future; however, it does allow us to understand the broader historical context and our ability to appreciate what is different about our current circumstances. This important observation helps establish why the study of financial history has such important practical significance in the current economic environment.

Part 1: Risk and Return over the Long Run

1. Long-Term Asset Returns

Elroy Dimson
Chairman of the Centre for Endowment Asset Management at Cambridge Judge Business School, emeritus professor of finance at London Business School, and adviser to the board of FTSE International

Paul Marsh
Emeritus professor of finance at London Business School

Mike Staunton
Director of the London Share Price Database, a research resource of London Business School

> *This chapter summarizes the long-run global historical evidence on the returns from stocks, bonds, bills, and exchange rates, all adjusted for inflation, over the 116 years since 1900. It updates and expands the data originally published in our 2002 book,* Triumph of the Optimists. *Given that returns are volatile, long-run historical data are important for understanding security returns and long time series are needed both to reduce measurement errors and to span the broadest possible range of historical market conditions.*

The Dimson–Marsh–Staunton (DMS) Dataset

Our database of annual returns (DMS 2016c) has expanded to cover 23 countries from the beginning of 1900 to the beginning of 2016. It comprises annual returns for stocks, bonds, and bills, plus inflation and exchange rates. It now covers two North American markets (the United States and Canada), ten markets from the Eurozone (Austria, Belgium, Finland, France, Germany, Ireland, Italy, the Netherlands, Portugal, and Spain), six European markets that are outside the Eurozone (Denmark, Norway, Russia, Sweden, Switzerland, and the United Kingdom), four Asia-Pacific markets (Australia, China, Japan, and New Zealand), and one African market (South Africa). As of the start of 2016, these countries make up 92% of the investable universe for a global investor, based on free-float market capitalizations. Our database also includes three global indices (World, World ex-USA, and Europe) denominated in a common currency (US dollars). The equity indices are weighted by market capitalization, and the bond indices are weighted by GDP.

General Methodology

The DMS database is based on the best-quality capital appreciation and income series available for each country, drawing heavily on previous studies and existing sources. Where possible, data are taken from peer-reviewed academic papers or highly rated professional studies that are listed in DMS (2002, 2007, 2016b). Many of the underlying studies are also listed by Annaert, Buelens, and Riva (2016). We update these studies by linking their return series to the best, most comprehensive commercial return indices available. To span the entire period from 1900, we link multiple index series. The best index is chosen for each period, switching when feasible to better alternatives as they become available. Other factors equal, we have chosen equity indices that afford the broadest coverage of their market. The DMS series are all total return series, including reinvested income (dividends for stocks; coupons for bonds).

The creation of the DMS database was in large part an investigative and assembly operation. Most of the series already existed, but some were long forgotten, unpublished, or came from research in progress. In other cases, the task was to estimate total returns by linking dividends to existing capital gains indices. For several countries, there were periods when no adequate series existed. In these cases, we compiled our own indices from archival records of the underlying securities. A detailed description of the sources used for each country, together with references to the multitude of researchers to whom we are indebted and whose studies we have drawn on, is provided in the *Global Investment Returns Sourcebook* (DMS 2016b).

The DMS series all start in 1900, a common start date that facilitates international comparisons. Data availability and quality dictated this choice of start date, and for practical purposes, 1900 was the earliest plausible start date for a comparative international database with broad coverage (see DMS 2007).

Every one of the 23 countries experienced market closures at some point, typically during wartime. However, in all but two cases, it is possible to bridge these interruptions and construct an investment returns history that spans the closure period. For 21 countries, therefore, we have a complete 116-year history of investment returns. For Russia and China, market closure was followed by expropriation of investors' assets, so we have market returns only for the pre- and post-communist eras. We incorporate these returns into the world and regional indices, showing a total loss on both Russian and Chinese stocks and bonds at the start of the communist eras. A brief history for each market is included in DMS (2016a).

3

Then and Now

Figure 1.1 shows the relative sizes of world equity markets at our starting date of New Year's Day 1900 (Panel A) and how they had changed by 2016 (Panel B). Panel B is based on free-float market capitalizations within the FTSE All-World Index and hence shows the investable universe for a global investor. Note that emerging markets, especially China, would have a higher weighting if measured using full market-cap weights and if restrictions and quotas for global investors were ignored (see DMS 2014).

Panel A of Figure 1.1 shows the national breakdown at the start of the DMS database. The UK stock market was the largest in the world, accounting for a quarter of world capitalization and dominating the United States, Germany, and France, each of which represented some 12%–15% of global equities. The next two markets, each accounting for 5%–6%, are those of Russia and Austria. They are followed by two Benelux countries (Belgium and the Netherlands) and two then-British colonies (Australia and South Africa), which are in turn trailed by 12 smaller markets. In total, the DMS database covers 98.3% of global equity market capitalization at the start of 1900.

Early in the 20th century, the United States overtook the United Kingdom to become the world's dominant stock market (although from the start of 1988 until the start of 1990, Japan was briefly the largest, with a weighting of almost 45% of the World Index at the start of 1989 compared with 29% for the United States). The changing fortunes of individual countries, which we evaluate in detail in DMS (2013), raise two important issues. The first is survivorship bias. While investors in some countries were lucky, others suffered financial disaster. Incorporating China and Russia into our database—the two best-known cases of markets that failed to survive—addresses this issue. China was a small market in 1900 and in subsequent decades, but Russia accounted for some 6% of world market capitalization in 1900. Similarly, Austria–Hungary had a 5% weighting in the 1900 World Index, and although it was not a total catastrophe, it was the worst-performing equity market and the second-worst bond market among the 21 countries with continuous investment histories. Incorporating Austria, China, and Russia drastically reduces the potential for bias in world market returns from ignoring non-surviving and deeply unsuccessful markets.

Panel B of Figure 1.1 shows that today the US market dominates its closest rivals, accounting for more than half of global stock market value. Japan and the United Kingdom are next, each representing 7%–9% of global equities. Switzerland, France, and Germany each represent about 3% of the global market, and Canada, Australia, and China now represent around 2% each. These markets are followed by 14 smaller markets. The areas in the pie charts

Figure 1.1.   Relative Sizes of World Stock Markets, 1 January 1900 versus 1 January 2016

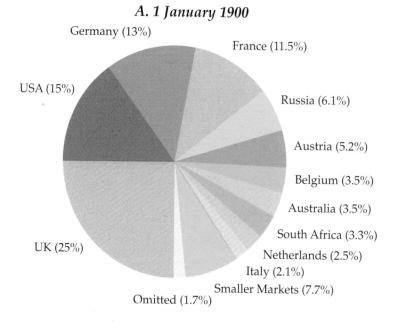

A. 1 January 1900

Germany (13%)

France (11.5%)

USA (15%)

Russia (6.1%)

Austria (5.2%)

Belgium (3.5%)

Australia (3.5%)

South Africa (3.3%)

Netherlands (2.5%)

UK (25%)

Italy (2.1%)

Smaller Markets (7.7%)

Omitted (1.7%)

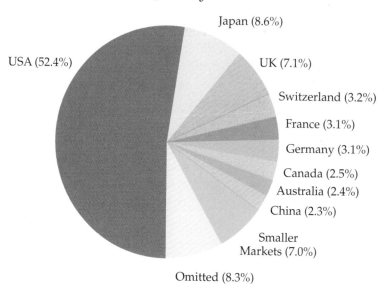

B. 1 January 2016

Japan (8.6%)

USA (52.4%)

UK (7.1%)

Switzerland (3.2%)

France (3.1%)

Germany (3.1%)

Canada (2.5%)

Australia (2.4%)

China (2.3%)

Smaller Markets (7.0%)

Omitted (8.3%)

Sources: DMS (2002, 2016b); FTSE Russell (2015).

labelled "omitted" represent countries that are excluded because the available data do not extend all the way forward from 1900 to 2016 or all the way backward from 2016 to 1900. The former are small markets that failed to prosper ("submerging markets"); the latter are mostly markets that came into existence after 1900 ("emerging markets").

An issue more serious than survivorship bias is success bias. The United States is the world's best-documented capital market, and prior to assembly of the DMS database, the evidence cited on long-run asset returns was predominantly US-based, mostly from Ibbotson Associates (see, for example, Ibbotson Associates 1999). Extrapolating from an unusually successful market—ignoring the fact that the economic and financial performance of that nation was exceptional—introduces success bias. That is mitigated by making inferences from the experience of a broad sample of countries.

The Great Transformation[1]

At the beginning of 1900—the start date of our global returns database—virtually no one had driven a car, made a phone call, used an electric light, heard recorded music, or seen a movie; no one had flown in an aircraft, listened to the radio, watched TV, used a computer, sent an e-mail, or used a smartphone. There were no x-rays, body scans, DNA tests, or transplants, and no one had taken an antibiotic; as a result, many would die young.

Mankind has enjoyed a wave of transformative innovation dating from the Industrial Revolution, continuing through the Golden Age of Invention in the late 19th century, and extending into today's information revolution. These transformations have given rise to entire new industries: electricity and power generation, automobiles, aerospace, airlines, telecommunications, oil and gas, pharmaceuticals and biotechnology, computers, information technology, and media and entertainment. Meanwhile, makers of horse-drawn carriages and wagons, canal boats, steam locomotives, candles, and matches have seen their industries decline. There have been profound changes in what is produced, how it is made, and the way in which people live and work.

These changes can be seen in the shifting composition of the firms listed on world stock markets. **Figure 1.2** shows the industrial composition of listed companies in the United States and the United Kingdom. The upper two pie charts show the position at the beginning of 1900, while the lower two show the beginning of 2015. Markets at the start of the 20th century were dominated by railroads, which accounted for 63% of US stock market value and almost 50% in the United Kingdom. More than a century later, railroads

---

[1]Material in this section from Dimson, Marsh, and Staunton (2015).

Figure 1.2. Industry Weightings in the USA and UK, 1900 Compared with 2015

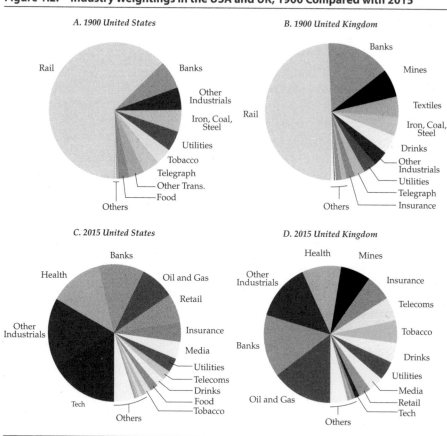

Note: For 1900, UK data are based on the top 100 companies and US data on the total market.
Sources: DMS (2002, 2015); FTSE Russell 2015.

declined almost to the point of stock market extinction, representing less than 1% of the US market and close to zero in the UK market.

Of the US firms listed in 1900, more than 80% of their value was in industries that are today small or extinct; the UK figure is 65%. Besides railroads, other industries that have declined precipitously are textiles, iron, coal, and steel. These industries still exist but have moved to lower-cost locations in the emerging world. Yet, similarities between 1900 and today are also apparent. The banking and insurance industries continue to be important. Similarly, such industries as food, beverages (including alcohol), tobacco, and utilities were present in 1900 just as they are today. And, in the United

Kingdom, quoted mining companies were important in 1900 just as they are in London today.

But even industries that initially seem similar have often altered radically. For example, compare telegraphy in 1900 with smartphones today. Both were high-tech at the time. Or contrast other transport in 1900—shipping lines, trams, and docks—with their modern counterparts, airlines, buses, and trucking. Similarly, within manufacturing and industrials, the 1900 list of companies includes the world's then-largest candle maker and the world's largest manufacturer of matches.

Another statistic that stands out from Figure 1.2 is the high proportion of today's companies whose business is in industries that were small or non-existent in 1900, 62% by value for the United States and 47% for the United Kingdom. The largest industries today are technology (notably in the United States), oil and gas, banking, healthcare, the catch-all group of other industrials, mining (for the United Kingdom), telecommunications, insurance, and retail. Of these, oil and gas, technology, and health care (including pharmaceuticals and biotechnology) were almost totally absent in 1900. Telecoms and media, at least as we know them now, are also new industries.

Our analysis relates only to exchange-listed businesses. Some industries existed throughout the period but were not always listed. For example, there were many retailers in 1900, but apart from the major department stores, these were often small, local outlets rather than national and global retail chains like Walmart or Tesco. Similarly, in 1900 a higher proportion of manufacturing firms were family owned and unlisted. In the United Kingdom and other countries, nationalization has also caused entire industries—railroads, utilities, telecoms, steel, airlines, airports—to be delisted, often to be re-privatized at a later date. We included listed railroads, for example, while omitting highways that remain largely state-owned. The evolving composition of the corporate sector highlights the importance of avoiding survivorship bias within a stock market index, as well as across indices (see DMS 2002).

Long-Run Asset Returns

Figure 1.3 shows the cumulative real total return for the main asset categories in the United States and the United Kingdom. Returns include reinvested income, are measured in local currency, and are adjusted for inflation. In each country, equities performed best, long-term government bonds less well, and Treasury bills the worst. In the United States, an initial investment of $1 grew in real value to $1,271 if invested in equities, $10 in bonds, and $2.7 in bills. In the United Kingdom, an initial investment of £1 grew in real value to £445 if invested in equities, £7 in bonds, and £3.3 in bills.

Figure 1.3.   Cumulative Returns on US and UK Asset Classes in Real Terms, 1900–2015

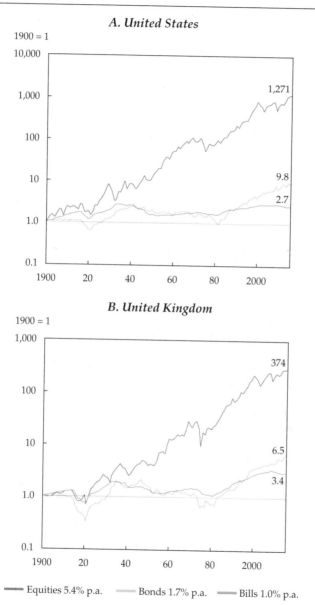

Sources: DMS (2016b, 2016c).

We previously noted the need for caution when generalizing from the United States, which, with hindsight, emerged as the world's premier economic power. We have already shown the acceptable, but lower, long-term performance of the United Kingdom. For a more complete view, we examine investment returns in other countries. **Figure 1.4** shows annualized real equity, bond, and bill returns over the period 1900–2015 for the 21 countries with continuous index histories, plus the World Index (Wld), the World ex-USA (WxU), and Europe (Eur). The abbreviations for each market are listed in Appendix 1.1. Markets are ranked in ascending order of real (inflation-adjusted) equity market returns, which were positive in every location, typically at a level of 3% to 6% per year. Equities were the best-performing asset class everywhere. Bonds beat bills in every country.

In most countries, bonds gave a positive real return over the 116 years, with just four exceptions: Austria, Italy, Germany, and Japan. These countries also delivered poor equity performance, the origins of which date from the first half of the 20th century. These were the countries that suffered most from the ravages of war and from ensuing periods of high or hyperinflation.

Figure 1.4 shows that the United States performed well, ranking third for equity performance (6.4% per year) and sixth for bonds (2.0% per year). This confirms the conjecture that US returns would be above average. However, the differences in annualized performance are moderate. Although its stock

Figure 1.4. Real Annualized Returns (%) on Equities versus Bonds and Bills Internationally, 1900–2015

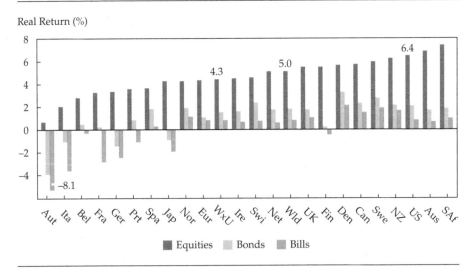

Sources: Appendices 1.2, 1.4, and 1.5 in this chapter.

market performance was good, the United States was not the top performer and its return was not especially high relative to the world averages. The real return on US equities of 6.4% contrasts with the real US dollar return of 4.3% on the World ex-USA Index. A common factor among the best-performing equity markets over the last 116 years is that they tended to be resource-rich and/or New World countries.

Although risky equities, viewed as an asset class, performed better than less-volatile bonds or bills, investors did not benefit from investing in more-volatile stock markets as compared to more-stable markets. US equities had a standard deviation of returns of 20.1%, placing the United States among the lower-risk markets ranking sixth after Canada (17.0%), Australia (17.7%), New Zealand (19.4%), Switzerland (19.5%), and the United Kingdom (19.7%). The World Index, with a standard deviation of just 17.5%, shows the risk reduction obtained from international diversification. The most volatile markets were Portugal (34.4%), Germany (31.7%), Austria (30.0%), Finland (30.0%), Japan (29.6%), and Italy (28.5%), which were the countries most seriously affected by the depredations of war, civil strife, and inflation, and (in Finland's case) also reflecting the risk of a concentrated market in more-recent periods. Further details on the risk and return from equity investing are presented in Appendix 1.2.

Inflation, Bills, and Bonds

Inflation was a major force in the 20th century. In the United States, annualized inflation was 2.9% per year, versus 3.7% in the United Kingdom. This apparently small difference means that, since 1900, US consumer prices rose by a factor of 27 and UK prices rose 69-fold. Prices did not rise steadily over the 116 years, and all the DMS countries experienced deflation at some stage in the 1920s and early 1930s. In the United States, consumer prices fell by almost a third in the years after 1920 and did not regain their 1920 level until 1947. In three-quarters of the years since the mid-1990s, one or more of our 21 countries experienced (generally mild) deflation. Over the last 116 years, there were seven high inflation countries: Germany, Austria, Portugal, Finland, France, Japan, and Spain. There were two runners-up, Belgium and South Africa, and one low-inflation country, Switzerland. Further details on historical inflation rates are provided in Appendix 1.3. Note that the true 116-year mean and standard deviation for Germany are far higher than Appendix 1.3 shows because the hyperinflationary years of 1922–23 are omitted from the table.

Treasury bills provide a benchmark for the risk-free rate of interest. Since 1900, US and UK investors earned annualized real (inflation-adjusted) returns of 0.8% and 1.0%, respectively. Over the period, there were negative real returns on bills in eight countries: Austria, Belgium, Finland, France, Germany, Italy, Japan, and Portugal. If we include the hyperinflation of 1922–23, German bill (and bond) investors lost virtually everything in real terms. Further details on real interest rates over the long term are in Appendix 1.4.

Government bonds were on average disappointing for investors over the 116 years from 1900 to 2015. Across the 21 countries, the average annualized real return was 1.0% (1.2% excluding Austria's very low figure). Although this exceeds the return on cash by 1.3%, bonds had much higher risk. As already noted, real bond returns were negative in four countries, with German bonds doing worst once the 1922–23 hyperinflation is incorporated. In the United Kingdom, the annualized real bond return was 1.7%, while US bondholders did better with a real return of 2.0% per year. Over the full period, Denmark, Sweden, Switzerland, Canada, and New Zealand did better than the USA, with real bond returns of 3.2%, 2.7%, 2.4%, 2.3%, and 2.1%, respectively. Note that Danish bond returns were estimated from mortgage bonds over part of their history (see DMS 2016b) and were thus exposed to some credit risk. The best-performing country in terms of pure government bonds was therefore Sweden, with an annualized real return of 2.7%. Since 1900, the average standard deviation of real bond returns was 13.1%, versus 23.6% for equities and 7.7% for bills (these averages exclude Austria). US real bond returns had a standard deviation of 10.4%, versus 20.1% for equities and 4.6% for bills. Further details on real bond returns are in Appendix 1.5.

Exchange Rates

For decades, investors have been exhorted to diversify internationally so they can benefit from the "free lunch" of risk reduction through diversification. It is an old idea: More than a century ago when capital flowed freely, London, New York, Amsterdam, and Paris facilitated the development of transport systems, utilities, and natural resources around the world. In those days, many currencies were linked to the price of gold and foreign exchange risk seemed unimportant. However, that was to change as the 20th century unfolded. **Figure 1.5** compares our 21 countries' exchange rates against the US dollar. On the left of the graph, we show the dollar value of 5.38 Swiss francs, 0.21 British pounds, and the sums in other currencies that equated to one dollar at the beginning of 1900. That is, we re-based the exchange rates at the start of 1900 to a value of 1.0. The vertical axis displays the number of dollars required to purchase one local currency unit (after re-basing). A depreciating currency trends downward, while an appreciating currency trends upward.

Figure 1.5.   Nominal Exchange Rates, 1900–2015, in US Dollars per Unit of Local Currency (rebased to 1900=1)

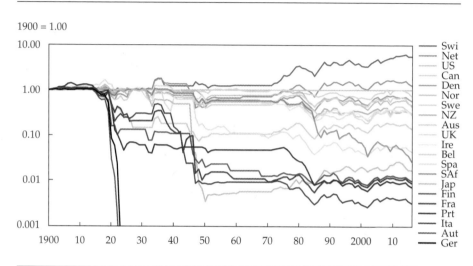

Sources: DMS (2002, 2016b, 2016c).

Because of Austria's ultrahigh inflation that peaked in 1922 and Germany's hyperinflation that peaked in 1923, the currencies of these two countries were debased to a negligible value. Other currencies took longer to move less. By the beginning of 2016, the currencies in the diagram had depreciated to the point where the number of Italian currency units (lira, followed by euros) that could be bought for one dollar was 314 times as large as in 1900; the number of yen was 59 times larger; and the number of British pounds was 3.3 times larger. The strongest currency was the Swiss franc, which had appreciated until, by today, one dollar could buy only 18 rappen (Swiss centimes)—that is, 0.18 Swiss francs, one-sixth of the number of francs that the dollar could have bought in 1900.

At the start of 1900, the exchange rate between US dollars and British pounds was $1 = £0.208, almost five dollars to the pound. By the end of 2015, the pound had weakened to $1 = £0.67—only 1.48 dollars for each pound, a fall of 1% per year. But the strengthening of the dollar against the pound was accompanied by lower inflation in the United States than in the United Kingdom. So, to determine the "real" movement in the exchange rate, we must adjust the exchange rate for inflation in the United States relative to the United Kingdom. The inflation-adjusted, or real, exchange rate is defined as the nominal exchange rate multiplied by the ratio of the two countries' inflation indices. Over the long run, the real dollar/pound exchange rate moved by much less than the nominal exchange rate, increasing by 0.22% per year.

Figure 1.6 presents the real exchange rates for the 21 countries with a complete history over the period from 1900 onward. Note that the vertical scale is quite different from the previous chart of nominal exchange rates. As with the real dollar/pound rate discussed above, these inflation-adjusted currency values have been comparatively stable over this long interval, albeit with large spikes for countries that emerged from wartime defeat. Consistent with the findings in Taylor (2002), real exchange rates do not appear to exhibit a long-term upward or downward trend but are clearly volatile. Over the long term, it is remarkable that no country had a currency that in real terms appreciated against the US dollar by as much as 1% per year (the strongest, the Swiss franc, appreciated by 0.76% per year). Only one country had a currency that depreciated by as much as 1% per year (the weakest, the South African rand, depreciated by –1.15% per year). Detailed real exchange rate statistics for 1900–2015 are provided in Appendix 1.7.

Figure 1.6. Real Exchange Rates, 1900–2015, in US Dollars per Unit of Local Currency (rebased to 1900=1)

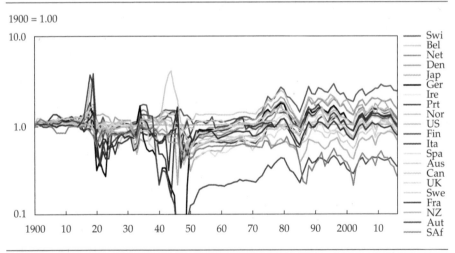

Sources: DMS (2002, 2016b, 2016c).

Common-Currency Returns

We have displayed the real returns to a domestic equity investor based on local purchasing power in that investor's home country (see Figure 1.4 and Appendix 1.2). For example, over the period 1900–2015, the annualized real return to an American buying US equities was 6.4%, and for a Swiss investor buying Swiss equities it was 4.5%. However, when considering cross-border investment, we also need to account for exchange rate movements. To illustrate, consider an American buying Swiss equities and a Swiss investor buying US equities. Each investor now has two exposures, one to foreign equities and the other to foreign currency. We thus convert each investor's return into his or her reference currency.

To convert nominal returns, we use changes in the nominal exchange rate. By analogy, to convert real returns in one currency into real returns in another, we simply adjust by the change in the real exchange rate. Over the period 1900–2015, Appendix 1.7 shows that the real (inflation-adjusted) Swiss franc was stronger than the US dollar by 0.76% per year. Thus, the American who invested in Switzerland had a real return of 4.48% (from Swiss equities) plus 0.76% (from the Swiss franc), giving an overall return of (1+4.48%) × (1+0.76%) − 1 = 5.28% (all numbers rounded). In contrast, the Swiss investor who invested in America had a real return of 6.36% (from US equities) minus 0.76% (from the US dollar), namely (1+6.36%) × (1−0.76%) − 1 = 5.55% (again, rounded).

To provide a common-currency view of stock market investing, **Figure 1.7** therefore converts local-currency real returns into US dollar-denominated real returns. It simply involves adding each country's real exchange rate movement to the local real returns we presented in Figure 1.4. In the case of Switzerland, for example, the domestic real return is 4.5% and the real exchange rate movement is +0.76%. Adding these (geometrically) gives the real dollar return of 5.3% that we just discussed. It is clear that, over the long haul, the cross section of stock market returns reflects differing real equity performances far more than differing real exchange rates.

15

Figure 1.7. Real Annualized Equity Returns (%) in Local Currency and US Dollars, 1900–2015

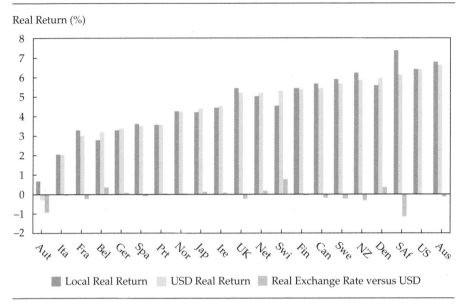

Real Return (%)

Local Real Return   USD Real Return   Real Exchange Rate versus USD

Sources: DMS (2002, 2016b, 2016c).

Conclusion

Since 1900, there have been transformational changes in the relative sizes of stock markets around the world. Coinciding with these developments, there has been a fundamental change in the industries represented on major stock exchanges. Although there have been setbacks, over the 116 years, equities beat bonds and bills in all 21 countries for which we have a continuous stock market history. For the world as a whole, equities outperformed bills by 4.2% per year and bonds by 3.2% per year. Over the long run, there was a reward for the higher risk of investing in stocks.

Currencies fluctuated considerably between 1900 and 2015. Over this long interval, most currencies weakened against the US dollar and only a few, led by the Swiss franc, strengthened. Yet during this 116-year period, foreign exchange fluctuations were largely a response to relative inflation. Over more than a century, real exchange rates against the US dollar changed by an annualized amount that was, in almost every case, below 1% per year. Common-currency returns have thus been quite close to, and have a very similar ranking to, real returns expressed in local currency terms.

We have provided an update on long-run rates of return on stocks, bonds, bills, currencies, and inflation in the 21 countries with continuous histories since 1900. We have updated and commented on the key statistics, charts, and findings from *Triumph of the Optimists* (DMS 2002). Interested readers also are referred to the *Global Investment Returns Sourcebook* (DMS 2016b) for additional analysis.

References

Annaert, Jan, Frans Buelens, and Angelo Riva. 2016. "Financial History Databases." In *Financial Market History*. Edited by David Chambers and Elroy Dimson. Charlottesville, VA: CFA Institute Research Foundation.

Dimson, Elroy, Paul Marsh, and Mike Staunton. 2002. *Triumph of the Optimists: 101 Years of Global Investment Returns*. New Jersey: Princeton University Press.

———. 2007. "The Worldwide Equity Premium: A Smaller Puzzle." In *The Handbook of the Equity Risk Premium*. Edited by R. Mehra. Amsterdam: Elsevier.

———. 2013. "The Low Return World." In *Global Investment Returns Yearbook 2013*. Edited by DMS. Zurich: Credit Suisse Research Institute.

———. 2014. "Emerging Markets Revisited." In *Global Investment Returns Yearbook 2014*. Edited by DMS. Zurich: Credit Suisse Research Institute.

———. 2015. "Industries: Their Rise and Fall." In *Global Investment Returns Yearbook 2015*. Edited by DMS. Zurich: Credit Suisse Research Institute.

———. 2016a. *Global Investment Returns Yearbook 2016*. Zurich: Credit Suisse Research Institute.

———. 2016b. *Global Investment Returns Sourcebook 2016*. Zurich: Credit Suisse Research Institute.

———. 2016c. "The Dimson-Marsh-Staunton Global Investment Returns Database" (the "DMS Database"). Morningstar Inc.

FTSE Russell. 2015. "FTSE All-World Index Series Monthly Review" (December).

Ibbotson Associates. 1999. *SBBI Yearbook*. Chicago: Ibbotson Associates.

Taylor, Alan. 2002. "A Century of Purchasing-Power Parity." *Review of Economics and Statistics*, vol. 84, no. 2: 139–150.

Appendices

The appendices below provide summary statistics on the return series for 21 countries and three regions with a continuous history. The markets are identified by the abbreviated names listed in **Appendix 1.1**. **Appendix 1.2** summarizes global equity returns; **Appendix 1.3** reports inflation rates; **Appendices 1.4** and **1.5** present real interest rates and real bond returns; and **Appendices 1.6** and **1.7** present nominal and real exchange rate changes. The data sources are the DMS dataset distributed by Morningstar (DMS 2016c) and the *Global Investment Returns Sourcebook* (DMS 2016b), which updates and extends the statistics presented in *Triumph of the Optimists* (DMS 2002).

The structure of Appendices 1.2–1.7 is as follows. The geometric means in the second column show the 116-year annualized returns achieved by investors; these are the figures that are plotted for selected asset-class returns in Figure 1.4. The arithmetic means in the third column show the average of the 116 annual returns for each market. The arithmetic mean of a sequence of different returns is always larger than the geometric mean, and the more volatile the sequence of returns, the greater the amount by which the arithmetic mean exceeds the geometric mean. This is verified by the fifth column, which shows the standard deviation of each market's returns. The fourth column presents the standard error of the arithmetic mean return (the lower the standard error, the more precise the estimate of the mean return). The sixth and eighth columns present the lowest and highest annual return for each market, respectively, and those returns are accompanied in the seventh and ninth columns by the years in which these extreme events occurred.

Note that Appendices 1.6 and 1.7 report each country's annualized rate of currency appreciation or depreciation in terms of the dollar value of local currency units. A strong currency (e.g., the Swiss franc) is shown by a positive rate of change in column two: More dollars are needed to buy one franc. A weak currency has a negative rate of change: Fewer dollars are needed to buy a unit of the currency.

Appendix 1.1.   Markets Presented in This Study and Their Abbreviations

Country	Abbreviation	Country	Abbreviation	Country/Region	Abbreviation
Australia	Aus	Ireland	Ire	Spain	Spa
Austria	Aut	Italy	Ita	Sweden	Swe
Belgium	Bel	Japan	Jap	Switzerland	Swi
Canada	Can	The Netherlands	Net	United Kingdom	UK
Denmark	Den	New Zealand	NZ	United States	US
Finland	Fin	Norway	Nor	Europe	Eur
France	Fra	Portugal	Prt	World ex-USA	WxU
Germany	Ger	South Africa	SAf	World	Wld

Appendix 1.2. Real (Inflation-Adjusted) Equity Returns around the World, 1900–2015

Country	Geometric mean%	Arithmetic mean%	Standard error%	Standard deviation%	Minimum return%	Minimum year	Maximum return%	Maximum year
Aus	6.7	8.3	1.6	17.7	−42.5	2008	51.5	1983
Aut	0.7	4.7	2.8	30.0	−60.1	2008	127.1	1985
Bel	2.8	5.4	2.2	23.7	−48.9	2008	105.1	1919
Can	5.6	7.0	1.6	17.0	−33.8	2008	55.2	1933
Den	5.5	7.4	1.9	20.9	−49.2	2008	107.8	1983
Fin	5.4	9.3	2.8	30.0	−60.8	1918	161.7	1999
Fra	3.2	5.8	2.1	23.1	−41.5	2008	66.1	1954
Ger	3.3	8.2	2.9	31.7	−90.8	1948	154.6	1949
Ire	4.4	7.0	2.1	23.0	−65.4	2008	68.4	1977
Ita	2.0	6.0	2.7	28.5	−72.9	1945	120.7	1946
Jap	4.2	8.8	2.7	29.6	−85.5	1946	121.1	1952
Net	5.0	7.1	2.0	21.4	−50.4	2008	101.6	1940
NZ	6.2	7.9	1.8	19.4	−54.7	1987	105.3	1983
Nor	4.2	7.1	2.5	26.9	−53.6	2008	166.9	1979
Prt	3.5	8.5	3.2	34.4	−76.6	1978	151.8	1986
SAf	7.3	9.4	2.1	22.1	−52.2	1920	102.9	1933
Spa	3.6	5.8	2.0	22.0	−43.3	1977	99.4	1986
Swe	5.9	8.0	2.0	21.2	−42.5	1918	67.5	1999
Swi	4.5	6.3	1.8	19.5	−37.8	1974	59.4	1922
UK	5.4	7.2	1.8	19.7	−57.1	1974	96.7	1975
US	6.4	8.3	1.9	20.1	−38.4	1931	56.2	1933
Eur	4.2	6.1	1.8	19.8	−47.5	2008	75.7	1933
WxU	4.3	6.0	1.8	19.0	−44.2	2008	80.0	1933
Wld	5.0	6.5	1.6	17.5	−41.4	2008	68.0	1933

Sources: DMS (2002, 2016b, 2016c).

Appendix 1.3. Inflation Rates around the World, 1900–2015

Country	Geometric mean%	Arithmetic mean%	Standard error%	Standard devia-tion%	Minimum return%	Minimum year	Maximum return%	Maximum year
Aus	3.8	3.9	0.5	5.1	−12.6	1921	19.3	1951
Aut	12.7	32.0	16.7	180.1	−5.0	1931	1748.1	1922
Bel	5.0	6.1	1.5	16.5	−37.9	1919	96.3	1917
Can	3.0	3.1	0.4	4.5	−15.8	1921	15.1	1917
Den	3.8	3.9	0.6	6.0	−15.1	1926	24.4	1940
Fin	7.1	8.8	2.4	26.2	−11.3	1919	241.4	1918
Fra	6.9	7.5	1.1	12.1	−18.4	1921	65.1	1946
Ger*	4.6	5.4	1.4	14.8	−9.5	1932	209 bn	1923
Ire	4.1	4.3	0.6	6.9	−26.0	1921	23.3	1981
Ita	8.1	10.4	3.2	34.3	−9.7	1931	344.4	1944
Jap	6.7	10.0	3.8	40.9	−18.7	1930	361.1	1946
Net	2.9	3.0	0.4	4.7	−13.4	1921	18.7	1918
NZ	3.6	3.7	0.4	4.6	−12.0	1932	14.7	1980
Nor	3.6	3.9	0.7	7.2	−19.5	1921	40.3	1918
Prt	7.4	8.2	1.4	14.7	−17.6	1948	80.9	1918
SAf	4.9	5.2	0.7	7.3	−17.2	1921	47.5	1920
Spa	5.6	5.8	0.6	6.8	−6.7	1928	36.5	1946
Swe	3.4	3.6	0.6	6.6	−25.2	1921	39.4	1918
Swi	2.2	2.3	0.5	5.2	−17.7	1922	25.7	1918
UK	3.7	3.9	0.6	6.5	−26.0	1921	24.9	1975
US	2.9	3.0	0.4	4.8	−10.7	1921	20.5	1918

*For Germany, the means, standard deviation, and standard error are based on 114 years, excluding 1922–23.
Sources: DMS (2002, 2016b, 2016c).

Appendix 1.4. Real Interest Rates around the World, 1900–2015

Country	Geometric mean%	Arithmetic mean%	Standard error%	Standard devia-tion%	Minimum return%	Minimum year	Maximum return%	Maximum year
Aus	0.7	0.8	0.5	5.3	−15.5	1951	18.5	1921
Aut	−8.0	−3.9	1.7	18.6	−94.2	1922	12.6	1931
Bel	−0.3	0.6	1.2	12.7	−46.6	1941	69.0	1919
Can	1.5	1.6	0.4	4.8	−12.5	1947	27.1	1921
Den	2.1	2.3	0.6	6.0	−15.8	1940	25.1	1921
Fin	−0.4	0.5	1.1	11.6	−69.2	1918	19.9	1919
Fra	−2.7	−2.2	0.9	9.4	−38.5	1946	29.7	1921
Ger*	−2.4	−0.4	1.2	13.0	−100.0	1923	38.8	1924
Ire	0.7	0.9	0.6	6.5	−15.5	1915	42.2	1921
Ita	−3.5	−2.5	1.0	11.3	−76.6	1944	14.2	1931
Jap	−1.9	−0.3	1.3	13.6	−77.5	1946	29.8	1930
Net	0.6	0.7	0.5	4.9	−12.7	1918	19.6	1921
NZ	1.7	1.8	0.4	4.6	−8.1	1951	21.1	1932
Nor	1.1	1.3	0.7	7.0	−25.4	1918	31.2	1921
Prt	−1.1	−0.5	0.9	9.7	−41.6	1918	23.8	1948
SAf	1.0	1.2	0.6	6.1	−27.8	1920	27.3	1921
Spa	0.3	0.5	0.5	5.7	−23.8	1946	12.6	1928
Swe	1.9	2.1	0.6	6.5	−23.2	1918	42.7	1921
Swi	0.8	0.9	0.5	4.9	−16.5	1918	25.8	1922
UK	1.0	1.2	0.6	6.3	−15.7	1915	43.0	1921
US	0.8	1.0	0.4	4.6	−15.1	1946	20.0	1921

*For Germany, the means, standard deviation, and standard error are based on 114 years, excluding 1922–23.
Sources: DMS (2002, 2016b, 2016c).

Appendix 1.5.   Real Bond Returns around the World, 1900–2015

Country	Geometric mean%	Arithmetic mean%	Standard error%	Standard devia-tion%	Minimum return%	Minimum year	Maximum return%	Maximum year
Aus	1.7	2.5	1.2	13.2	−26.6	1951	62.2	1932
Aut	−3.8	4.8	4.8	51.2	−94.4	1945	441.6	1926
Bel	0.4	1.6	1.4	15.0	−45.6	1917	62.3	1919
Can	2.3	2.8	1.0	10.4	−25.9	1915	41.7	1921
Den	3.2	3.8	1.1	11.9	−18.2	1919	50.1	1983
Fin	0.2	1.4	1.3	13.7	−69.5	1918	30.2	1921
Fra	0.2	1.1	1.2	13.0	−43.5	1947	35.9	1927
Ger*	−1.4	1.3	1.5	15.8	−100.0	1923	62.5	1932
Ire	1.5	2.6	1.4	15.1	−34.1	1915	61.2	1921
Ita	−1.1	0.3	1.4	14.8	−64.3	1944	35.5	1993
Jap	−0.9	1.7	1.8	19.7	−77.5	1946	69.8	1954
Net	1.7	2.1	0.9	9.8	−18.1	1915	32.8	1932
NZ	2.1	2.5	0.8	9.0	−23.7	1984	34.1	1991
Nor	1.9	2.6	1.1	12.0	−48.0	1918	62.1	1921
Prt	0.8	2.6	1.7	18.7	−49.7	1994	82.4	1922
SAf	1.8	2.3	1.0	10.5	−32.6	1920	37.1	1921
Spa	1.8	2.5	1.2	12.6	−30.2	1920	53.2	1942
Swe	2.7	3.4	1.2	12.7	−37.0	1939	68.2	1921
Swi	2.4	2.7	0.9	9.4	−21.4	1918	56.1	1922
UK	1.7	2.6	1.3	13.7	−30.7	1974	59.4	1921
US	2.0	2.5	1.0	10.4	−18.4	1917	35.1	1982
Eur	1.1	2.4	1.5	16.2	−52.4	1919	72.8	1933
WxU	1.5	2.5	1.4	14.7	−45.5	1919	76.1	1933
Wld	1.8	2.4	1.0	11.3	−32.0	1919	46.7	1933

*For Germany, the means, standard deviation, and standard error are based on 114 years, excluding 1922–23.
Sources: DMS (2002, 2016b, 2016c).

Appendix 1.6. Nominal Exchange Rate Changes against the US Dollar, 1900–2015

Country	Geometric mean%	Arithmetic mean%	Standard error%	Standard devia- tion%	Minimum change%	Minimum year	Maximum change%	Maximum year
Aus	−1.0	−0.4	1.0	11.1	−39.4	1931	53.4	1933
Aut	−9.6	−4.0	2.1	22.1	−96.2	1922	53.0	1940
Bel	−1.7	−0.7	1.2	13.3	−41.9	1919	55.8	1933
Can	−0.3	−0.1	0.5	5.8	−20.0	2008	22.3	2003
Den	−0.5	0.2	1.1	11.4	−37.6	1946	40.2	1925
Fin	−3.9	−2.4	1.4	15.1	−73.3	1919	54.4	1933
Fra	−4.0	−1.5	1.8	19.4	−85.3	1946	91.3	1943
Ger*	−2.5	8.6	9.6	102.5	−100.0	1923	1046.3	1948
Ire	−1.1	−0.5	1.0	10.7	−30.2	1931	53.4	1933
Ita	−4.8	−3.0	1.5	16.7	−64.8	1946	59.1	1933
Jap	−3.5	−0.7	1.6	16.9	−91.7	1945	47.8	1933
Net	0.2	1.0	1.1	11.9	−59.1	1946	55.1	1933
NZ	−1.0	−0.3	1.2	12.5	−36.0	1942	74.2	1933
Nor	−0.7	0.0	1.1	12.0	−30.5	1931	49.5	1933
Prt	−4.2	−2.9	1.3	14.3	−70.5	1920	52.5	1933
SAf	−3.1	−2.0	1.3	14.1	−46.0	1985	46.1	1987
Spa	−2.7	−1.2	1.6	16.9	−62.2	1946	99.2	1939
Swe	−0.7	−0.1	1.0	10.5	−29.2	1931	44.7	1933
Swi	1.5	2.0	1.0	11.1	−29.4	1936	56.0	1933
UK	−1.0	−0.4	1.0	10.8	−30.2	1931	53.4	1933
US	0.0	0.0	0.0	0.0	0.0		0.0	

*For Germany, the means, standard deviation, and standard error are based on 114 years, excluding 1922–23.
Sources: DMS (2002, 2016b, 2016c).

Appendix 1.7.   Real Exchange Rate Changes against the US Dollar, 1900–2015

Country	Geometric mean%	Arithmetic mean%	Standard error%	Standard deviation%	Minimum change%	Minimum year	Maximum change%	Maximum year
Aus	−0.16	0.52	1.1	11.7	−39.9	1931	46.4	1933
Aut	−0.93	2.06	2.0	21.9	−83.2	1919	74.7	1917
Bel	0.37	2.23	1.8	19.1	−68.6	1919	77.8	1917
Can	−0.21	−0.03	0.6	6.1	−19.2	2008	22.5	2003
Den	0.35	1.07	1.1	11.8	−47.6	1946	35.0	1933
Fin	−0.04	2.10	1.9	21.0	−79.4	1919	146.8	1918
Fra	−0.24	2.34	2.1	22.6	−79.4	1946	135.9	1943
Ger	0.10	13.45	11.7	125.8	−75.0	1945	1302.0	1948
Ire	0.09	0.70	1.0	11.1	−38.1	1946	53.6	1933
Ita	0.00	3.73	3.4	37.0	−64.9	1946	335.2	1944
Jap	0.14	2.98	2.9	30.7	−77.9	1945	290.2	1946
Ne	0.16	1.01	1.1	12.4	−61.6	1946	54.3	1933
NZ	−0.33	0.48	1.2	13.1	−39.7	1942	66.1	1933
Nor	0.01	0.75	1.1	12.1	−37.4	1946	46.4	1933
Prt	0.01	1.36	1.6	17.0	−52.1	1919	91.1	1924
SAf	−1.15	−0.01	1.4	15.4	−38.3	1985	60.5	1987
Spa	−0.09	1.33	1.7	18.0	−56.4	1946	128.7	1939
Swe	−0.21	0.40	1.0	11.0	−39.2	1919	41.0	1933
Swi	0.76	1.35	1.0	11.2	−29.1	1936	51.6	1933
UK	−0.22	0.43	1.1	11.4	−36.7	1946	52.6	1933
US	0.00	0.00	0.0	0.0	0.0		0.0	

Sources: DMS (2002, 2016b, 2016c).

2. A Historical Perspective on Time-Varying Expected Returns

Antti Ilmanen
AQR Capital Management, LLC[1]

Investors naturally think about the expected returns of bonds based on their market yields, thus assuming time-varying expected returns. Yet when it comes to equities, investors and academics have traditionally assumed constant expected returns and have estimated prospective returns based on long-run historical realized returns. Since the turn of the millennium, however, expected equity market returns have been increasingly seen as time varying. But can investors capture this predictability over time using real-time indicators? If the answer is yes, it seems natural to engage in market timing. As this chapter shows, however, market timing is not easy.

Introduction

This chapter discusses the evolving thinking about time-varying expected returns, the reasons behind it, and its practical relevance in today's environment of low expected returns. The increased availability of long return histories and predictive data of consistent quality enables academics and practitioners to re-examine the case for market timing. However, I argue that the pendulum may have shifted too far if investors now think that market timing (and the predictability of future returns) is easy instead of impossible.

I focus on time variation in expected *equity* market returns because equity risk dominates most investor portfolios. I show, in particular, that although contrarian indicators exhibit an apparently promising ability to predict market returns over long horizons, real-world applications using such tactical market-timing rules have a surprisingly poor empirical track record.

I draw upon history in two ways: first, to describe how financial economic thought about time-varying equity returns has evolved in recent decades;

---

[1]The views and opinions expressed herein are those of the author and do not necessarily reflect the views of AQR Capital Management, LLC (AQR), its affiliates, or its employees. This document does not represent valuation judgments, investment advice, or research with respect to any financial instrument, issuer, security, or sector that may be described or referenced herein and does not represent a formal or official view of AQR.

and second, to make use of long-run historical data on equity valuations and equity returns to assess return predictability.

Shifting Conventional Wisdom from Constant to Time-Varying Expected Returns

Bond investors may study historical returns, but for logical and empirical reasons, their estimates of prospective long-run returns almost always start from market yields.[2] In contrast, equity investors rarely use starting (dividend) yields when assessing long-run expected returns. This makes perfect sense if they assume expected returns to be constant over time: The future return could be best estimated from the long-run average of the realized return (i.e., unexpected returns should wash out over a broadly representative historical period). Long sample periods give better estimates because they mitigate sampling variation in returns, assuming that there are no structural/regime changes.

Equity market researchers have taken this approach for decades. Most of the early empirical work focused on US equity market returns: Edgar Lawrence Smith (1924); Alfred Cowles (1938); Larry Fisher and Jim Lorie (1964), linked to the creation of the CRSP (Center for Research in Security Prices) database at the University of Chicago; Roger Ibbotson and Rex Sinquefield (1976), and subsequent Ibbotson/Morningstar Yearbooks continued the tradition. Then Jorion and Goetzmann (1999) as well as Dimson, Marsh, and Staunton (2002) brought the global perspective.

Over time, the historical average return approach was refined to allow for time-varying expected cash or bond yields or inflation, plus a constant equity premium. Chapter 1 in this monograph (by Dimson, Marsh, and Staunton)[3] documents a compound annual real return of 5.0% for world equities between 1900 and 2015 and an equity premium of 3.2% over global bonds (4.2% over US Treasury bills). Thus, if the historical average real return is 5%, this is also our best forecast for the future *assuming constant expected real returns.*

---

[2]They may adjust yields for roll-down effects; mean reversion effects; or, in high credit-risk bonds, for expected default effects to get better estimates of expected returns. But yields rather than realized past returns are a natural anchor for forward-looking return estimates. If long-term bonds delivered 8% average returns in recent decades due to high starting yields and windfall gains when bond yields fell, no reasonable bond investor will assume 8% future returns if today's bond yield is 2%. (The 10-year Treasury yield was near 10% at end-1985, averaged near 5% since then, and ended 2015 near 2.2%. The average annual return over this 30-year period was near 8%.)

[3]This chapter also covers other relevant topics on estimating the historical equity premium, such as the use of arithmetic and geometric average returns, currency effects, and the impact of survivorship and success biases.

The standard asset pricing model in financial theory, Bill Sharpe's (1964) capital asset pricing model (CAPM), was a one-period model that automatically implied a constant equity premium. More directly, the random walk model of asset prices (Fama 1965; Samuelson 1965) implied unpredictable returns and constant expected returns. Fama's (1976) classic finance textbook set out the efficient market hypothesis. (Yet, despite this theory often being associated with random walk price behavior and constant expected returns, the textbook mentions the possibility of time-varying expected returns.) The academic consensus migrated toward the trinity of one-factor CAPM, efficient markets, and no return predictability.

In the 1980s, this consensus was increasingly subject to challenge based on evidence of cross-sectional "anomalies" inconsistent with the CAPM, irrational investor and behavioral explanations of market inefficiencies, and empirical evidence in favor of return predictability over time. The leading proponents of behavioral explanations included Yale's Robert Shiller and Harvard's Larry Summers (with many co-authors). Although there seemed to be little short-term predictability in market returns, claims of long-term predictability appeared much more promising—for example, stock prices that mean-revert and equity market returns predicted by dividend yields. Eugene Fama and Kenneth French (1989) argued that observed return predictability was related to business cycle fluctuations. Low stock prices and high dividend yields near cyclical troughs could be explained as rationally time-varying risk premiums. As with cross-sectional anomalies, rational and irrational camps often agreed on the empirical evidence but disagreed on its interpretation and the underlying causes.

Theoretical literature in the 1990s developed both rational (risk-based) models and irrational (behavioral) models, although most of these focused on such cross-sectional anomalies as the long-run outperformance of value stocks. Robert Shiller's book *Irrational Exuberance* (2000) highlighted the predictive (timing) ability of a market valuation indicator known as the "cyclically-adjusted price/earnings," also called the "Shiller P/E" or "CAPE" (see Campbell and Shiller 1998). This ratio smooths earnings over 10 years and inflation-adjusts prices and earnings.

Over the same two decades, market timing had developed a bad name among practitioners. The long bull market in the 1980s and 1990s made it important to be fully invested. In one famous example of "being early equals being wrong," Fidelity Magellan's portfolio manager Jeff Vinik shifted a large part of his equity fund into cash in 1995. He left Magellan a year later.

The tech boom and bust cycle around the turn of the millennium was important in shifting the conventional wisdom. As the 1990s bull market continued, estimates of the long-run equity premium based on historical average returns kept inching higher. Yet, any valuation measures based on lower starting yields should imply lower future returns (even if one does not assume mean-reverting valuations). Periods of sustained declines in required returns boost contemporaneous returns (the so-called discount rate effect) and are especially dangerous for investors who believe in constant expected returns: A rearview-mirror perspective made the equity premium seem highest at the end of a long bull market, just when market valuation ratios were flashing red. After the bust in the early 2000s, it was evident that forward-looking valuation measures had given an empirically and logically better signal than had historical average returns.

In academic circles, the behavioral school of thought was gaining ground at the expense of the efficient markets school. Robert Shiller was hailed in the news media as a prophet because he had published his book just when the NASDAQ Index peaked. In 2001, CFA Institute convened a forum of experts on the equity risk premium, and the importance of forward-looking analysis was one of the key topics.[4] In 2002, Robert Arnott and Peter Bernstein published an influential article, "What Risk Premium Is 'Normal'?" (2002), which analyzes forward-looking measures of real equity returns over two centuries and documents extreme time variation.

As often happens, reactions may lead to overreactions. It is no coincidence that market-timing strategies become popular soon after such market crashes as in 1987, 2000–2002, and 2008. Partly, this reflects hindsight bias. Such events seem more probable and predictable after a few years' hindsight than they were in real time. Crystal balls that were cloudy are forgotten, and many investors feel that they knew all along that there was a bubble (and maybe even the timing of its bursting...). When investors think that market timing is easy, the pendulum has shifted too far. Academic research on return predictability ballooned again, and among practitioners the Shiller P/E became the most widely cited market-timing measure.

The debate between constant and time-varying expected returns can also be couched as the debate regarding the perceived information in market yields (valuation ratios). Does a low market dividend yield predict low future returns (reflecting low required risk premiums or investor irrationality) or

---

[4]See CFA Institute (2002) for proceedings of this forum. The report from a follow-up event a decade later by the CFA Institute Research Foundation (*Rethinking the Equity Risk Premium* 2011) includes my chapter, "Time Variation in the Equity Risk Premium," which has some overlap to the current contribution. Also, my book *Expected Returns* (Ilmanen 2011) emphasizes the role of time-varying expected returns while calling for humility on the part of investors in their attempts to exploit them.

high future cash flow growth (reflecting growth optimism)? It must be one or the other or some combination of the two. Empirical research has shown that low dividend yields tend to precede subpar market returns rather than above-average growth. In the American Finance Association's presidential address in January 2011, Professor John Cochrane argued that there has been a full reversal in academic thinking on this question in the past 20 to 30 years:

> The equity premium is no longer thought to be constant over time. All time variation in market valuation ratios was once thought to reflect changing growth expectations (with an unchanging *ex ante* required risk premium), while now all such variation is thought to reflect changing required returns.

Not all academics agree that expected returns vary over time in a way that is captured by real-time valuation ratios. An influential study by Welch and Goyal (2008) presented a comprehensive study of numerous market predictors used in the academic literature, including the dividend yield. They concluded that these well-known predictors do not outperform a passive buy-and-hold investment when used "out of sample." In the rest of this chapter, I review some of the evidence on return predictability, focusing on value or contrarian signals.

Another strand of literature studied time-varying expected returns and market-timing opportunities through the lens of boom/bust episodes—such as tulip mania, the South Sea Bubble, and the 1907, 1929, and 1974 equity market crashes—mainly using descriptive rather than statistical analysis. This approach is clearly contrarian. Implicitly, this timing approach involved identifying unsustainable bubbles and selling risky assets before the bust materialized (see Kindleberger 1978; see also Goetzmann's Chapter 9 in this monograph, where he emphasizes the role of hindsight in bubble identification).

An opposite, procyclical approach to market timing can be dated back to at least 1819, when David Ricardo captured the spirit of trend following in his advice: "Cut short your losses. Let your profits run on." As a famous practitioner example, William Peter Hamilton's Dow theory had a procyclical flavor. Alfred Cowles (1933) concluded that Hamilton's editorials in the *Wall Street Journal* between 1902 and 1929 had a poor track record in market timing, but later research by Brown et al. (1998) drew a contrary conclusion: Risk-adjusting his performance vindicates Hamilton as a market timer.

State of the Art: How to Predict Asset Returns?

In *Expected Returns: An Investor's Guide to Harvesting Market Rewards* (Ilmanen 2011), I argue that the assessment of expected returns is as much art as science. The challenge is to refine the art of prediction. Investors should exploit all our knowledge about historical experience, theories, and current market yields and valuations without being overly dependent on any one of these three anchors.

What does financial theory say about why expected returns should vary over time? As is the case with cross-sectional strategies (average return differences between assets), any time variation in expected returns can be explained by either rational or irrational theories.

- Rational explanations include time-varying volatility, time-varying risk aversion, and time-varying risk of rare disasters. Time-series analysis borrows one main intuition from cross-sectional analysis: Assets that perform poorly in bad times should earn higher returns as a form of compensation. Hence, forward-looking required risk premiums should be higher after bad times; for example, the equity premium should be higher after recessions and financial crises. (These explanations are mainly cyclical. Note, however, that there are also secular explanations for the apparent decline in required equity market returns: lower macro volatility, lower trading costs, and easier investor access to passive global equity portfolios.)

- Irrational explanations often rely on time-varying investor sentiment, cycles of greed and fear, as well as social interactions (see, for example, Shiller 2000).

It is almost impossible to disentangle these explanations for predictable returns, but survey-based evidence clearly sides with irrational explanations. The consensus in survey-based return expectations is often bullish when rational valuation measures suggest low required (and thus rationally expected) returns (see Ilmanen 2011, Chapter 8.5; Greenwood and Shleifer 2014).

As noted, valuation-based indicators are the most widely used measures of market conditions and timing signals, but the literature is filled with other indicators.

- Arguably, the second-most important indicator is recent price momentum, or trend. Across assets and over time, recent outperformance tends to persist (for time-series evidence, see Moskowitz, Ooi, and Pedersen 2012). Good performance in recent months (up to a year but not over multiple years) tends to be followed by further good performance, and vice versa. Value and momentum signals tend to be negatively correlated because often an asset that is cheap today tends to have performed poorly in the past. When the two signals agree—for example, in the market-timing context when the market is cheap and has recently begun to improve—the double signal is especially strong.

- There are timing indicators other than value and momentum, but these often resemble either long-run value or short-term momentum. For example, both too-loose credit conditions (value-like) and tightening credit conditions (momentum-like) are bearish market indicators.

- Over long horizons, value and yield indicators tend to have the best predictive ability; over short horizons, momentum and macro indicators are more helpful. No tactical indicators are particularly reliable for near-term market timing. Although predictability results look more promising over longer horizons, their practical usefulness is limited.

Focus on Value- or Yield-Based Expected Returns

Even when restricted to yield-based expected returns, there are many candidates. Given that no uniquely correct measure exists, I present two commonly used measures. The first is the expected real return based on the *inverse* of the Shiller P/E (E/P or earnings yield, using past-decade earnings). The second is based on the dividend discount model (DDM): a sum of dividend yield and the real trend growth of dividends-per-share (DPS) or earnings-per-share (EPS), where I simply used a constant growth of 1.5% to reflect the long-run real growth in DPS and EPS. Conceptually, the DDM includes a third term besides yield and growth: the expected change in market valuations. Assume that this term is zero, or in other words, that today's above-average valuations could be sustainable in the future. At the end of 2014, both metrics suggest expected long-run real returns of 3–4% for US equities, near 4% for the Shiller E/P, and 3.2% (1.7% D/P + 1.5% growth) for the DDM. Assuming mean-reverting valuations would make the predictions more bearish. Other forecasters could be more bullish if they assume faster growth or boost the dividend yield due to net buybacks.

Figure 2.1 traces these two expected real return proxies all the way back to 1900 and compares them with the next-decade average realized real return for the US equity market. There are several things to point out in the chart:

- Both expected return series exhibit wide variations over time with similar contours. Equities offered especially high expected returns (i.e., their valuations were low) in the early 1920s, through the Great Depression of the 1930s, and in the stagflationary 1970s/80s. Equities offered especially low expected returns in the late 1920s, mid-1960s, late 1990s, and recently. There is a secular downtrend, and the latest

Figure 2.1. Two Proxies for the Expected Real Return of US Stocks and the Next-Decade Realized Real Return, January 1900–December 2014

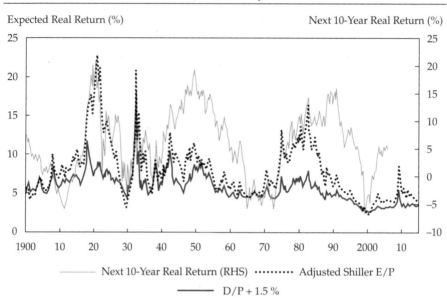

Sources: The adjusted Shiller E/P and dividend yield are from Robert Shiller's website. The adjusted Shiller E/P scales up the normal Shiller E/P by 1.075 to correct for the fact that the 10-year average of an EPS series that grows over time will systematically underestimate its current value (the scalar reflects assumed real trend growth of 1.5% and 5-year average staleness). US equity market returns are from the S&P 500 Index, and its predecessors are from Global Financial Data (GFD), Ibbotson/Morningstar, and Datastream. Realized equity return calculations are from AQR.

observations are among the lowest 10% of the full history (i.e., equity valuations look rich historically).

- Both expected return series appear to predict next-decade realized returns of the S&P 500 Index (or its predecessor large-cap indices). The forecasts were especially good during the first half of the sample. The biggest forecast failure occurred in the 1990s, when both predictors forecasted low returns but the bull market extended until the year 2000 before reversing.

Promising Forecasting Ability and Disappointing Reality

Figure 2.1 looks visually promising in terms of return-forecasting ability and may entice investors to use these yield-based measures as contrarian market-timing indicators. Indeed, the full-sample correlation between the timing indicators and next-decade returns is 0.57 for the Shiller E/P and 0.42 for "dividend yield plus growth." From now on, I focus only on the stronger of the two predictors, the Shiller E/P.

Figure 2.2 displays a common way to summarize the strength of the predictive relation in a bar chart. Every quarter since 1900 is sorted into one of five quintiles based on the ranking of starting yields (Shiller E/Ps), and the average real return over the subsequent decade for all observations within each quintile is then computed. The monotonic pattern in Figure 2.2 shows that periods with low starting yields (quintile 1, expensive valuations) tend to be followed by low future returns; periods with high starting yields (quintile 5, cheap valuations) tend to be followed by high future returns. Arguably, this situation looks even more promising for putative market timers than that shown in Figure 2.1.

However, let's get more realistic. First, this evidence is "in-sample," and second, it may not work as well over shorter horizons.

- Using in-sample data means to assume investors knew, in real-time, in which quintile the indicator is for the full 1900–2014 period. For example, it would have been valuable to know in the 1930s that markets will be on average much more expensive in future decades. This is called

Figure 2.2. Next-Decade Real US Equity Return Sorted by Starting Yield (Shiller E/P), 1900–2014

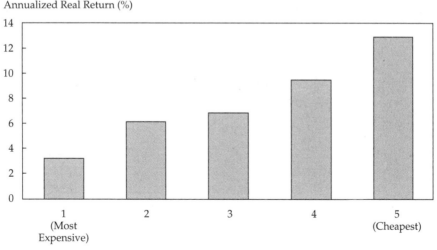

Sources: The smoothed earnings yield is from Robert Shiller's website. US equity market returns are from GFD, Ibbotson/Morningstar, and Datastream. Realized equity return calculations are from AQR. These are not the returns of actual AQR portfolios and are for illustrative purposes only.

hindsight bias. A more realistic "out-of-sample" approach involves sorting starting yields by comparing the current starting yield with, say, the *preceding* 60 years' rolling average level.

- Moreover, few market timers would consider trading once a decade based on their chosen market-timing signal and then leaving their portfolios untouched for the next decade. Asness, Ilmanen, and Maloney (Forthcoming 2016) explores a monthly trading horizon and many other variants of trading rules that try to address how a tactical market timer can use information in the Shiller E/P. They find that with various specifications, contrarian market timing could not meaningfully outperform the buy-and-hold strategy and often even lagged it. I provide similar evidence below for a slightly simpler trading rule.

Removing the hindsight bias and shortening the horizon reveal a more realistic picture. Predictability patterns are weaker if "out-of-sample" data are used, more so if a shorter horizon is used. Still, there is a positive relation over the full sample. The real disappointment comes when data are presented in a different way.

Figure 2.3 compares the cumulative performance (over cash) of a buy-and-hold investment in US stocks with a contrarian timing strategy. The contrarian timing strategy overweights stocks when starting yields are high (150% allocation when yields are in the top quintile, 125% when in the second quintile) and underweights them when starting yields are low (50% allocation when in the bottom quintile, 75% when in the fourth quintile), with quarterly rebalancing. The contrarian timing strategy did outperform the buy-and-hold strategy mildly over the full 115-year period, but the edge is not visually impressive (and the contrarian strategy, which uses leverage, turned out to have higher volatility and thus a slightly lower Sharpe ratio). Perhaps worse, the lowest line shows that all the outperformance relative to the buy-and-hold strategy occurred in the first half of the sample; most readers can say that the contrarian strategy has underperformed buy-and-hold during our lifetime! (You can specify such trading rules in a variety of ways; I tried numerous variants with somewhat varying results but never found compelling success.) Welch and Goyal (2008), Dimson et al. (2013), and Asness et al. (Forthcoming 2016) all document underwhelming out-of-sample performance of contrarian equity market-timing signals.)

This result was surprising, especially given that bar charts like in Figure 2.2 seemed promising, so I drilled deeper to understand the reasons for the underwhelming success. I identified three key reasons.

Figure 2.3. **Cumulative Excess Return of US Equity Timing Strategy Based on Shiller E/P, 1900–2014**

A. Cumulative Excess Return of Buy-and-Hold and Contrarian Timing Strategies

Cumulative Excess Return

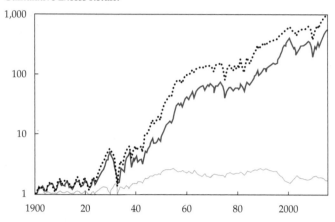

B. Timing Stategy's Proposed Weight on US Equity Market

Timing Signal (%)

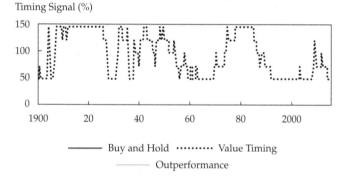

——— Buy and Hold ·········· Value Timing
——— Outperformance

Sources: The smoothed earnings yields are from Robert Shiller's website. US equity market returns are from GFD, Ibbotson/Morningstar, and Datastream. Realized equity return calculations are from AQR. These are not the returns of actual AQR portfolios. Value timing is a hypothetical US equity timing strategy that rebalances each quarter, applying a tactical weight of 0.5, 0.75, 1.0, 1.25, or 1.5 depending on the latest Shiller E/P quintile and based on a rolling 60-year sample (with an expanding window until 1940). Returns are gross of transaction costs and fees.

1. *An adverse window for contrarian investing.* The underperformance since the 1950s partly reflects the fact that the contrarian timing strategy resulted in an underinvestment in equities, on average. US equity market valuations experienced a gradual rerating in the second half of the 20th century (the E/P more than halved), which meant that a contrarian market timer would have been "waiting for the market to come back to him or her," but it rarely did. As a result, the average holding in the equity index since the mid-1950s was 80% instead of the expected 100%, so the market-timer forfeited one fifth of the realized equity premium.

2. *The difficulty of getting the timing right.* Had the market-timing signals been accurate enough over equity market cycles, they could have easily offset the secular headwinds from the underinvestment in equities due to their long-term rerating. However, market-timing signals are accurate only with the benefit of hindsight, where it may have been easy to buy near market lows and sell near highs. In reality, contrarian indicators give relatively coarse signals and too often recommend buying or selling too early in a cycle. Our favorite data point is to stress that if a market timer would have decided to stay in the equity market most of the time but exit it when the valuation signal showed worst-quintile richness, he/she would have sold stocks already in 1992 when the Shiller E/P fell below the 20th percentile (the lower panel in Figure 2.3 shows the evolution of the percentile since 1900). It is likely that no professional investor would have survived in the job during the roaring 1990s with that position. Even the tech bust in the early 2000s or the later global financial crisis did not bring equity markets back to their 1992 levels. The "early equals wrong" lesson from this story is highly relevant today when bonds, stocks, and most other asset classes appear historically rich (offering abnormally low real yields). Investors tempted to move risky asset holdings into cash should ask themselves if they have the patience to stay in cash for several years in the plausible scenario where the current low-yield environment persists several more years.

3. *Headwinds from short-term momentum.* Recall that financial assets tend to exhibit trending behavior (return persistence) over multi-month windows. This partly explains why contrarian signals are more often than not "too early." Momentum implies that cheap things tend to get cheaper before they normalize (and vice versa for rich things). Contrarian value signals tend to be most efficient at prediction when used over a 2- to 3-year horizon when the momentum headwinds have passed and before the value signal begins to decay.

How Can Investors Better Take Advantage of Time-Varying Expected Returns?

One constructive approach for tactical market timers is to combine both contrarian and momentum signals; for example, when market valuations signal cheapness, it may be worth waiting for a confirmatory signal from momentum that the market has turned. Investors could broaden the set of predictors even beyond these two central signals to various macro and sentiment indicators. Others prefer a discretionary approach instead of the systematic methods covered here.

If investors had to choose only one type of market-timing approach, historical experience would, surprisingly to many, suggest ignoring valuations and applying instead the opposite of contrarian strategies—that is, procyclical strategies. Trend-following certainly has a better historical track record than contrarian timing. Trend-following is a directional strategy that invests in a diverse set of liquid assets based on the past 1 to 12 months' performance, and it has given positive long-run average returns in dozens of assets studied (with interim losses, of course, and always missing the market turn). The edge when timing any single asset tends to be modest, but the risk-adjusted return on a diversified trend-following portfolio looks attractive over histories longer than arguably any other investment can claim. Hurst, Ooi, and Pedersen (2014) use "only" a century of data on trend-following. Lempérière et al. (2014) do better with two centuries, and Greyserman and Kaminski (2014) boast a history of 700 years! Despite such evidence, many institutional investors find this strategy a poor cultural fit, unlike the contrarian approach, and also worry that its profits will not be sustainable (and will be soon arbitraged away) because the main explanations for these profits are behavioral and not rational or risk based.

Even the most realistic market-timing models analyzed (the unrealistic ones rely heavily on data mining and overfitting) do not suggest that timing is easy. At best, they can provide some edge with which investors can modify their strategic asset allocations with appropriate humility. The challenge is formidable because short-term return predictability is limited; holding on to underperforming positions is difficult, and the risk in market-directional positions is concentrated.

The last point emphasizes the general problem with market-timing strategies: lack of diversification. This aspect may have motivated Paul Samuelson's dictum that financial markets may be micro-efficient but macro-inefficient because it is so hazardous to battle (or "arbitrage") mispriced markets by timing strategies. The reasons go back to the famous comment, usually attributed to John Maynard Keynes, that "the market can stay irrational longer than you can remain solvent." Thus, strategic diversification may be a better path to investment success than tactical timing.[5]

Conclusion

The first part of this chapter described the important shift in academic and practitioner thinking to the point of view that expected returns are not constant but time varying. The later sections then delivered the sobering message that exploiting this time variation is so difficult that most investors are better off resisting the temptation to try. Thus, while we have focused on the predictability of equity markets, we finish with a call for better diversification: Well-diversified strategic exposures across many rewarded factors may be the most reliable way to earn consistent long-term returns.

---

[5]This chapter focuses on the equity premium, which according to the CAPM is the only long-run source of excess returns. Newer research emphasizes that we live in a multi-factor world instead of the CAPM's one-factor world. Some risks are not rewarded in the long run—such as stock-specific risk or industry risk—so we should try to diversify them away in line with the CAPM's prescriptions. But some factors are well rewarded in the long run. We should diversify across several of them, harvesting not just the equity premium but also other asset class premiums (such as the term premium for bonds), illiquidity premiums (such as possible rewards for illiquid alternative assets), and style premiums (such as the long-run outperformance of value stocks and momentum stocks over their peers). Each of these factors might offer time-varying expected rewards just as the equity premium does, so we might consider using similar value and momentum indicators for timing them. Yet, deeper analysis shows that tactical timing of these other return sources is no easier than tactical timing of equity markets. Assuming constant long-run rewards for factors you believe in may be a reasonable basis for strategic diversification.

Bibliography

Arnott, Robert D., and Peter L. Bernstein. 2002. "What Risk Premium Is 'Normal'?" *Financial Analysts Journal*, vol. 58, no. 2: 64–85.

Asness, Clifford S., Antti Ilmanen, and Thomas Maloney. Forthcoming 2016. "Market Timing: Sin a Little." AQR white paper.

Brown, Stephen J., William N. Goetzmann, and Alok Kumar. 1998. "The Dow Theory: William Peter Hamilton's Track Record Reconsidered." *Journal of Finance*, vol. 53, no. 4: 1311–1333.

Campbell, John Y., and Robert J. Shiller. 1998. "Valuation Ratios and the Long-Run Stock Market Outlook." *Journal of Portfolio Management*, vol. 24: 11–26.

CFA Institute. 2002. "Proceedings of the Equity Risk Premium Forum." Association for Investment Management and Research (now CFA Institute) and TIAA-CREF (www.cfapubs.org/toc/cp.1/2002/7).

Cochrane, John. 2011. "'Discount Rates.' Presidential Address at the American Finance Association meeting." *Journal of Finance*, vol. 66: 1047–1108.

Cowles, Alfred. 1933. "Can Stock Market Forecasters Forecast?" *Econometrica*, vol. 1, no. 3: 309–324.

———. 1938. *Common Stock Indices, 1871–1937*. Cowles Commission for Research in Economics, Monograph No. 3. Bloomington, IN: Principia Press.

Dimson, Elroy, Paul Marsh, and Mike Staunton. 2002. *Triumph of the Optimists: 101 Years of Global Investment Returns*. Princeton, NJ: Princeton University Press.

———. 2013. *Global Investment Returns Yearbook 2013*. Zurich: Credit Suisse Research Institute.

———. 2016. "Long-Term Asset Returns." In *Financial Market History*. Edited by David Chambers and Elroy Dimson. Charlottesville, VA: CFA Institute Research Foundation.

Fama, Eugene F. 1965. "The Behavior of Stock Market Prices." *Journal of Business*, vol. 38, no. 1: 34–105.

———. 1976. *Foundations of Finance: Portfolio Decisions and Securities Prices.* New York: Basic Books.

Fama, Eugene F., and Kenneth R. French. 1989. "Business Conditions and Expected Returns on Stocks and Bonds." *Journal of Financial Economics*, vol. 25, no. 1: 23–49.

Fisher, Lawrence, and James H. Lorie. 1964. "Rates of Return on Investments in Common Stocks." *Journal of Business*, vol. 37, no. 1: 1–21.

Goetzmann, William N. 2016. "Bubble Investing: Learning from History." In *Financial Market History*. Edited by David Chambers and Elroy Dimson. Charlottesville, VA: CFA Institute Research Foundation.

Greenwood, Robin, and Andrei Shleifer. 2014. "Expectations of Returns and Expected Returns." *Review of Financial Studies*, vol. 27, no. 3: 714–746.

Greyserman, Alex, and Kathryn Kaminski. 2014. *Trend Following with Managed Futures.* Wiley Trading.

Hammond, P. Brett, Martin L. Leibowitz, and Laurence B. Siegel, eds. 2011. *Rethinking the Equity Risk Premium.* Charlottesville, VA: CFA Institute Research Foundation.

Hurst, Brian, Yao Hua Ooi, and Lasse Heje Pedersen. 2014. "A Century of Evidence on Trend-Following Investing." AQR white paper.

Ibbotson, Roger G., and Rex A. Sinquefield. 1976. "Stocks, Bonds, Bills and Inflation: Simulations of the Future 1976-2000." *Journal of Business*, vol. 49, no. 3: 313–338.

Ilmanen, Antti. 2011. *Expected Returns: An Investor's Guide to Harvesting Market Rewards.* Chichester, West Sussex, UK: Wiley.

Jorion, Philippe, and William N. Goetzmann. 1999. "Global Stock Markets in the Twentieth Century." *Journal of Finance*, vol. 54, no. 3: 953–980.

Kindleberger, Charles P. 1978. *Manias, Panics, and Crashes: A History of Financial Crises.* New York: Basic Books.

Lempérière, Yves, Cyril Deremble, Philip Seager, Marc Potters, and Jean Philippe Bouchaud. 2014. "Two Centuries of Trend Following." Capital Fund Management white paper.

Moskowitz, Tobias, Yao Hua Ooi, and Lasse Heje Pedersen. 2012. "Time Series Momentum." *Journal of Financial Economics*, vol. 104, no. 2: 228–250.

Samuelson, Paul A. 1965. "Proof That Properly Anticipated Prices Fluctuate Randomly." *Industrial Management Review*, vol. 6, no. 2: 41–49.

Sharpe, William F. 1964. "Capital Asset Prices: A Theory of Market Equilibrium under Conditions of Risk." *Journal of Finance*, vol. 19, no. 3: 425–442.

Shiller, Robert. 2000. *Irrational Exuberance.* Princeton, NJ: Princeton University Press.

Smith, Edgar Lawrence. 1924. *Common Stocks as Long-Term Investments.* New York: MacMillan.

Welch, Ivo, and Amit Goyal. 2008. "A Comprehensive Look at the Empirical Performance of Equity Premium Prediction." *Review of Financial Studies*, vol. 21: 1455–1508.

3. Financial History Databases: Old Data, Old Issues, New Insights?

Jan Annaert
Professor, University of Antwerp and Antwerp Management School

Frans Buelens
Senior Researcher, University of Antwerp

Angelo Riva
Private Professor, European Business School—Paris and Affiliate Researcher, Paris School of Economics

In this chapter, we draw attention to the potential flaws historical financial data sets might embed. The way in which historical financial data have been gathered and constructed is even more important than for recent data. For data users, overlooking these potential flaws can affect the reliability of the underlying analysis. For data collectors, considering them can lead to data of better quality. To illustrate, we first discuss the general issues that may affect stock and bond data. Next, we examine in more detail the data items needed to construct equity and bond market indices as well as the consequences of not having these items. An appendix provides an overview of the existing cross-sectional historical datasets

Introduction

The recent financial crisis again highlighted the weak empirical foundations of the economic and financial analytical models used to study stakeholder expectations, financial innovation, regulations, and investment strategies. One reason for this shortcoming is the scarcity of long-run financial micro-data available to test the theoretical models, especially when allowing for structural changes, which are vital to evaluating the impact of financial regulation, the causes of economic fluctuations, and interactions between economic (if not demographic and social) changes and the financial system. But long-run financial micro-data are even more useful for both traders and investors looking for synoptic, accurate, and easily accessible information on securities markets to outline, explain, and backtest their strategies. Both security market indices and cross-sectional information on individual securities are therefore crucial to economists as well as financial market participants.

As a consequence, interest and efforts in building long-run securities market data and indices have grown rapidly over recent years. However, databases containing security-specific information over broader time periods are still remarkably scarce and scattered in the literature. Country indices reflecting the performance of bond and equity markets are more easily available, thanks to the contributions of Jorion and Goetzmann (1999); Dimson, Marsh, and Staunton (DMS 2002); and Global Financial Data (2005). Rather than constructing these series from primary sources, usually several existing series have been spliced. Unfortunately, these underlying series were not all constructed with the same objective, so their coverage is heterogeneous. Moreover, a variety of construction rules were used, some of which no longer meet present-day standards. Comparisons across time and space are therefore difficult and potentially hazardous to unaware users. Nevertheless, with a few remarkable exceptions,[1] the methodology of indices is too little discussed today in both the academic and business worlds.

This chapter, therefore, examines the main issues facing economists and practitioners when dealing with long-run financial indices. The way in which historical financial data have been gathered and constructed is even more important than for recent data. For data users, overlooking the potential flaws in the construction of indices can affect the reliability of the analysis. For data collectors, considering them when designing their work can lead to data of better quality. After discussing the general issues affecting broad market indices, we turn to specific issues related to equity indices and then to bond indices. In the appendix, we summarize the available cross-sectional data sets. We conclude that, with a few exceptions, it is difficult and problematic to compare the performance of broad indices correctly, both over time and across countries. We would therefore welcome additional efforts to increase the coverage of existing series, both cross-sectionally and further back in time. We also believe that, given the variety of purposes market indices may be used for, increasing the availability of high quality micro-data is crucial: It will allow for the construction of the pertinent index for the given purpose.

General Issues

When studying the long-run performance of stock and bond indices, attention should be paid to several issues that may affect research, particularly in diachronic and comparative perspectives.

According to DMS (2000a, p. 6), the more pervasive problem in existing long-run financial data is the "easy data" bias. Scholars often focus on

---

[1] See DMS (2000a; 2002).

easily available historical sources and omit troubled periods from their analysis. Historical sources that publish securities data are often hidden in distant archives with stringent rules and are thus difficult to access. This increases the cost of data collection and explains why secondary sources are relied on. Unfortunately, these secondary sources are also "second best," because they summarize the data without explicitly stating the methodology employed or informing the user about potential biases.

For instance, prices may not reflect the most relevant market. Take the case of Paris, where some securities were listed both on the official and the over-the-counter (OTC) market in the 19th century (Hautcoeur, Rezaee, and Riva 2010). However, even though the OTC market was by far the more important market for many securities, including the French consols, secondary sources still used prices from the official market (see Rist 1913). Even scholars building historical series often focus on the primary sources of the official market because they are more easily accessible (e.g., Vaslin 2007).

In addition, such troubled periods as wars, times of political unrest, and radical changes in economic regimes are often omitted. First, sources are often rare and difficult to interpret for these periods. Second, the rapid institutional changes (e.g., periods of nationalizations) often require huge efforts to make data coherent with the previous ones. Third, markets are typically closed during these troubled times and/or stringent regulations prevent market forces from acting. As a consequence, many return series start after these events but are nevertheless considered to be representative of the entire period. For example, the UK Barclays de Zoete Wedd Equity Index (BZW) starting in 1919, after World War I, overstates UK returns during the period 1919–1954 by 2.34% relative to the DMS Index beginning in 1900. Furthermore, markets can be closed for many years. The Portuguese case is a good example (DMS 2000b). The Lisbon Exchange closed down in the aftermath of the Carnation Revolution in April 1974 and didn't resume trading until March 1977. As a result, some assumptions are needed to compute a long-run Portuguese index (Da Costa, Mata, and Justino 2012).

Another problem involves selection bias. Generally speaking, it refers to the corruption of statistical analysis resulting from the sampling process. In finance, the tendency to focus on the larger companies may lead to underestimated returns as analysts miss the higher returns offered by firms with low market value (Banz 1981). It is the approach chosen, for example, by Le Bris and Hautcoeur (2010) for France when they focused on the largest 40 companies. However, such bias may be sample or period specific as Annaert, Buelens, Cuyvers, De Ceuster, Deloof, and De Schepper (2011) show, with data from the Brussels Stock Exchange, that a return index of the 20 largest stocks produces results broadly similar to those of an all-share return index in terms of average returns, risk, and industrial composition over the period 1833–2005. The selection of value stocks with high fundamentals-to-price ratios (or their opposite, glamour stocks with low ratios) can also significantly alter returns (Chan, Jegadeesh, Lakonishok 1995; Desai, Rajgopal, and Venkatachalam 2004). When from the outset some industries are omitted from the selection, returns may be affected. For example, DMS (2000a) report that standard UK equity indices do not take into account the railroad sector, although it represented about one-half of the UK capitalization in 1900.

Survivorship bias is a special case of selection bias. It concerns both companies and markets. As far as companies are concerned, it is the tendency in performance studies to consider only the securities of issuers that survived up to the end of the period studied. By excluding delisted securities, backtests of investment strategies can lead to optimistic results simply because a majority of delistings result from failures. As a consequence, survival bias may contribute to the equity premium puzzle. This is an empirical matter: Brown, Goetzmann, and Ross (1995) argue that survivorship bias can explain much of the US equity premium, although Li and Xu (2002) argue that this bias is not significant in the US case. In terms of markets, survivorship bias refers to the fact that the historical experience of markets that disappeared is usually neglected. For instance, with 5.2% of estimated world equity market capitalization, Austria–Hungary was the 6th largest market in 1900; however, its series was only added to the DMS database in 2013 (DMS 2015). Likewise, indices of markets that re-emerged or completely disappeared also warrant attention. Recently, efforts have been made to reconstruct Russian (Goetzmann and Huang 2015) and Chinese indices (Fan 2010). Having similar data on such formerly important or promising markets as Argentina, India, or Hong Kong would be beneficial for risk–return studies.

Delisting often influences returns of securities when it is not taken into account by existing historical financial databases, resulting in delisting bias. Delisting is usually associated with specific firm events—such as bankruptcy, liquidation, mergers and acquisitions, or migration to another exchange—that often negatively affect the returns of the security. Furthermore, the variation in the liquidity of the delisted securities may structurally alter the returns and prices at which investors are willing to transact. Without including the return after delisting, it is not possible to calculate returns of a feasible portfolio. The sources often are mute on the reasons for a delisting, as is the case for the *Investor's Monthly Manual* (IMM), the London Stock Exchange yearbook.[2] To adjust the British equity index for this bias, Grossman (2002) formulates and discusses no fewer than four hypotheses. The bias also affects CRSP (Center for Research in Security Prices) data. Shumway (1997) and Shumway and Warther (1999) find that the size of missing delisting returns in CRSP data is significant. Annaert, Buelens, and De Ceuster (2012) identify 477 delistings from the Brussels Stock Exchange between 1832 and 1914. If one assumes that all delistings for unknown reasons have a delisting return of –100%, the compound average index return drops from 5.33% to 5.09% per year. Compounded over the entire period, this small annual difference reduces the end-of-period wealth by 23%.

The indices that are available are not necessarily representative of the investable universe. Because market capitalizations are not easily available for earlier periods (related sources are often scarce, scattered, and heavy to handle), indices often use equal or price weights (Goetzmann, Ibbotson, and Peng 2001) and therefore do not fully capture the average investor's investment experience. Indeed, Annaert et al. (2012) show that there are important differences between market cap-weighted returns, equal-weighted returns, and price-weighted returns in Brussels from 1832 to 1914.

Another concern is the non-synchronous trading effect, which has two elements. The first occurs *within* a single market: Scholars often rely on the first or the last price of the day for their analysis, but these events do not systematically occur at the same time for each security. According to Campbell, Lo, and MacKinlay (1997), this effect creates a non-negligible bias in the moments and co-moments of returns (means, variances, covariances, betas, and autocorrelation and cross-autocorrelation coefficients). The second element arises when the relationships *among* several markets are examined. Not only are the opening and closing times different among markets in the same time zone, but markets are also located in different time zones. In addition, markets are often closed because of different national and religious holidays, unexpected bank holidays, etc. As a consequence, return observations are not synchronous (Eun and Shim 1989; Olbrys and Majewska 2014). Of course, this is less of an issue at lower data frequencies.

The informational content and the behavior of securities' prices can vary according to the price discovery system adopted by the exchange. Different

---

[2] According to the International Center of Finance (ICF), Yale School of Management: "The *Investor's Monthly Manual* (IMM), a record of The London Exchange, exists in hard copy for the period from 1871 to 1930, the peak of the colonial era... The ICF received a grant from a generous donor to transform this data into an electronic database that can be downloaded, manipulated and analyzed by scholars." See http://som.yale.edu/faculty-research/our-centers-initiatives/international-center-finance/data/historical-financial-research-data/london-stock-exchange.

securities can be traded according to different systems. Not only do the systems vary within the same exchange, but particularly before the diffusion of the electronic order book, the price discovery systems varied strongly among exchanges. For example, the different levels of transparency can affect price behavior. Similarly, the adoption of an order-driven market instead of a price-driven market may influence price formation, the former being typically more transparent but less immediate than the latter. The adoption of fixings, which are the concentration and matching of orders at one moment in time, may smooth volatility relative to continuous trading. Furthermore, some securities can be traded not only on the spot market but also on the forward and option markets, which may result in higher liquidity on the spot market and lower volatility than for securities traded only on spot. Hautcoeur et al. (2010) find such effects when analyzing prices from the Paris official and OTC markets. Likewise, listing requirements affect the characteristics of the quoted securities and consequently price behavior.

Prices and dividends are stated as nominal values, while inflation is a big issue over the course of time. For long historical time series, nominal values are almost useless and have to be corrected for inflation. Good inflation data are crucial for transforming nominal data into real data. The standards used to compute them vary widely across countries. Past inflation data are often of poor quality for many countries, especially during such periods as world wars, when inflation measures are highly questionable.

Stocks

Issues of data quality vary according to which data item is being studied. Issues with prices, dividends, capital operations, exchange rates, number of shares outstanding, and inflation can profoundly influence calculations. As indicated previously, returns are usually computed from end-of-period to end-of-period, but not always. For example, in studying the Boston market, Atack and Rousseau (1999) construct price and return indices for 1835–1869 from annual highest and lowest prices. Due to the imprecise timing of returns constructed in this way, the corresponding price and return indices are hardly comparable to those using precisely timed data. In the same way, the famous Cowles U.S. 1871–1937 Indices are based on an average of the lowest and highest monthly prices (Goetzmann et al. 2001, p. 3), a method that introduces autocorrelation and reduces apparent volatility.

When transcribing prices from original sources, care should be taken to correctly interpret the numbers. Indeed, occasionally prices are reported as a profit or loss compared to initial or par value, as with insurance companies on the Paris stock exchange where prices were quoted as "...% Profits (Bénéfice)" or "...% Losses (Perte)" in the early 19th century (Compagnie des Agents de change près de la Bourse de Paris, 1796-1848; Duneau and Rietsch 2008). Moreover, the way in which prices are reported may switch over time from absolute value to percentages or vice versa. Additionally, the prices can be based on the share's par value, whereas only 10% or 20% was paid-up (with the obligation to pay the remaining amount on demand). Such a stock is, in fact, a combination of a stock and an option (Acheson, Hickson, Turner, and Ye 2009).

Reported prices are not necessarily transaction prices. Sources can publish the average of some or all prices of the day or quoted bid and ask as the *Investor's Monthly Manual* does. If no transaction took place, either bid or ask prices or the previous transaction price may be reported. If this problem lasts for a longer period, the issue of sticky or stale prices arises. In addition, the currency of denomination may change over time, as for example in France, where in 1960 the French franc changed to the "new French franc" at a rate of 100 old to 1 new. Stocks may even be simultaneously quoted in different currencies, as was the case in China for the Shanghai Stock Exchange Indices, 1870–1940, with pounds, dollars, and local currencies all being quoted at the same time (Fan 2010).

The availability of dividends is often a bigger problem than the availability of prices, although dividends are extremely important given that the larger part of total return is from dividend income rather than capital gains. Missing dividends, therefore, give rise to all kinds of second-best estimation methods. For example, the Dutch return data used in the DMS dataset (based on Eichholtz, Koedijk, and Otten 2000) were constructed as follows: For 1900–1919, prices and dividends were taken from only 30 stocks listed on the Amsterdam stock exchange (of which a majority were companies in the Dutch East Indies). In addition, missing dividends for 1919–1951 were estimated to be 5.2% per year; that is, the average dividend yield for the periods 1890–1920 and 1952–1999 was used as the estimate for the missing years. In other cases, an average dividend yield was computed using only dividend-paying shares, biasing the dividend yield estimate upward (because many companies did not pay dividends). Similar heroic assumptions have been made for some periods in Australia (Brailsford, Handley, and Maheswaran 2008).

Needless to say, such methods can only proxy for actual returns. But even if dividends are available, they may be reported as annual dividends per book year without knowing the ex-coupon day. Or they are reported as percentages of nominal value for the year as a whole without dividing them into different ex-coupon days (it was quite common to have two or even four ex-coupon days a year). In that case, dividends are often simply added to the return in the calendar year, at year end, or spread *pro rata temporis* across the year. Although this procedure may not harm long-run average return estimates, it can impact volatility calculations and may even spuriously introduce seasonality. Moreover, sources sometimes report dividends in other currencies, requiring the availability of corresponding exchange rates. For example, Russian stocks quoted on Western European stock exchanges before 1917 often paid out dividends in rubles. The fact that several kinds of rubles coexisted only complicates correct return computation. Finally, dividends can be net or gross of taxation. Because taxation differs across countries, varies among investors, and changes over time, it is usually best to calculate returns before taxes.

Correct calculation of returns also crucially depends on the availability of information on securities events, such as (reverse) stock splits, inscription rights, or bonus rights. Unfortunately, such information is neither always easily available nor documented for long historical periods. For example, based on looking for suspicious one-month price drops of, say, 50% (as evidence of a split), Goetzmann et al. (2001) report finding no splits before 1900, although the phenomenon is quite well observed in other markets. Moreover, those events cannot always be inferred from price data alone because they tend to occur simultaneously. For example, in 1927 the National Bank of Belgium had 50,000 shares listed. An important operation affecting the bank's equity capital took place in April 1927, and the price went down from 7,950 to 2,670 Belgian francs (BEF). But, based on this price information only, it is not possible to identify the event because it was a combination of a secondary equity offering (50,000 new shares) and a one-to-three stock split (*Recueil Financier*[3]). Finally, the exact timing of a corporate action is important, even more than for dividend payments. For example, the Union Minière du Haut-Katanga stock[4] (quoted in Brussels) experienced a 1:10 split in January 1955. As a result, its price dropped from 48,600 BEF to 4,780 BEF; however, in exactly the same month, a dividend was reported of 600 BEF for each of the old shares. Obviously, the dividend needs to be divided by 10 when using the price of the new shares to compute returns.

Companies have often issued many types of stock, such as founders stock, privileged stocks, and multiple voting rights stocks. Their characteristics differ, with some having limited and/or special shareholder rights. Therefore, it is common practice to divide such types into two categories: common stocks and preferred stocks. Common stock is identified as having all the usual

---

[3] The Institute for Financial Archeology has digitalized the *Recueil Financier*, which is the only known yearbook to cover Brussels' finance and financiers from 1893–1975. This information was found at Recueil Financier 1930, I, p. 959. (See www.finarcheo.org.)
[4] "Mining Union of Upper Katanga," often abbreviated to UMHK.

residual cash flow (and other) rights for a shareholder. For comparative purposes, it is thus advisable to use only common stock and not to mix different types. But it is not always easy to make the distinction. For example, for the UK market, the IMM "did not include separate tables for equities and bonds" (Grossman 2002, p. 124). In Germany, however, it is advised to include both common stocks (*Stammaktien*) and what is typically translated as preferred stocks (*Vorzugsaktien*), because the latter also entitle their holders to residual cash flows but do not give them voting rights (Stehle and Schmidt 2015). Moreover, during the 19th century, the holders of common stocks often received both a fixed interest return and a variable dividend.

In contrast, cross-listings, which are often of large foreign multinational companies, are usually not included in indices. Indeed, in most cases and particularly for small exchanges, it does not make sense to add such stocks to domestic indices. Of course, this requires obtaining company information to allow such identification. As Grossman (2002) indicates:

> Several large French railways (for example, Northern of France, and Paris, Lyons, and Mediterranean) were excluded from the sample since the market capitalization information (price times number of shares) reported by the IMM included the total number of shares traded both in French and British markets. Since the majority of trading in these companies took place in France, including their total market capitalization would dramatically overstate their importance in the British index. (p. 124)

Similarly, in the case of Dublin, the inclusion of Guinness shares in a cap-weighted index would squash the rest of the market (Grossman, Lyons, O'Rourke, and Ursu 2014). It is a point of contention whether the company, which moved its headquarters from Dublin to London in 1932 in response to hostile legislation, is Irish or English.

Identifying the industry to which a company belongs necessitates access to additional information from secondary sources, because relying solely on the company's name may lead to erroneous classification. Yet, industry classifications can be quite important for some research (e.g., to identify industry effects or exclude holding companies that invest in other quoted companies to avoid double counting).

Bonds

Many of the issues raised in the previous sections also apply to the construction and interpretation of bond indices. But bond markets show even more diversity than equity markets, implying that most bond indices only focus on specific segments of the bond market that usually coincide with popular asset classes. Indices are constructed by the following:

- *Issuer.* Government bonds, which are usually considered to have limited credit risk, are often separated from corporate bonds. However, Siegel (1992) stresses that the absence of credit risk in central government bonds should not be taken for granted: Municipal bonds issued by the Commonwealth of Massachusetts and the City of Boston during the early 19th century were deemed to be of higher quality than those of the federal government, which traded at higher yields. Even today, some corporate bonds occasionally trade "through" (at lower yields than) government bonds issued in the same currency. But even further subdivisions are possible: bonds issued by the central government versus those issued by local authorities, corporate bonds segmented by estimated credit risk as measured by credit ratings, or the guarantees on both the payment of interest and reimbursement of capital. Unsurprisingly, scarcity or the sheer absence of historical information on both ratings and guarantees makes it difficult to build homogeneous long-run corporate bond indices.

- *Maturity.* Maturity is also an important investment characteristic. In addition to overall bond indices, which contain all issues from a given universe, sub-indices segmented by remaining term to maturity can be built. This criterion invokes the question of how to consider bonds with early redemption features or other optionality clauses. It goes without saying that the need to gather all such issue-specific information imposes a significant burden.

- *Coupon payment.* Not all bonds pay fixed coupons. Coupons can be floating, or the "fixed" coupon may shift according to pre-specified schedules. Coupon payments can be specified in real rather than nominal terms or may be subject to optionality clauses. A well-known example is the bimetallism option, which allowed the US federal government to repay its bonds either in gold or silver (Garber 1986). It is no surprise that most indices are restricted to fixed coupon bonds.

- *Liquidity.* Liquidity is perhaps of even more importance to bonds than to stocks because a larger share of them is typically held to maturity and therefore not available for trading, worsening the stale price problem. Moreover, much more than stocks, bonds are more likely to trade OTC, making price data less accessible.

It is not surprising that only a few long-run databases based on individual bond returns are found in the literature. Among them, Vaslin (2007) built a French public bond weekly index and Rezaee (2013) a monthly weighted corporate bond index, both covering the 19th century.[5] Most available bond indices are derived from yield series—often from a limited sample of bonds and sometimes even a single bond—deemed to be sufficiently liquid and representative of the investable universe.

Focusing on yields of a restricted set of bonds obviously greatly reduces the archival workload and the stale price issue, but it comes at a potential cost:

- Yield series are often provided from secondary sources. This alleviates the data collection efforts, but yields are calculated from the bond price and the issue's characteristics. Care should be taken to make sure the correct bond prices were used: Do they include accrued interest ("dirty price") or not ("clean price")? If dirty prices were used, knowledge of the ex-coupon date becomes important. Also, the likelihood of early redemption needs to be considered. Klovland (1994) points out that these issues (amongst others) have plagued the estimation of even British consol yields in the second half of the 19th century. In addition, some sources rely on interpolated yields because of lack of appropriate data (e.g., Ibbotson and Sinquefield 1976).

- The yield needs to be taken from a representative bond (sample). To the extent that yields of all bonds are highly correlated, this may be a lesser issue. Yet, most empirical research indicates that yields are not perfectly correlated, and the correlations are not necessarily constant over time. The yield recorded may therefore fail to capture the investment experience of the average bond investor.

- To build a return index, yields have to be transformed into returns. Without having full price information, this transformation relies on approximations.

We turn to the US Datastream Calculated Government Bond Indices (Thomson Reuters 2008) to appreciate some of the approximation errors that are introduced by relying on partial information. Three sets of indices are calculated: the All Bond series, which are value-weighted total return indices of all eligible government bonds; the Tracker series, which focuses on the largest issues such that at least 25% of the total market value is covered; and the

---

[5]In a different vein, macroeconomists have built databases covering mainly public bonds, often with annual data, for a wide range of countries (e.g., the Global Finance database by Accominotti, Flandreau, and Rezzik 2011; see http://eh.net/database/global-finance/). Scholars interested in financial development have constructed low-frequency, long-run bond databases to grasp the evolution of this market (see Coyle and Turner 2013; Musacchio 2008).

Benchmark series. The latter contain only the bond deemed to be the most liquid with a term to maturity close to the index's target maturity.

First, we investigate the correlation among several yield series. Using monthly data for the Benchmark indices with terms to maturity 5, 7, 10, and 30 years over the period January 1980–June 2015, we compute correlation coefficients for yields and yield changes. The levels are virtually perfectly correlated: The lowest correlation coefficient is 0.98. For yield *changes*, correlations are somewhat lower (the lowest is 0.87). A principal component analysis shows that loadings onto the first principal component, which account for no less than 95% of common variation, are very similar for the four benchmark indices. This clearly motivates using one set of yield changes to capture returns of bonds with various terms to maturity.

Second, we look into the approximation errors introduced when going from yields to returns. We focus on the Duration and the Shiller (1979) approximations. The Duration approximation involves

$$R_{t+1} = \frac{y_t}{12} - \frac{D_t}{1+y_t}\left(y_{t+1} - y_t\right),$$

where R_{t+1} is the bond return from month t to $t+1$, y_t is its annualized yield to maturity at the end of month t, and D_t is its Macaulay duration at the end of month t. Clearly, this formula needs information about the bond's yield, coupon rate, and maturity to compute its duration. This may be cumbersome in some cases. The Shiller approximation assumes a par yield bond, which is repriced at the end of the month at the new yield to maturity.[6] Assuming a par yield bond avoids the need to assemble coupon information.

To save space, we illustrate the results using some representative cases. In Panel A of **Table 3.1**, we focus on the very broad All Bonds Index (all maturities) and the single bond Benchmark 10 Years Index. For the single bond index, both approximations work well: Average return as well as volatilities are close to their actual values, and the correlation with the exact return series varies around 99%. The differences are somewhat larger for the All Bonds Index because of its broader coverage. The Duration approximation is better, but it needs more information. Nevertheless, both series correlate highly with the original return series.

Of course, the approximations require knowledge of the (average) bond characteristics. To study the impact of not knowing the exact index maturity, we focus in Panel B on the Tracker 10 Years and More Index because it shows the highest

---

[6] It is used by Ibbotson and Sinquefield (1976). Shiller (1979) also derives a log-linear approximation. However, in our illustrations it always performs worse than the two others.

Table 3.1. Return Approximations, Some Illustrations

	Benchmark 10 Year			All Bonds		
	Actual	Duration	Shiller	Actual	Duration	Shiller
A. All bond index and single bond 10-year benchmark						
Average	0.66%	0.66%	0.69%	0.63%	0.63%	0.66%
Std.	2.44	2.45	2.53	1.60	1.55	2.02
Correlation		98.98	99.05		99.79	99.31
Tracking error volatility		0.37	0.38		0.13	0.48

	Actual	Actual Maturity	Average Maturity	Average − 1 Std.	Average + 1 Std.
B. Tracker 10 years and more: Shiller approximation					
Average	0.80%	0.82%	0.82%	0.80%	0.84%
Std.	3.33	3.65	3.68	3.44	3.88
Correlation		99.43	99.01	99.02	98.93
Tracking error volatility		0.52	0.63	0.51	0.78

	Actual	10 Years	10-Year Average Maturity	7 Years	7-Year Average Maturity
C. All bonds: Shiller approximation with benchmark index					
Average	0.63%	0.69%	0.66%	0.64%	0.65%
Std.	1.60	2.53	2.11	2.09	2.26
Correlation		97.09	97.26	97.88	97.84
Tracking error volatility		1.06	0.68	0.63	0.78

volatility of the term to maturity over the period studied: It is, on average, 22.88 years with a standard deviation of 3.11 years. The Shiller approximation is computed using respectively the exact maturities, the average index maturity and a maturity one standard deviation above or below the average maturity. Again, all four approximations correlate very strongly with the actual series, and deviations in average return are quite small. Volatility estimates are somewhat higher than the actual one, but the differences are still reasonable.

Finally, what happens if another yield series than the one in which we are interested is used? In Panel C, the broad All Bonds Index return is proxied by either the Benchmark 7 or 10 Years Index. For each index, the maturity is alternatively set equal to the actual maturity of the benchmark bond or to the average maturity of the All Bonds Index (7.54 years). The best approximation is given by the Benchmark 7 Years series, which has a maturity that closely matches that of the All Bond Index. Using the Benchmark 10 Years series results in larger tracking error volatility, which can be remedied to some extent by imposing the average maturity of the All Bonds Index. In any case, all proxies result in return series with higher volatility than the actual series. Although the correlations are somewhat lower than in the previous panels, they are still satisfactorily high.

All in all, these illustrations show that even with limited information, overall bond returns can be reconstructed as long as the term to maturity of the proxy does not deviate too much from the market.

Conclusions

This brief survey of potential biases affecting historical financial data shows that when studying long-run performances of stocks and bonds (indices), attention must be paid to several issues that may impact the results of the data analysis, particularly in diachronic and comparative perspectives. These issues should be kept in mind by data collectors to improve the quality of their data.

With a few exceptions, available indices can be only partially compared across time and space. Although several research teams have made tremendous efforts to reconstruct long and broad data sets, we feel that additional important efforts are required to obtain a truly comparable set of indices. Moreover, given the variety of purposes market indices may be used for, availability of high-quality micro-data turns out to be crucial: It allows for the construction of the pertinent index for the given purpose.

The scarcity of long-run financial micro-data is particularly glaring at the European level. Most European scholars have no choice but to use the American financial micro-databases, which are, with a few such remarkable exceptions as the SCOB database of Antwerp University, the only ones in existence suited to their research. The most widely used database is produced by CRSP (the Center for Research in Security Prices), a production platform managed by the University of Chicago. Considerable progress could be made by setting up high-quality harmonized financial databases for Europe, generating the potential for an extensive revision of current knowledge of the financial markets. Nowadays, some ongoing European research projects are trying to fill the gap, such as the "Data

Appendix

An Overview of Historical Cross-Sectional Equity Databases.

In **Table A**, we present an overview of the different cross-sectional equity databases we encountered in the literature.[7] We did not include "contemporaneous" databases—such as the CRSP database, Datastream, or Bloomberg—and we omitted the DMS database, which is described in Chapter 1 of this monograph. Rather, we focus on data sets covering a relatively broad cross section of equity returns for a considerable pre–World War II sample. We did not mention explicitly Global Financial Data, but several compiled historical series can be retrieved from its website (www.globalfinancialdata.com/index.html).

The table is ordered by country and provides the following information:

- The data period and market covered as well as the data frequency.

- A reference of the publication.

- Information about the prices collected, including their timing, the nature of the price quotes, and the extent of the sample.

- Information about the return calculation, including

  - whether returns are inclusive of dividends (total) or only reflect price appreciation (price); and

  - whether market indices are computed, and, if so, how their components' returns have been weighted (EW=equal weights, PW=price weights, VW=value weights).

- A short overview of the price sources used.

- When dividends have been included in the return calculation (if that information is available).

- Whether and how information on the amounts of shares outstanding has been used to compute return indices.

- Additional sources that have been used to retrieve dividends, shares outstanding, corporate actions, etc.

---

[7] The full version of the table can be found online at cfapubs.org in supplemental material.

Table A.   Selected Historical Equity Databases

Country	Period	Frequency	Paper	Type Index	Weighting
Australia	1900:01– 1925:12	M	Moore (2006)	Total	VW
Austria	1900:01– 1925:12	M	Moore (2006)	Total	VW
Canada	1900:01– 1925:12	M	Moore (2006)	Total	VW
China	1871–1940	A	Fan (2010)	Price, Total	EW, VW
Finland	1912:10– 1970:03	M	Nyberg & Vaihekoski (2010)	Total	VW, EW
Finland	1970:01– 1987:12	M	Nyberg & Vaihekoski (2014)	Total	VW, EW
France	1900:01– 1925:12	M	Moore (2006)	Total	VW
France	1854–1998	M	Le Bris & Hautcoeur (2010)	Price, Total	VW
Germany	1900:01– 1925:12	M	Moore (2006)	Total	VW
Germany	1954:01– 2013:12	M	Stehle & Schmidt (2015)	Total	VW
Germany	1870–1914	M	Eube (1998) & Weigt (2005)		
Germany	1870–1959	M	Ronge U. (2002)		
Ireland	1864:10– 1930:06	M	Grossman et al. (2014)	Price	VW, EW
Japan	1900:01– 1925:12	M	Moore (2006)	Total	VW
Netherlands	1900:10– 1925:12	M	Moore (2006)	Total	VW
Russia	1865:01– 1914:07	M	Goetzmann & Huang (2015)	Price, Total	PW
South Africa	1900:01– 1925:12	M	Moore (2006)	Total	VW

(continued)

Table A.   Selected Historical Equity Databases (continued)

Country	Period	Frequency	Paper	Type Index	Weighting
Spain	1900:01–1925:12	M	Moore (2006)	Total	VW
Switzerland	1900:01–1925:12	M	Moore (2006)	Total	VW
UK	1900:01–1925:12	M	Moore (2006)	Total	VW
UK	1870–1913	A	Grossman (2002)	Price, Total	EW, VW
UK	1825–1870	M	Acheson et al. (2009)	Price, Total	EW, VW
UK	1867–1907	M	Chabot et al. (2014)	Total	VW
USA	1900:01–1925:12	M	Moore (2006)	Total	VW
USA	1850:01–1925:12	M	Goetzmann et al. (2001)	Price, Total	EW, VW

Notes: M = monthly; A = annual; EW = equal weighted; VW = value weighted; and PW = price weighted.

Sources: Acheson, Hickson, Turner, and Ye (2009); Brailsford, Handley, and Maheswaran (2008); Fan (2010); Goetzmann and Huang (2015); Goetzmann, Ibbotson, and Peng (2001); Grossman (2002); Grossman, Lyons, O'Rourke, and Ursu (2014); Ibbotson and Sinquefield (1976); Le Bris and Hautcoeur (2010); Rezaee (2013); Stehle and Schmidt (2015); Vaslin (2007).

References

Accominotti, O. Marc Flandreau, and Riad Rezzik. 2011. "The Spread of Empire: Clio and the Measurement of Colonial Borrowing Costs." *Economic History Review*, vol. 64, no. 2 (May): 385–407.

Acheson, Graeme G., Charles R. Hickson, John D. Turner, and Qing Ye. 2009. "Rule Britannia! British Stock Market Returns, 1825–1870." *Journal of Economic History*, vol. 69, no. 4 (December): 1107–1136.

Annaert, Jan, Frans Buelens, Ludo Cuyvers, Marc De Ceuster, Marc Deloof, and Ann De Schepper. 2011. "Are Blue Chip Stock Market Indices Good Proxies for All-Shares Market Indices? The Case of the Brussels Stock Exchange 1833–2005." *Financial History Review*, vol. 18, no. 3 (December): 277–308.

Annaert, Jan, Frans Buelens, and Marc De Ceuster. 2012. "New Belgian Stock Market Returns: 1832–1914." *Explorations in Economic History*, vol. 49, no. 2 (April): 189–204.

Atack, Jeremy, and Peter L. Rousseau. 1999. "Business Activity and the Boston Stock Market, 1835–1869." *Explorations in Economic History*, vol. 36, no. 2 (April): 144–179.

Banz, R.W. 1981. "The Relationship between Return and Market Value of Common Stocks." *Journal of Financial Economics*, vol. 9, no. 1 (March): 3–18.

Brailsford, Tim, John C. Handley, and Krishnan Maheswaran. 2008. "Re-Examination of the Historical Equity Risk Premium in Australia." *Accounting and Finance*, vol. 48, no. 1 (March): 73–97.

Brown, S.J., W.N. Goetzmann, and S.A. Ross. 1995. "Survival." *Journal of Finance*, vol. 50, no. 3, Papers and Proceedings Fifty-Fifth Annual Meeting, American Finance, Washington, DC, 6–8 January (July): 853–873.

Campbell, J.Y., A. Lo, and A.C. MacKinlay. 1997. *The Econometrics of Financial Markets*. Princeton, NJ: Princeton University Press.

Chan, L.K., N. Jegadeesh, and J. Lakonishok. 1995. "Evaluating the Performance of Value versus Glamour Stocks: The Impact of Selection Bias." *Journal of Financial Economics*, vol. 38, no. 3 (July): 269–296.

Compagnie des Agents de Change près de la Bourse de Paris, Cours Authentique, 1796–1848.

Coyle, C., and J. Turner. 2013. "Law, Politics, and Financial Development: The Great Reversal of the UK Corporate Debt Market." *Journal of Economic History*, vol. 73, no. 3 (September): 810–846.

Da Costa, J.R., M.E. Mata, and D. Justino. 2012. "Estimating the Portuguese Average Cost of Capital." *Historical Social Research*, vol. 37, no. 2 (140): 326–361.

Desai, H., S. Rajgopal, and M. Venkatachalam. 2004. "Value-Glamour and Accruals Mispricing: One Anomaly or Two?" *Accounting Review*, vol. 79, no. 2 (April): 355–385.

Dimson, E., P. Marsh, and M. Staunton. 2000a. *The Millennium Book: A Century of Investment Returns*. UK: ABN AMRO and London Business School.

———. 2000b. "Risk and Return in the 20th and 21st Centuries." *Business Strategy Review*, vol. 11, no. 2: 1–18.

———. 2002. *Triumph of the Optimists: 101 Years of Global Investment Returns*. Princeton, NJ: Princeton University Press.

———. 2015. *Crédit Suisse Global Investment Return Sourcebook 2015*. Zurich: Crédit Suisse Research Institute.

Duneau, F., and C. Rietsch. 2008. "Les compagnies d'assurance sur le marché financier français jusqu'en 1870. " In *Le marché financier français au XIXème siècle*, vol. 2. Edited by G. Gallais-Hamonno. Paris: Publications de la Sorbonne: 507-570.

Eichholtz, P.M.A., C.G. Koedijk, and R. Otten. 2000. "De eeuw van het aandeel." *Economisch-Statistische Berichten*, vol. 85, no. 4238: 24–27.

Eun, C.S., and S. Shim. 1989. "International Transmission of Stock Market Movements." *Journal of Financial and Quantitative Analysis*, vol. 24, no. 2 (June): 241–256.

Fan, W. 2010. "Construction Methods for the Shanghai Stock Exchange Indexes: 1870–1940." Shanghai Stock Exchange Project, Yale School of Management (http://som.yale.edu/faculty-research/our-centers-initiatives/international-center-finance/data/historical-financial-research-data/shanghai-stock-exchange-project).

Garber, P.M. 1986. "Nominal Contracts in a Bimetallic Standard." *American Economic Review*, vol. 76, no. 5 (December): 1012–1030.

Global Financial Data. 2005. *GFD Encyclopedia of Global Financial Markets*. 10th ed.

Goetzmann, W., and S. Huang. 2015. "Momentum in Imperial Russia." NBER Working Paper No. 21700.

Goetzmann, W., R. Ibbotson, and Liang Peng. 2001. "A New Historical Database for the NYSE 1815 to 1925: Performance and Predictability." *Journal of Financial Markets*, vol. 4, no. 1 (January): 1–32.

Grossman, R.S. 2002. "New Indices of British Equity Prices, 1870–1913." *Journal of Economic History*, vol. 62, no. 1 (March): 121–146.

Grossman, R.S., R.C. Lyons, K.H. O'Rourke, and M.A. Ursu. 2014. "A Monthly Stock Exchange Index for Ireland, 1864–1930." *European Review of Economic History*, vol. 18, no. 3 (June): 248–276.

Hautcoeur, P.-C., A. Rezaee, and A. Riva. 2010. "How to Regulate a Financial Market? The Impact of the 1893-1898 Regulatory Reforms on the Paris Bourse." Paris School of Economics WP 2010-01.

Ibbotson, R.B., and R.A. Sinquefield. 1976. "Stocks, Bonds, Bills, and Inflation: Year-by-Year Historical Returns (1926–1974)." *Journal of Business*, vol. 49, no. 1 (January): 11–47.

Jorion, P., and W. Goetzmann. 1999. "Global Stock Markets in the Twentieth Century." *Journal of Finance*, vol. 54, no. 3 (June): 953–980.

Klovland, J.T. 1994. "Pitfalls in the Estimation of the Yield on British Consols, 1850–1914." *Journal of Economic History*, vol. 54, no. 1 (March): 164–187.

Le Bris, D., and P.-C. Hautcoeur. 2010. "A Challenge to Triumphant Optimists? A Blue Chips Index for the Paris Stock Exchange, 1854–2007." *Financial History Review*, vol. 17, no. 2: 141–183.

Li, H., and Y. Xu. 2002. "Survival Bias and the Equity Premium Puzzle." *Journal of Finance*, vol. 57, no. 5 (October): 1981–1995.

Musacchio, A. 2008. "Can Civil Law Countries Get Good Institutions? Lessons from the History of Creditor Rights and Bond Markets in Brazil." *Journal of Economic History*, vol. 68, no. 1 (March): 80–108.

Olbrys, J., and E. Majewska. 2014. "On Some Empirical Problems in Financial Databases." *La Pensee*, vol. 76, no. 9 (September): 2–9.

Rezaee, A. 2013. "Creation and Development of a Market: The Paris Corporate Bond Market in the 19th Century." *Entreprises et Histoire*, vol. 2, no. 67 (June): 24–36.

Rist, C. 1913. "Graphiques relatifs à la hausse du taux d'intérêt." *Revue d'Economie Politique*, vol. 27, no. 1: 462–473.

Shiller, R.J. 1979. "The Volatility of Long-Term Interest Rates and Expectations Models of the Term Structure." *Journal of Political Economy*, vol. 87, no. 6 (December): 1190–1219.

Shumway, T. 1997. "The Delisting Bias in CRSP Data." *Journal of Finance*, vol. 52, no. 1 (March): 327–340.

Shumway, T., and V.A. Warther. 1999. "The Delisting Bias in CRSP's Nasdaq Data and Its Implications for the Size Effect." *Journal of Finance*, vol. 54, no. 6 (December): 2361–2379.

Siegel, J.J. 1992. "The Equity Premium: Stock and Bond Returns since 1802." *Financial Analysts Journal*, vol. 48, no. 1 (January/February): 28–38.

Stehle, R., and M.H. Schmidt. 2015. "Returns on German Stocks 1954 to 2013." *Credit and Capital Markets*, vol. 48, no. 3: 427–476.

Thomson Reuters. 2008. *Datastream Calculated Government Bond Indices Issue 4.* Thomson Reuters.

Vaslin, J.M. 2007. "Le siècle d'or de la rente perpétuelle française." In *Le marché financier français au XIXᵉ siècle*, vol. 2. Edited by G. Gallais-Hamonno. Paris: Publications de la Sorbonne:117–208.

4. Foreign Exchange Markets and Currency Speculation: Historical Perspectives

Olivier Accominotti

Associate Professor, London School of Economics
Research Affiliate, Centre for Economic Policy Research (CEPR)

This chapter presents a short history of currency speculation and examines currency returns over the long run. I first review the main institutional developments in foreign exchange markets from the Middle Ages to the modern period. Next, I discuss the existing evidence on the long-run profitability of currency speculation strategies. Finally, I examine selected historical case studies of currency investors. The historical evidence suggests that foreign exchange traders can generate high profits but that any trading strategy also involves substantial risk. This is consistent with the view that the returns to currency speculation compensate investors for risk-taking.

Introduction

Between 2001 and 2016, global turnover on currency markets increased from 1.2 to 5.1 trillion US dollars per day (Bank for International Settlements, BIS, 2016). The foreign exchange market is now considered the largest financial market in the world. Recently, an increasing number of institutional investors and hedge funds have engaged in currency trading.[1] The once dominant form of dealings, spot transactions, have now been surpassed by such derivatives as foreign exchange swaps, outright forwards, and currency options. Derivatives are now the most actively traded currency instruments.[2]

The recent growth in foreign exchange turnover has also been accompanied by a reassessment of the returns to currency speculation in the academic literature. Economists have long been skeptical about investors' abilities to make sustainable profits from trading in foreign exchange markets. They

---

[1] According to the BIS 2016 *Triennial Central Bank Survey*, large commercial and investment banks known as reporting FX dealers accounted for 42% of global foreign exchange turnover. Other financial institutions (including small banks not identified as reporting dealers, institutional investors, hedge funds, and proprietary trading firms) and non-financial institutions (including corporations and retail traders) accounted for, respectively, 51% and 7% of turnover. See BIS (2016, p. 7).

[2] In 2016, spot transactions represented 33% of all foreign exchange transactions—compared to 47% for foreign exchange swaps, 14% for outright forwards, 5% for currency options, and 2% for currency swaps (BIS 2016, p. 6).

have traditionally considered exchange rates to be difficult to predict and thus thought that foreign exchange instruments are only useful to hedge the currency risk of other transactions and investments.[3] Of course, currency speculators occasionally make money—as anecdotes in the press frequently relate—but such gains might be the result of luck rather than skill (or biased reporting may exaggerate successes and ignore failures).

Yet, recent empirical research has shown that some currency managers and retail traders have performed strongly over the last 20 years and that their profits arise from more than pure chance (Pojarliev and Levich 2008, 2010, 2012a, 2012b; Abbey and Doukas 2015). Researchers also have documented the strong performance of several zero-investment speculation strategies—such as carry trade, momentum, and value—on currency markets over the last 30 years, and they have proposed explanations for these returns.[4]

This chapter provides some historical perspectives on the development of foreign exchange markets and speculation and on the returns to currency investing. I first describe the main institutional evolutions on the foreign exchange market from the Middle Ages to the modern period. Second, I review the existing evidence on the returns to currency speculation strategies over the last 100 years. Finally, I discuss a few historical case studies of currency investors. The historical evidence suggests that returns to currency speculation can be high but are also time varying and that any currency trading strategy entails substantial risks. This is consistent with the idea that returns to currency speculation arise from limits to arbitrage and reward investors who are willing to take such risks.

Foreign Exchange Markets and Speculation in History

Foreign exchange markets have been in existence since the Middle Ages. Transactions in metallic currencies and bills of exchange dominated for centuries, but then 1900s technological advances started changing how transactions were done. The foreign exchange markets went digital, via cable or telephone, and then different exchange rate regimes arose. This section briefly describes these changes and what they mean for today's market.

---

[3]See Pojarliev and Levich (2012a, pp. 2–4) for the reasons underlying the traditional skepticism toward currency investing.

[4]See, for example, Lustig and Verdelhan (2007); Brunnermeier et al. (2008); Burnside et al. (2011); Berge, Jordà, and Taylor (2011); Jordà and Taylor (2011, 2012); Lustig, Roussanov, and Verdelhan (2011, 2014); Asness et al. (2013); Menkhoff et al. (2012a, 2012b, 2016).

Currency Markets from the Middle Ages to the Early Modern Period.[5] For centuries, foreign exchange markets were dominated by transactions in metallic currencies and bills of exchange. A bill of exchange is an unconditional order of payment through which one person (the *drawer*) commands another person (the *drawee*) to make a payment to the bill's beneficiary (the *payee*) in a given place and a given currency either on sight or at a future date.[6] The bill of exchange became the most widely used instrument for international payments in Europe in the 13th century, becoming the cornerstone of the medieval foreign exchange markets (Einzig 1962). Bills provided a cheap and safe way of transferring funds between countries.

Let us suppose, for example, that a Genoese merchant needed to make a payment in Paris in French *livres tournois*. The merchant could buy a bill of exchange from a banker in Genoa (the *drawer*) at an agreed price in Genoese pounds. Through this bill, the Genoese banker would order her correspondent (the *drawee*) to pay the merchant's correspondent in Paris the equivalent amount in *livres tournois* of the sum initially received in Genoese pounds. The merchant could, therefore, obtain foreign currency (French *livres tournois*) in exchange for local currency (Genoese pounds) without having to exchange or mint coins. Evidently, sending a bill of exchange was cheaper and less risky than shipping metallic coins abroad and having those coins assessed by a money changer.

Aside from their convenience, bills also allowed circumvention of the Catholic Church's anti-usury laws, which prohibited loans at interest. The buyer of a bill payable some time in the future (a *long bill*) was in effect lending cash to the seller between the date at which the bill was purchased and the date at which it matured. Therefore, *long* bills of exchange were always cheaper than similar bills payable on sight, because purchasers charged a disguised interest rate (de Roover 1944, 1953; Flandreau, Galimard, Jobst, and Nogues-Marco 2009). As the Belgian historian Raymond de Roover (1953) has described, the sale or purchase of a bill always involved a foreign exchange transaction and a credit operation, and these two functions were not dissociated clearly.

The Church tolerated the use of bills of exchange on the basis that their return was influenced by exchange rate movements and therefore remained uncertain, which was in contrast to the fixed interest rate earned on straight

---

[5]This section is, of course, a drastic simplification of the early history of foreign exchange markets. For fuller accounts, see de Roover (1953) and Einzig (1962), from which this survey is largely inspired.
[6]Neal (1991, pp. 5–7) provides a schematic description of the functioning of foreign bills of exchange.

loans. The canon law did not condemn traders for betting on exchange rates, and profits from currency speculation were considered licit because they could not be known in advance and compensated investors for bearing an exchange rate risk (de Roover 1944, p. 258). Bankers frequently used bills of exchange in order to speculate. They tried to exploit seasonal variations in exchange rates and predict changes in economic and political conditions as well as in the coinages of the different currencies (Einzig 1962, pp. 85–86; de Roover 1946).

Developments in the 19th and 20th Centuries. Until the end of the 19th century, the foreign exchange market remained principally a market for bills. With the emergence of endorsement in England in the 17th century, bills became negotiable and discountable instruments, which enhanced their liquidity (de Roover 1953). From the 17th century until the Napoleonic Wars (1803–1815), the Dutch guilder was the leading international currency before it was superseded by the pound sterling. As world trade expanded in the 19th century, the number of bills quoted in the different international financial centers increased considerably. Sterling bills were the most widely quoted in 1900, followed by French francs and German marks (Flandreau and Jobst 2005, 2009).

The new transatlantic cable completed in 1866 facilitated foreign exchange dealings via telegraphic transfers, and as a result, the importance of bills of exchange progressively declined. However, it was only after World War I that transfers via cables and telephone became widespread and outstripped transfers of bills via mail. The new cable lines set up by governments during the war and the improvement of telegraphy contributed to this development (Phillips 1926, p. 53; Atkin 2005). Foreign exchange transactions were then undertaken directly via telephone between the main banks and through brokers. In the interwar years, the microstructure of the foreign exchange market was already very similar to that with which traders are familiar today.[7]

The Emergence of Foreign Exchange Derivatives. The 19th and 20th centuries also saw the emergence of organized markets for foreign exchange derivatives, especially forward contracts and currency options. Forward exchange transactions must certainly have taken place over-the-counter between merchants and bankers well before the 19th century. For example, bankers lending their capital through the purchase of bills of exchange drawn on foreign centers needed to repatriate the funds received abroad—a practice known as *re-change*. As mentioned in several trading manuals of the time, the

---

[7]See Lyons (2001) for a description of the microstructure of the modern foreign exchange market.

price of *re-change* bills was often agreed in advance so that exchange risk was covered (Einzig 1962, p. 86; Flandreau et al., 2009). However, the first organized forward exchange markets only made their appearance at the end of the 19th century in Berlin and Vienna (Einzig 1937; Flandreau and Komlos 2006). Central European currencies were at that time on flexible exchange rates, and investors engaging in international securities arbitrage needed forward contracts in order to hedge the exchange rate risk inherent in these operations. In Vienna, quotations of the florin/reichsmark forward exchange rate were published in local newspapers from 1876 to 1914 (Flandreau and Komlos 2006).

In the post-World War I period, a large forward exchange market developed for the first time in London. British newspapers started reporting forward quotations for all major currencies of the time (the US dollar, French franc, German mark, Dutch guilder, Italian lira, Spanish peseta, Belgian franc, Swiss franc) against the sterling pound (Accominotti and Chambers 2016). Turnover increased considerably on the London forward market during the floating exchange rate era of the 1920s, and contemporaries described a "veritable orgy of dealing" (Phillips 1926, p. 54). Other forward currency markets also emerged at the same time in New York and Paris (Einzig 1937).

In parallel with the development of forward markets, a market for currency options developed in New York in the immediate post-World War I years. Mixon (2011) describes how leading newspapers, such as the *New York Times* and *Wall Street Journal*, advertised options on the Russian ruble, French franc, and German mark between 1917 and 1921. The most actively traded options appear to have been call options on the German mark, which were sold to investors of German ancestry eager to speculate on a mark appreciation. However, dealings in options remained subdued compared to those in forwards, and currency options were not traded again on a large scale until the 1970s.

Fixed and Floating Exchange Rate Regimes. Opportunities for currency speculation, of course, vary according to the exchange rate regime. Early monetary systems were commodity based. Following the Franco–Prussian War of 1870–1871, many countries adopted the gold standard (Eichengreen 1996). Opportunities to speculate were thus reduced in the decades preceding World War I, but they did not completely vanish because certain countries also remained off gold.

Belligerent countries introduced capital controls and suspended gold convertibility during World War I. At the end of the war, an era of floating exchange rates opened up, marked by dramatic exchange rate volatility.

Most countries, however, stabilized their currencies against gold during the 1920s. But the interwar gold standard system did not ultimately survive the waves of speculative attacks that characterized the Great Depression (Eichengreen 1992).

After World War II, representatives of the victor countries at the Bretton Woods Conference designed a new international monetary order based on fixed exchange rates and capital controls. The Bretton Woods system remained in operation for almost 30 years. But even after its collapse in 1971–1973, many countries have still been prone to "fear of floating" and continue to peg to another major currency (Calvo and Reinhart 2002). **Figure 4.1** displays the proportion of countries, out of a 17-country sample, that maintained

Figure 4.1. Pegged versus Floating Exchange Rates, 1880–2010

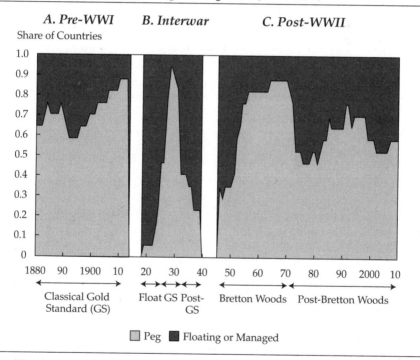

Notes: The 17 countries are Austria (Austria–Hungary up to 1914), Argentina, Belgium, Brazil, Denmark, France, Germany, Greece, Italy, the Netherlands, Norway, Portugal, Spain, Sweden, Switzerland, the United Kingdom, and the United States.
Sources: 1880–1913: Flandreau and Zumer (2004); 1919–1939: Eichengreen (1992) and League of Nations (1926–1944 period); 1946–2015: Reinhart and Rogoff (2004), updated dataset available at www.carmenreinhart.com/data/browse-by-topic/topics/11.

pegged exchange rates, as opposed to floating or managed floating exchange rates, in each year from 1880 to 2010. The euro is treated as a fixed exchange rate among its members.

Long-Run Evidence on Currency Returns

Investors have always used available foreign exchange instruments in order to speculate on exchange rate movements. This section reviews the existing empirical evidence on the returns to currency investing and speculation over the last 100 years.

Macroeconomists have long viewed currency investing with skepticism for two reasons. First, one of the most well-known theories in international economics—the uncovered interest rate parity condition—states that high interest rate currencies depreciate on average relative to low interest rate currencies at a rate that eliminates the interest rate differential. Therefore, borrowing in one currency to invest in another (which is equivalent to exchanging one currency against another on the forward market)[8] should not yield positive returns in the long run. Second, the poor performance of macroeconomic models in forecasting short-term currency movements implies that predicting changes in exchange rates is an extremely difficult task.[9]

Currency Speculation Strategies in the Post-Bretton Woods Period. The recent literature in empirical finance, however, shows that some simple currency speculation strategies have performed strongly during the post-Bretton Woods period. The most famous of these investment strategies is the so-called carry trade, which consists of borrowing in low interest rate currencies and investing in high interest rate ones. This strategy has become increasingly popular among traders. Lustig, Roussanov, and Verdelhan (2011) and Menkhoff, Sarno, Schmeling, and Shrimpf (2012a) find that this strategy yielded an annualized excess rate of return of approximately 6% and a Sharpe ratio (a measure of risk-adjusted performance) close to 0.6 (before transaction costs) when implemented on developed countries' currencies from 1983 to 2009. This performance is stronger than that of US stocks during the same period.

---

[8]The covered interest parity condition holds that borrowing in one currency to invest in another while hedging the exchange rate risk through a forward contract should yield zero expected return. When covered interest parity holds, borrowing in currency A to invest in currency B is equivalent to selling currency A against currency B on the forward market.

[9]Meese and Rogoff (1983) show that standard macroeconomic models do not perform better than a random walk model at forecasting exchange rates out-of-sample.

Researchers have interpreted the returns to the carry trade as compensation for risk-taking. For example, Lustig and Verdelhan (2007) have argued that the high returns earned by carry traders on average compensate them for taking the risk of incurring significant losses in bad times (when consumption growth is low).[10] Brunnermeier, Nagel, and Pedersen (2008); Burnside, Eichenbaum, Kleshchelski, and Rebelo (2011); and Farhi, Fraiberger, Gabaix, Rancière, and Verdelhan (2009) argue that carry traders are exposed to rare disaster or crash risk because at times they incur dramatic losses. Lustig, Roussanov, and Verdelhan (2011) and Menkhoff et al. (2012a) also show that the carry trade performs poorly in times of unexpectedly high global equity market volatility and unexpectedly high global foreign exchange volatility. Mancini, Ranaldo, and Wrampelmayer (2013) provide evidence that this strategy yields low returns when the liquidity of the foreign exchange market deteriorates.

Another simple strategy that has performed strongly is momentum, which consists of borrowing in currencies with low recent returns and investing in currencies with high recent returns. Menkhoff, Sarno, Schmeling, and Shrimpf (2012b) show that returns to currency momentum strategies are high when implemented on a wide range of developed and emerging countries' currencies but that their performance varies over time, which might make these strategies unattractive for traders with short investment horizons. Limits to arbitrage, as described by Shleifer and Vishny (1997), could therefore explain the performance of currency momentum strategies over the last 30 years. Finally, researchers have documented the profitability of currency value strategies, which involve borrowing in overvalued currencies and investing in undervalued currencies based on an assessment of real exchange rates (see Jordà and Taylor 2011, 2012; Asness, Moskowitz, and Pedersen 2013; Menkhoff, Sarno, Schmeling, and Shrimpf 2016).

Currency Returns over the Last 100 Years. Investors appear to have exploited currency trading strategies well before their performance was documented and studied. Before the term "carry trade" was coined, traders were familiar with the practice of borrowing in low interest rate currencies and investing in high interest ones, a strategy that interwar economists came to call uncovered interest arbitrage. For example, de Roover (1946, p. 159) describes how the Medici Bank in the 15th century attempted to buy bills of exchange (lend money) in places where they were cheap (interest rates were high) and sell them (borrow money) where they were expensive (interest rates were low), while acknowledging that such operations involved substantial

---

[10]See Burnside (2011) and Lustig and Verdelhan (2011) for a discussion of this argument.

risks. Interwar speculators also identified patterns in stock prices and tried to exploit them using trend-following and momentum techniques (Schabacker 1932; Gartley 1935).

Relatively little is known, however, about the performance of currency speculation strategies in periods other than the last 40 years.[11] Recently, Doskov and Swinkels (2015) explored the long-run profitability of the carry trade using annual data on spot exchange rates and Treasury bill rates for 20 industrialized countries between 1900 and 2012. They found that the strategy yields a lower Sharpe ratio (0.2–0.4) when considering the entire period rather than only the post-Bretton Woods period (0.6). Their results also highlight the fact that the carry trade incurred large occasional losses, which supports explanations of its performance in terms of compensation for risk-taking.

Accominotti and Chambers (2014, 2016) and Cen and Marsh (2013) look at the performance of carry and momentum strategies during an era of high exchange rate volatility: the 1920s and 1930s. They use monthly data on spot and forward exchange rates for the main currencies of the time against the pound sterling and find that both strategies performed strongly during the interwar period. Accominotti and Chambers (2014, 2016) find that transaction costs (measured through bid–ask spreads) only accounted for one-third of their returns over the interwar period. However, they also find that both strategies' performance varied greatly over time and depended on the exchange rate regime.

Table 4.1 summarizes the performance of carry and momentum strategies implemented on a sample of nine currencies and shows their log annualized (sterling) excess returns, annualized standard deviation of returns, annualized Sharpe ratio, and skewness and kurtosis of monthly returns during the interwar float (January 1920–December 1927), the interwar gold standard (January 1928–August 1931), and the managed floating period of the 1930s (September 1931–July 1939).[12] The table also displays log (dollar) excess returns to the same strategies implemented on the G10 currencies during the January 1985–December 2012 period.[13] Currencies in the sample are

---

[11]Lustig and Verdelhan (2007) explore the returns to the carry trade on annual data starting in 1953.

[12]The German mark is excluded from the sample during the hyperinflation period of 1922:02–1924:10. Although forward exchange rate quotations of the German mark were reported in newspapers in 1922:02–1923:08, trading restrictions and the escalation in counterparty risk made it almost impossible to trade this currency.

[13]The G10 currencies are the Australian dollar, British pound, Canadian dollar, German mark (or euro as of January 1999), Japanese yen, Norwegian krone, New Zealand dollar, Swedish krona, Swiss franc and US dollar.

Table 4.1. Carry and Momentum Strategies' Returns, 1920–1939 and 1985–2012

	CARRY		MOM	
	Before TC	After TC	Before TC	After TC
Sterling Returns on BEF, CHF, DEM, ESP, FRF, GBP, ITL, NLG, and USD				
Interwar float: 1920:01–1927:12				
Mean annualized return (%)	24.73	20.89	21.61	17.91
t-Statistic	(2.47)	(2.12)	(2.22)	(1.85)
Annualized std. dev. (%)	23.76	23.65	27.49	27.43
Sharpe Ratio	1.04	0.88	0.79	0.65
Skewness	0.51	0.44	−0.12	−0.17
Kurtosis	1.93	2.00	1.55	1.50
Interwar gold standard: 1928:01–1931:08				
Mean annualized return (%)	8.10	6.73	5.48	4.00
t-Statistic	(3.06)	(2.57)	(1.43)	(1.04)
Annualized std. dev. (%)	5.2	5.09	8.23	8.22
Sharpe Ratio	1.58	1.32	0.67	0.49
Skewness	0.99	0.97	2.18	2.17
Kurtosis	1.41	1.45	9.13	9.08
Interwar managed float: 1931:09–1939:07				
Mean annualized return (%)	−3.73	−7.77	6.48	2.81
t-Statistic	(−0.84)	(−1.75)	(1.44)	(0.62)
Annualized std. dev. (%)	12.57	12.58	12.72	12.88
Sharpe Ratio	−0.30	−0.62	0.51	0.22
Skewness	−4.99	−4.94	3.40	3.18
Kurtosis	33.25	32.53	29.75	29.13

(continued)

Table 4.1. Carry and Momentum Strategies' Returns, 1920–1939 and 1985–2012 (continued)

	CARRY		MOM	
	Before TC	After TC	Before TC	After TC
Dollar Returns on G-10 Currencies				
Modern float: 1985:01–2012:12				
Mean annualized return (%)	6.17	3.36	2.47	0.08
t-Statistic	(2.79)	(1.61)	(1.28)	(0.04)
Annualized std. dev. (%)	11.07	11.06	10.34	10.34
Sharpe Ratio	0.56	0.30	0.24	0.01
Skewness	−0.92	−0.94	0.33	0.31
Kurtosis	2.06	2.08	2.56	2.53

Notes: Currencies included in the sample for 1920–1939 are the Belgian franc, BEF (1921:02–1939:07); British pound, GBP (1920:01–1939:07); Dutch guilder, NLG (1921:02–1939:07); French franc, FRF (1920:01– 1939:07); German mark, DEM (1920:04–1922:01, 1924:11–1931:06); Italian lira, ITL (1920:01–1934:05); Spanish peseta, ESP (1925:12–1931:05); Swiss franc, CHF (1922:01–1939:07); and US dollar, USD (1920:01–1939:07). The sample for the 1985–2012 period is composed of the G-10 currencies (Australian dollar, British pound, Canadian dollar, German mark or euro as of January 1999, Japanese yen, Norwegian krone, New Zealand dollar, Swedish krona, Swiss franc, and US dollar). Log excess returns to each strategy are expressed in sterling for the 1920–1939 period and in dollars for the 1985–2012 period. Newey–West (1987) t-statistics computed with the optimal number of lags according to Andrews (1991) are in parentheses.
Sources: Log excess returns to CARRY and MOM strategies (before and after transaction costs, TC) are from Accominotti and Chambers (2016) for 1920–1939 and Accominotti and Chambers (2014) for 1985–2012.

ranked at the end of each month according to their interest rate differential, proxied by their forward discount[14] (CARRY) and by their previous month's spot exchange rate appreciation (MOM). The strategies then go long the two highest ranked currencies and short the two lowest ranked currencies on the forward market at the end of each month.

Table 4.1 reveals that the carry trade yielded high risk-adjusted returns during the floating exchange rates periods of 1920–1927 and 1985–2012 but performed much less well during the managed float period of the 1930s. The performance of the momentum strategy was also much stronger in the 1920s than in any other period, including the modern period (when implemented

---

[14]When covered interest rate parity holds, the forward discount of one currency against another is equal to the interest rate differential between the two currencies.

on G10 currencies only).[15] Both strategies also incurred huge losses in certain months in both the interwar and modern periods. The high variability in returns over time is, therefore, consistent with the recent literature, which interprets these strategies' performance as compensation for the substantial risks involved in following them.

Currency Investor Case Studies

History abounds with anecdotes about successful and less successful currency speculators. However, because detailed data on individual investors' currency trading record are rarely available, there is little evidence on how speculators implemented their trading strategies in different historical periods. This section examines a few historical case studies of currency investors. It first looks at central banks' management of their foreign exchange reserves in the 19th and 20th centuries before analyzing the currency trading strategy of John Maynard Keynes in the 1920s and 1930s.

Central Banks. The largest currency investors of the 19th and 20th centuries were probably central banks, which held substantial amounts of foreign exchange reserves. Before World War II, most central banks were owned by private shareholders. Therefore, even though their mandate required them to consider such objectives as the maintenance of specie convertibility, central banks had to keep an eye on their profitability when managing their foreign assets. Recently, researchers have dug into archival records in order to describe the currency composition of different countries' foreign exchange reserves over the 19th and 20th centuries and have provided new insights into how central banks managed their foreign exchange portfolio.[16]

Ugolini (2012) describes how the National Bank of Belgium, one of the first central banks to manage large amounts of foreign exchange reserves in the 1850s, chose the currency composition of its foreign bills portfolio by looking at both interest rate differentials and expected changes in exchange rates. Jobst (2009) finds that the Austro-Hungarian Bank intervened directly on the newly emerged Vienna forward exchange market in 1896–1913 and even engaged in sophisticated transactions, such as foreign exchange swaps. One of the purposes of these operations was to increase the bank's profitability.

Accominotti (2009) analyzes the foreign reserve management strategy of the Bank of France from 1928 to 1936. At that time, France was the world's

---

[15]Extending the sample to emerging countries' currencies would result in obtaining higher momentum returns in the modern period. See Menkhoff et al. (2012b).

[16]Eichengreen and Flandreau (2009) describe the currency composition of central banks' foreign exchange reserves during the interwar period.

largest holder of currency reserves. In 1926–1928, the French government had mandated the Bank of France to purchase huge amounts of US dollars and pounds sterling in order to avoid a French franc appreciation and stabilize the currency against gold. Foreign exchange reserves were held in the form of short-term deposits placed with the main banks in London and New York, as well as in commercial and Treasury bills. Both the US dollar and the pound sterling had fixed exchange rates with the French franc during this period, because they were all pegged to gold. However, since short-term interest rates were higher in London and New York than in Paris during 1928–1930, foreign currency assets yielded higher returns than domestic bills for the Bank of France. Even though the Bank did not borrow in other foreign currencies, the fact that it invested in relatively high interest rate ones rather than (noninterest bearing) gold implied that it was partly exposed to carry trade risks.

Sterling and dollar assets first boosted the Bank's profitability, and it was able to increase its dividend. However, the Bank's staff members were also wary of taking substantial risks and of being exposed to high losses in the case of a sterling or dollar devaluation. In the late 1920s, the United Kingdom struggled to remain on the gold standard. In 1929–1931, the Bank of France progressively reallocated its foreign portfolio toward the US dollar; however, it did so smoothly in order to avoid weakening the pound on the foreign exchange market. The risks eventually materialized in September 1931, when the pound sterling was devalued and the Bank of France made a huge loss on its remaining sterling assets. The loss amounted to twice the value of its capital, and the Bank had to be bailed out by the French government.[17] Therefore, the Bank of France appears to have been a victim of one of the large losses foreign exchange and carry traders sometimes experience.

Currency Speculators: The Example of John Maynard Keynes. The most famous retail traders in the foreign exchange market of the 1920s and 1930s were probably Winston Churchill and the economist John Maynard Keynes himself.[18] The latter, in particular, traded on the London foreign exchange market from its very inception in 1919 up to the outbreak of World War II in 1939, with an interruption in the years 1927–1932 when exchange rate fluctuations were dampened by countries returning to the gold standard.

---

[17]The arrangement with the Treasury to compensate the Bank of France for its exchange loss faced strong opposition in the French Parliament. See Mouré (1991, pp. 65–79) on the Bank of France's attitude during the sterling crisis and on the subsequent negotiations with the French government.

[18]Clarke (2014, p. 148) relates that Winston Churchill speculated on the US dollar in the early 1930s. Moggridge (1992) and Skidelsky (1992) describe how John Maynard Keynes speculated in currencies.

Using detailed archival records of Keynes' currency transactions, Accominotti and Chambers (2016) describe his strategy during this period and analyze his performance. Keynes did not follow any technical strategy, such as the carry trade or momentum, but instead tried to exploit fundamental misalignments in exchange rates that he identified by monitoring the macroeconomic and political situation. Although his currency speculation strategy generated positive cumulative returns in both periods he traded, he also suffered large losses during the 1920s and 1930s.

In May 1920, Keynes had a gigantic loss speculating against continental European currencies, especially the German mark, and those currencies initially appreciated relative to sterling. The loss left Keynes technically bankrupt, and he could only survive by borrowing through his social network. But Keynes then borrowed more money, maintained his positions, and recovered from this loss after two years. His predictions about continental European currencies were eventually proven right, and he ended up with a positive cumulative profit in 1927 at the end of his first trading period.

When he came back to currency trading in 1932, Keynes was skeptical about some countries' abilities to remain on the gold standard. He anticipated that France and the Netherlands would devalue after the United States abandoned the gold anchor in 1933. However, his shorting of these two currencies led him to go through two years of losses in 1934–1936 before he was proven right. In September 1936, the French franc and Dutch guilder were eventually devalued, allowing Keynes to generate positive cumulative profits.

Overall, Accominotti and Chambers (2016) find that Keynes' risk-adjusted performance as a currency speculator did not look astonishingly good over the 1920s and 1930s. His endeavor to exploit the fundamental misalignments in exchange rates of the interwar period required a willingness to weather large drawdowns. Keynes' example illustrates that the profits from currency speculation also come with substantial risks and may represent the compensation required by investors for bearing such risks.

Conclusion

This chapter provides a historical perspective on currency speculation and currency returns. Although relatively little research has been done on currency trading outside the modern period, a few interesting facts can be highlighted. First, foreign exchange speculation is not a modern phenomenon. Investors have always used available currency instruments in order to speculate on exchange rate movements and have followed strategies similar to those implemented by modern traders. Second, the evidence from the last 100 years shows that the returns to simple currency speculation strategies, such as the

References

Abbey, Boris S., and John A. Doukas. 2015. "Do Individual Currency Traders Make Money?" *Journal of International Money and Finance*, vol. 56 (September): 158–177.

Accominotti, Olivier. 2009. "The Sterling Trap: Foreign Reserves Management at the Bank of France, 1928–1936." *European Review of Economic History*, vol. 13, special issue no. 3 (December): 349–376.

Accominotti, Olivier, and David Chambers. 2014. "Out-of-Sample Evidence on the Returns to Currency Trading." CEPR Discussion Paper No. 9852 (March).

———. 2016. "If You're So Smart: John Maynard Keynes and Currency Speculation in the Interwar Years." *Journal of Economic History*, vol. 76, no. 2 (June): 342–386.

Andrews, Donald W.K. 1991. "Heteroskedasticity and Autocorrelation Consistent Covariance Matrix Estimation." *Econometrica*, vol. 59, no. 3 (May): 817–858.

Asness, Clifford S., Tobias J. Moskowitz, and Lasse Heje Pedersen. 2013. "Value and Momentum Everywhere." *Journal of Finance*, vol. 68, no. 3 (June): 929–985.

Atkin, John. 2005. *The Foreign Exchange Market of London*. New York: Routledge.

Bank for International Settlements (BIS). 2016. "Foreign Exchange Turnover in April 2016." BIS Triennial Central Bank Survey (September): www.bis.org/publ/rpfx16fx.pdf.

Berge, Travis, Òscar Jordà, and Alan M. Taylor. 2011. "Currency Carry Trades." *NBER International Seminar on Macroeconomics 2010*, vol. 7: 357–388.

Brunnermeier, Markus K., Stefan Nagel, and Lasse H. Pedersen. 2008. "Carry Trades and Currency Crashes." *NBER Macroeconomics Annual*, vol. 23: 313–348.

Burnside, Craig. 2011. "The Cross Section of Foreign Currency Risk Premia and Consumption Growth Risk: Comment." *American Economic Review*, vol. 101, no. 7 (December): 3456–3476.

Burnside, Craig, Martin Eichenbaum, Isaac Kleshchelski, and Sergio Rebelo. 2011. "Do Peso Problems Explain the Returns to the Carry Trade?" *Review of Financial Studies*, vol. 24, no. 3 (March): 853–891.

Calvo, Guillermo A., and Carmen M. Reinhart. 2002. "Fear of Floating." *Quarterly Journal of Economics*, vol. 117, no. 2 (May): 379–408.

Cen, Jason, and Ian W. Marsh. 2013. "Off the Golden Fetters: Examining Interwar Carry Trade and Momentum." Working paper (http://ssrn.com/abstract=2358456).

Clarke, Peter. 2014. *Mr. Churchill's Profession: Statesman, Orator, Writer.* London: Bloomsbury Publishing.

de Roover, Raymond. 1944. "What Is Dry Exchange? A Contribution to the Study of English Mercantilism." *Journal of Political Economy*, vol. 52, no. 3 (September): 250–266.

———. 1946. "The Medici Bank Financial and Commercial Operations." *Journal of Economic History*, vol. 6, no. 2 (November): 24–52.

———. 1953. *L'évolution de la Lettre de Change, XIVe–XVIIIe siècles.* Paris: Armand Colin.

Doskov, Nikolay, and Laurens Swinkels. 2015. "Empirical Evidence on the Currency Carry Trade, 1900–2012." *Journal of International Money and Finance*, vol. 51 (March): 370–389.

Eichengreen, Barry. 1992. *Golden Fetters: The Gold Standard and the Great Depression, 1919–1939.* New York: Oxford University Press.

———. 1996. *Globalizing Capital: A History of the International Monetary System.* Princeton, NJ: Princeton University Press.

Eichengreen, Barry, and Marc Flandreau. 2009. "The Rise and Fall of the Dollar (or When Did the Dollar Replace Sterling as the Leading Reserve Currency?)." *European Review of Economic History*, vol. 13, special issue no. 3 (December): 377–411.

Einzig, Paul. 1937. *The Theory of Forward Exchange.* London: Macmillan.

———. 1962. *The History of Foreign Exchange.* London: Macmillan.

Farhi, Emmanuel, Samuel P. Fraiberger, Xavier Gabaix, Romain Rancière, and Adrien Verdelhan. 2009. "Crash Risk in Currency Markets." NBER Working Paper No. 15062 (June).

Flandreau, Marc, and Clemens Jobst. 2005. "The Ties That Divide: A Network Analysis of the International Monetary System, 1890–1910." *Journal of Economic History*, vol. 65, no. 4 (December): 977–1007.

———. 2009. "The Empirics of International Currencies: Network Externalities, History, and Persistence." *Economic Journal*, vol. 119, no. 537 (April): 643–664.

Flandreau, Marc, and John Komlos. 2006. "Target Zones in Theory and History: Credibility, Efficiency, and Policy Autonomy." *Journal of Monetary Economics*, vol. 53, no. 8: 1979–1995.

Flandreau, Marc, and Frédéric Zumer. 2004. *The Making of Global Finance, 1880–1913*. Paris: OECD Development Centre Studies.

Flandreau, Marc, Christophe Galimard, Clemens Jobst, and Pilar Nogues-Marco. 2009. "The Bell Jar: Commercial Interest Rates between Two Revolutions, 1688–1789." In *The Origins and Developments of Financial Markets and Institutions from the Seventeenth Century to the Present*. Edited by Jeremy Attack and Larry Neal. Cambridge: Cambridge University Press.

Gartley, H.M. 1935. *Profits in the Stock Market*. Pomeroy, WA: Lambert-Gann Publishing Company.

Jobst, Clemens. 2009. "Market Leader: The Austro-Hungarian Bank and the Making of Foreign Exchange Intervention, 1896–1913." *European Review of Economic History*, vol. 13, special issue no. 3 (December): 287–318.

Jordà, Òscar, and Alan M. Taylor. 2011. "Performance Evaluation of Zero Net-Investment Strategies." NBER Working Paper No. 17150 (June).

———. 2012. "The Carry Trade and Fundamentals: Nothing to Fear but FEER Itself." *Journal of International Economics*, vol. 88, no. 1 (September): 74–90.

League of Nations. 1926–1944 period. *Statistical Year-Book, 1926-1944*, various issues.

Lustig, Hanno, and Adrien Verdelhan. 2007. "The Cross Section of Foreign Currency Risk Premia and Consumption Growth Risk." *American Economic Review*, vol. 97, no. 1 (March): 89–117.

———. 2011. "The Cross-Section of Foreign Currency Risk Premia and Consumption Growth Risk: Reply." *American Economic Review*, vol. 101, no. 7 (December): 3477–3500.

Lustig, Hanno, Nikolai Roussanov, and Adrien Verdelhan. 2011. "Common Risk Factors in Currency Markets." *Review of Financial Studies*, vol. 24, no. 11: 3731–3777.

————. 2014. "Countercyclical Currency Risk Premia." *Journal of Financial Economics*, vol. 111, no. 3 (March): 527–553.

Lyons, Richard. 2001. *The Microstructure Approach to Exchange Rates*. Cambridge: MIT Press.

Mancini, Loriano, Angelo Ranaldo, and Jan Wrampelmayer. 2013. "Liquidity in the Foreign Exchange Market: Measurement, Commonality and Risk Premiums." *Journal of Finance*, vol. 68, no. 5 (October): 1805–1841.

Meese, Richard A., and Kenneth Rogoff. 1983. "Empirical Exchange Rate Models of the Seventies: Do They Fit out of Sample?" *Journal of International Economics*, vol. 14, nos. 1–2 (February): 3–24.

Menkhoff, Lukas, Lucio Sarno, Maik Schmeling, and Andreas Schrimpf. 2012a. "Carry Trades and Global Foreign Exchange Volatility." *Journal of Finance*, vol. 67, no. 2 (April): 681–718.

————. 2012b. "Currency Momentum Strategies." *Journal of Financial Economics*, vol. 106, no. 3 (December): 660–684.

Menkhoff, Lukas, Lucio Sarno, Maik Schmeling, and Andreas Schrimpf. Forthcoming 2016. "Currency Value." *Review of Financial Studies*.

Mixon, Scott. 2011. "The Foreign Exchange Option Market, 1917–1921." Mimeo: http://econ.as.nyu.edu/docs/IO/23160/Mixon_0309012.pdf.

Moggridge, Donald E. 1992. *Maynard Keynes: An Economist's Biography*. London: Routledge.

Mouré, Kenneth. 1991. *Managing the Franc Poincaré: Economic Understanding and Political Constraint in French Monetary Policy, 1928–1936*. Cambridge, UK: Cambridge University Press.

Neal, Larry. 1991. *The Rise of Financial Capitalism: International Capital Markets in the Age of Reason*. Cambridge, UK: Cambridge University Press.

Newey, Whitney K., and Kenneth D. West. 1987. "A Simple, Positive Semi-Definite, Heteroskedasticity and Autocorrelation Consistent Covariance Matrix." *Econometrica*, vol. 55, no. 3 (May): 703–708.

Phillips, H.W. 1926. *Modern Foreign Exchange and Foreign Banking*. London: Macdonald and Evans.

Pojarliev, Momtchil, and Richard M. Levich. 2008. "Do Professional Currency Managers Beat the Benchmark?" *Financial Analysts Journal*, vol. 64, no. 5 (September/October): 18–32.

————. 2010. "Trades of the Living Dead: Style Differences, Style Persistence and Performance of Currency Fund Managers." *Journal of International Money and Finance*, vol. 29, no. 8 (December): 1752–1775.

————. 2012a. *A New Look at Currency Investing*. Charlottesville, VA: CFA Institute Research Foundation Publications.

————. 2012b. "Is There Skill or Alpha in Currency Investing?" In *The Handbook of Exchange Rates*. Edited by Jessica James, Ian Marsh, and Lucio Sarno. Hoboken, NJ: John Wiley and Sons.

Reinhart, Carmen M., and Kenneth S. Rogoff. 2004. "The Modern History of Exchange Rate Arrangements: A Reinterpretation." *Quarterly Journal of Economics*, vol. 119, no. 1 : 1–48.

Schabacker, Richard W. 1932. *Technical Analysis and Stock Market Profits*. Petersfield: Harriman House Ltd.

Shleifer, Andrei, and Robert W. Vishny. 1997. "The Limits of Arbitrage." *Journal of Finance*, vol. 52, no. 1 (March): 35–55.

Skidelsky, Robert. 1992. *John Maynard Keynes: The Economist as Saviour, 1920–1937*. London: Macmillan.

Ugolini, Stefano. 2012. "The Origins of Foreign Exchange Policy: The National Bank of Belgium and the Quest for Monetary Independence in the 1850s." *European Review of Economic History*, vol. 16, no. 1: 51–73.

5. The Long-Term Returns to Durable Assets

Christophe Spaenjers

Associate Professor, HEC Paris

Although a substantial amount of durable assets is included in many house-holds' investment portfolios, these assets are hard to measure. As a result, it is difficult to form return expectations based on a theoretical framework. This chapter examines what the investment performance of durable assets has been in the past to help make predictions about their future returns. It also shows how durable assets can help with diversification (but not inflation hedging) in investors' portfolios.

Introduction

Long-lasting non-financial assets—durable assets—feature prominently in households' investment portfolios. For many households, real estate is the most important component of their portfolio. Even high-net-worth individuals have more wealth invested in real estate (other than their primary residence) than in fixed income and only slightly less invested in real estate than in equities (Capgemini and RBC Wealth Management 2015). Moreover, such households typically have a substantial proportion of their wealth—almost 10%, on average, according to a survey done by Barclays (2012)—locked up in luxury collectibles (such as art and wine), precious metals, and diamonds. Likewise, endowments and other long-term institutional investors are increasingly looking to non-financial assets to diversify their portfolios and protect against inflation (e.g., Dhar and Goetzmann 2006).

Despite their economic importance, it can be challenging for academics and investment professionals to form expectations of the financial returns on durable assets. The risk exposures are hard to estimate, and a whole range of costs and benefits of "carry" may affect equilibrium expected returns. For example, both houses and artworks are indivisible (leading to investor under-diversification) and illiquid, and they are costly to maintain, store, and insure. Moreover, some of these assets also provide their owners with a non-financial utility dividend that can be hard to measure. Given the difficulty of forming return expectations based on a theoretical framework, it is useful to turn to history and examine what the investment performance of durable assets has been in the past. In financial asset markets, long-term historical returns are often used as a first proxy for expected returns going forward—even if expected returns are time varying and differ from the historical average (Ilmanen 2011).

In this chapter, I summarize the existing knowledge on the long-term price appreciation of three categories of durable assets: (1) housing and land; (2) collectibles; and (3) gold, silver, and diamonds. Where price indices are not available, I complement the literature with new data and analysis. Although this study focuses on capital gains, I comment on income yields where relevant. By considering more than a century of returns for each asset, I mitigate the worry that my findings are driven by fads or fashions. Finally, I also analyze the diversification and inflation-hedging properties of durable assets.

Housing and Land

Figure 5.1 presents long-term real (i.e., inflation-adjusted) price indices for US and UK real estate and land for the period 1900–2014. For the United States, I used a real home price index from Shiller (2015a, 2015b). (For the years since 1953, for which monthly data are available, I used the average of the June and July index values.) To create a land index starting in 1910, I adjusted average farmland values per acre (from Clifton and Crowley 1973; US Department of Agriculture 2015) for inflation using data from Dimson, Marsh, and Staunton (2002, 2015). In Figure 5.1, I set the starting value of this index equal to the value of the US home price index in 1910. For the United Kingdom, I used a real housing price index from Monnery (2011) chain-linked to four yearly average inflation-adjusted price levels from Nationwide (2015). I also constructed a real farmland value index based on trends in price per acre shared by the Rural Research team of the real estate service provider Savills. Figure 5.1 also compares the capital gains on housing and land to the investment performance of government bills since the beginning of 1900 for the two countries (Dimson, Marsh, and Staunton 2002, 2015).

Table 5.1 summarizes the real return distribution information, adding total equity and bond returns to the comparison. Both here and for the other durable assets in this chapter, the standard deviation (S.D.) may be underestimating the true volatility because the price indices typically aggregate information over 12-month periods (and because some indices use appraisal values, which are known to be "stickier" than transaction prices). For some assets, returns are computed as the average price appreciation *between* two calendar years (e.g., between 1999 and 2000) rather than *over* a calendar year (e.g., between the start and the end of 2000).

What can we learn from the data presented in Figure 5.1 and Table 5.1? It is clear that the long-term appreciation rates of housing and land have been

Figure 5.1. Housing and Land: Long-Term Price Indices 1900–2014 (in real USD and GBP)

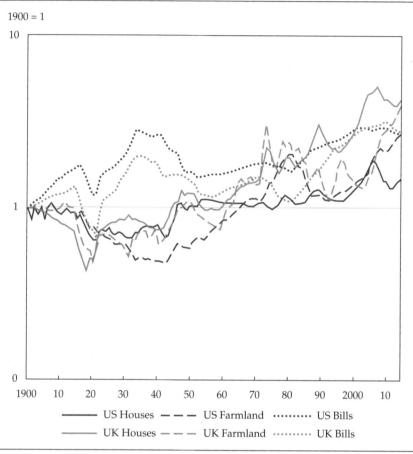

1900 = 1

————— US Houses — — — US Farmland ·········· US Bills
————— UK Houses — — — UK Farmland ·········· UK Bills

low; they are more or less comparable to the historical returns on government bills. In the first decades of the 20th century, housing and land even lost value in real terms. Between the 1940s and the 1990s, housing prices in the United States barely moved in real terms—despite substantial economic and demographic growth over this period—before showing a boom and bust that is exceptional by historical standards.

UK housing prices have appreciated somewhat more steadily since the end of World War II, but also during this period the price increases were interrupted by substantial setbacks. Turning to farmland values, we see that a temporary bubble occurred in the late 1970s, and recently prices have increased substantially.

Table 5.1. Housing and Land: Return Distributions 1900–2014 (in real USD and GBP)

	Mean Returns		Dispersion of Annual Returns				
	Geometric	Arithmetic	S.D.	Lowest	Year(s)	Highest	Year(s)
US houses	0.3%	0.5%	6.2%	–14.3%	1904–05	21.4%	1945–46
US farmland	0.9%	1.2%	5.5%	–14.4%	1984–85	16.4%	2004–05
US equities	6.5%	8.5%	20.1%	–37.6%	1931	56.3%	1933
US bonds	2.0%	2.5%	10.5%	–18.4%	1917	35.1%	1982
US bills	0.9%	1.0%	4.6%	–15.1%	1946	20.0%	1921
UK houses	1.3%	1.6%	7.7%	–14.8%	1914–15	27.7%	1921–22
UK farmland	1.2%	1.9%	12.6%	–34.5%	1973–74	67.3%	1971–72
UK equities	5.3%	7.1%	19.7%	–57.1%	1974	96.7%	1975
UK bonds	1.6%	2.4%	13.7%	–30.7%	1974	59.4%	1921
UK bills	0.9%	1.1%	6.3%	–15.7%	1915	43.0%	1921

Notes: For US farmland, the return data series starts in 1910 instead of 1900. Only capital gains are considered for houses and farmland.

The low capital gains on real estate have also been documented for other countries. For example, data collected by Eichholtz (1997, 2015) show that Amsterdam housing prices went up at an annualized real rate of 0.7% between 1900 and 2010. In Paris, the annualized rate of real appreciation has been estimated at 1.2% over the same period (CGEDD 2015). When evaluating these numbers, one should keep in mind that capital gains are typically even lower in rural areas than in such "superstar cities" (Gyourko, Mayer, and Sinai 2013).

It is important to highlight that this analysis only focuses on capital gains and ignores income yields. Housing rental income yields vary over time and in the cross-section—with higher relative prices typically being associated with lower yields—but can be substantial. Taking into account maintenance costs and other expenses, Weeken (2004) mentions an average net rental yield for UK residential properties of about 5% between 1967 and 2003. For UK farmland, high recent price growth seems to have brought down income yields to less than 2% (Savills 2015).

Collectibles

Figure 5.2 shows indices beginning in 1900 in real British pounds for four different types of collectibles. For art, the starting point is the long-term price index of Goetzmann, Renneboog, and Spaenjers (2011), which is largely based

Figure 5.2. Collectibles: Long-Term Price Indices 1900–2014 (in real GBP)

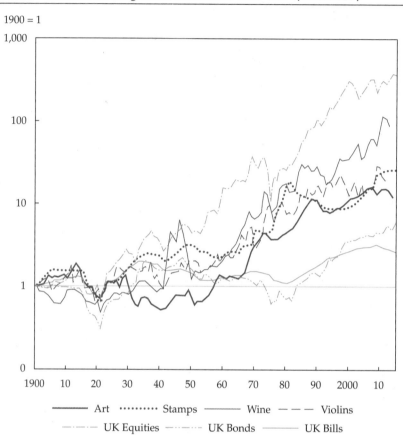

on London auction sales. I chain-linked this index to returns based on the mid-year values of the UK art market index, as calculated by Artprice.com (2015), to get a series that runs until 2014. For stamps, I chain-linked the index of Dimson and Spaenjers (2011), based on British stamp price catalogues from the dealer Stanley Gibbons, to the returns on Stanley Gibbons GB250 Stamp Index for the most recent year-ends. For wine, I used the index of Dimson, Rousseau, and Spaenjers (2015), which focuses on first-growth Bordeaux and is based on London price information from dealer Berry Bros. & Rudd and auction house Christie's. This index stops at the end of 2012. For violins, I converted the index constructed by Graddy and Margolis (2011, 2013), which uses a variety of sources but is largely based on sales by London-based dealer W.E. Hill & Sons, to real British pounds. This last price index also ends in 2012. Figure 5.2 also compares the long-term returns of the different collectibles to those of UK financial assets over the complete 1900–2014 period, again borrowing data from Dimson, Marsh, and Staunton (2002, 2015).

Table 5.2 shows statistics on the different return distributions.

We can draw a number of conclusions from the indices and data shown in Figure 5.2 and Table 5.2. First, the different collectible types have remarkably similar long-term returns. Art, stamps, wine, and violins outperformed government bonds but underperformed equities. Wine stands out somewhat, but Dimson, Rousseau, and Spaenjers (2015) note that the highest returns are observed on young high-quality wines that are still maturing. On older wines, which are more likely to be bought as collectibles, the returns are closer to those on art, stamps, and violins. Second, all collectibles have realized most of their increase in value over the last half century. Real appreciation was limited over the first six decades of the 20th century. Third, short-term returns can nevertheless differ substantially between different collectibles; the correlations between the return series are all below 0.22. Relatively high returns for a collectible category are typically followed by underperformance relative to other collectibles, suggesting some return predictability (Dimson, Rousseau, and Spaenjers 2015). Fourth, and finally, the price volatility of collectibles is relatively high, especially when considering that the standard deviations reported here may still underestimate true volatilities because of the time aggregation of data and the use of appraisal values.

It is important to note that the price indices reflect the estimated performance prior to transaction costs. Round-trip transaction costs can easily exceed 25%, both in auction and in dealer markets. Furthermore, only the wine index takes into account expenses associated with storage and insurance.

Table 5.2. Collectibles: Return Distributions 1900–2014 (in real GBP)

| | Mean Returns | | Dispersion of Annual Returns | | | | |
	Geometric	Arithmetic	S.D.	Lowest	Year(s)	Highest	Year(s)
Art	2.2%	3.0%	12.3%	−29.7%	1914–15	38.4%	1967–68
Stamps	2.9%	3.5%	12.2%	−19.2%	1915	56.3%	1979
Wine	4.1%	6.7%	26.3%	−37.1%	1949	145.6%	1942
Violins	2.7%	5.7%	25.4%	−47.7%	1970–71	105.0%	2009–10
UK equities	5.3%	7.1%	19.7%	−57.1%	1974	96.7%	1975
UK bonds	1.6%	2.4%	13.7%	−30.7%	1974	59.4%	1921
UK bills	0.9%	1.1%	6.3%	−15.7%	1915	43.0%	1921

Note: For wine and violins, the return data series end in 2012 instead of 2014.

Illiquidity is another factor that may play an even bigger role here than for the other durable assets covered in this chapter. Finally, it is clear that investors may face a number of pitfalls that they do not encounter when dealing with financial assets. Dimson and Spaenjers (2014) review these different expenses and investment risks in more depth. Still, most collector-investors also receive a significant (but elusive) emotional "yield" from ownership.

Gold, Silver, and Diamonds

Finally, I consider the long-term historical returns to gold, silver, and diamonds. **Figure 5.3** shows indices in real US dollars. Annual average gold prices for the years 1900–2014 were taken from Officer and Williamson (2015). Something to keep in mind is that for most of the 20th century, the price of gold was fixed in nominal terms. The convertibility of US dollars to gold was only cancelled in 1971. Real gold price changes before the early 1970s were thus driven by inflation and deflation or changes in the official nominal price of gold. (Moreover, private ownership of gold was outlawed in the United States between 1933 and 1974.) Silver prices are computed by using annual average silver-to-gold price ratios from Officer and Williamson (2015).

For diamonds, I constructed a price index for the period 1900–2012. I used data from the Minerals Yearbooks (US Geological Survey 2015) on the average import value per carat for a cut diamond for the years since 1929. Next, I took data from Sutton (1979) on the rough diamond price per carat for the periods 1900–1913 and 1926–1929; the resulting price index can be chain-linked to the one based on import values in 1929. For the years 1919–1921, I relied on imputations using the Minerals Yearbooks data that are also available for those years (and the year-1929 price ratio of cut diamonds relative to rough diamonds). For the periods 1914–1918 and 1922–1925, I geometrically interpolated the index values. Figure 5.3 also compares the performance of gold, silver, and diamonds to that of US bills.

Table 5.3 shows the return distributions and compares to US equities and bonds as well.

What do Figure 5.3 and Table 5.3 teach us about the dynamics of these assets? The most striking observation is that gold, silver, and diamonds all combine a low long-term real return with a high volatility. (Since the end of 1974, when gold could be traded freely again, gold has been more volatile than equities.) All three assets appreciated rapidly in the second half of the 1970s and in a 10-year period starting in 2002. However, strong price rises are typically followed by negative returns.

Figure 5.3. Gold, Silver, and Diamonds: Long-Term Price Indices 1900–2014 (in real USD)

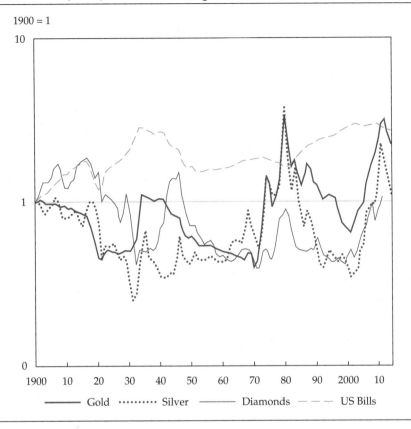

Table 5.3. Gold, Silver, and Diamonds: Return Distributions 1900–2014 (in real USD)

	Mean Returns		Dispersion of Annual Returns				
	Geometric	Arithmetic	S.D.	Lowest	Year(s)	Highest	Year(s)
Gold	0.7%	1.8%	16.2%	−33.2%	1980–81	75.8%	1979–80
Silver	0.1%	2.4%	22.7%	−54.6%	1980–81	88.4%	1978–79
Diamonds	0.0%	1.0%	13.9%	−33.3%	1946–47	42.4%	1941–42
US equities	6.5%	8.5%	20.1%	−37.6%	1931	56.3%	1933
US bonds	2.0%	2.5%	10.5%	−18.4%	1917	35.1%	1982
US bills	0.9%	1.0%	4.6%	−15.1%	1946	20.0%	1921

Note: For diamonds, the return data series ends in 2012 instead of 2014.

Diversification and Inflation Hedging

To better understand the potential diversification and inflation-hedging benefits of durable assets, I show how (real) durable asset returns have historically co-moved with (real) equity and bond returns and also with inflation. I estimated linear regression models that took into account the potential asynchrony in returns by including a lagged, a contemporaneous, and a leading independent variable (equity returns, bond returns, or inflation). I then aggregated the slope coefficients (Dimson 1979). For the durable asset series in GBP, I used UK financial market and inflation data; for the durable asset series in USD, I used US data. The results are shown in **Table 5.4**.

Table 5.4 shows positive but relatively small equity market betas for real estate and land. Consistent with the idea that demand for luxury assets is positively affected by wealth creation (Aït-Sahalia, Parker, and Yogo 2004), there is a relatively strong co-movement of art and wine with equities. Gold (for which I used return data since 1975) is the only asset that covaries negatively with equities. The bond market betas largely mirror the equity market sensitivities.

Deflated housing and land returns are negatively correlated with inflation (at least in the United Kingdom), and there is some evidence that real collectible returns are also negatively impacted by inflation. Interestingly, gold

Table 5.4. Estimates of Equity Market, Bond Market, and Inflation Betas

	Equities	Bonds	Inflation
US houses	0.15***	0.17*	−0.16
US farmland	0.06	−0.19**	0.10
UK houses	0.16**	0.27***	−0.44***
UK farmland	0.29**	0.41***	−0.50**
Art	0.52***	0.32**	−0.41*
Stamps	0.20*	0.26**	−0.22
Wine	0.54**	0.64**	−0.37
Violins	0.12	0.08	−0.15
Gold	−0.76*	−0.92*	1.55
Silver	−0.07	−0.28	0.56
Diamonds	0.14	0.00	0.14

Notes: For gold, I used return data starting in 1975. For the other assets, I used the longest possible series. All asset returns are in real GBP or USD.
*Significant at the 10 percent level.
**Significant at the 5 percent level.
***Significant at the 1 percent level.

and silver (and, to a lesser extent, diamonds) exhibit positive covariance with inflation. However, the regression coefficient is not statistically significant, and the very high short-term volatility in the real price of these assets makes them poor inflation hedges (Erb and Harvey 2013).

Conclusion

I have studied the returns to investments in durable assets since the start of the 20th century and have shown that these assets are generally characterized by relatively low capital gains and substantial price fluctuations. Collectibles have had higher rates of price appreciation, but transaction costs also are very high in such markets. However, rental income yield can add substantially to the returns on housing and land, whether the rental income is explicit or, as with owner-occupants, imputed. Likewise, owners of collectibles may receive a significant emotional dividend. Because of the lack of such an income or utility stream, gold, silver, and diamonds appear to have been particularly bad long-term investments (at least if not held in the form of jewelry). Finally, durable assets are unlikely to be good inflation hedges, but they may still help diversify a portfolio because of their imperfect correlations with financial assets.

I would like to thank Ian Bailey (Savills Rural Research), David Chambers, Elroy Dimson, Will Goetzmann, Katy Graddy, Paul Marsh, Neil Monnery, Peter Rousseau, Mike Staunton, Luc Renneboog, and Louise Reynolds (Stanley Gibbons) for data and comments. Any errors are mine.

References

Aït-Sahalia, Y., J. Parker, and M. Yogo. 2004. "Luxury Goods and the Equity Premium." *Journal of Finance*, vol. 59, no. 6 (December): 2959–3004.

Artprice.com. 2015. Artprice Global Indices: http://imgpublic.artprice.com/pdf/agi.xls (retrieved 2015).

Barclays. 2012. "Profit or Pleasure? Exploring the Motivations behind Treasure Trends." *Wealth Insights*, vol. 15: https://wealth.barclays.com/en_gb/home/research/research-centre/wealth-insights/volume-15.html.

Capgemini and RBC Wealth Management. 2015. *World Wealth Report 2015*: www.worldwealthreport.com.

CGEDD. 2015. "House Prices in France: Property Price Index, French Real Estate Market Trends in the Long Run" (www.cgedd.developpement-durable.gouv.fr/house-prices-in-france-property-price-index-french-a1117.html) (retrieved 2015).

Clifton, Ivery D., and William D. Crowley. 1973. "Farm Real Estate Historical Series Data: 1850–1970." Washington, DC: Economic Research Service, U.S. Department of Agriculture (June).

Dhar, R., and W. Goetzmann. 2006. "Institutional Perspectives on Real Estate Investing." *Journal of Portfolio Management*, vol. 32, no. 4 (Summer): 106–116.

Dimson, E. 1979. "Risk Measurement When Shares Are Subject to Infrequent Trading." *Journal of Financial Economics*, vol. 7, no. 2 (June): 197–226.

Dimson, E., and C. Spaenjers. 2011. "Ex Post: The Investment Performance of Collectible Stamps." *Journal of Financial Economics*, vol. 100, no. 2 (May): 443–458.

———. 2014. "Investing in Emotional Assets." *Financial Analysts Journal*, vol. 70, no. 2 (March/April): 20–25.

Dimson, E., P. Marsh, and M. Staunton. 2002. *Triumph of the Optimists: 101 Years of Global Investment Returns*. Princeton, NJ: Princeton University Press.

———. 2015. *Global Investment Returns Yearbook*. Zurich: Credit Suisse Research Institute.

Dimson, E., P. Rousseau, and C. Spaenjers. 2015. "The Price of Wine." *Journal of Financial Economics*, vol. 118, no. 2 (November): 431–449.

Eichholtz, P. 1997. "A Long Run House Price Index: The Herengracht Index, 1628–1973." *Real Estate Economics*, vol. 25, no. 2 (June): 175–192.

———. 2015. Herengracht Index.

Erb, C., and C. Harvey. 2013. "The Golden Dilemma." *Financial Analysts Journal*, vol. 69, no. 4 (July/August): 10–42.

Goetzmann, W., L. Renneboog, and C. Spaenjers. 2011. "Art and Money." *American Economic Review*, vol. 101, no. 3 (May): 222–226.

Graddy, K., and P. Margolis. 2011. "Fiddling with Value: Violins as an Investment?" *Economic Inquiry*, vol. 49, no. 4 (October): 1083–1097.

———. 2013. "Old Italian Violins: A New Investment Strategy?" *Global Finance Brief*, Rosenberg Institute of Global Finance, Brandeis International Business School (8 August).

Gyourko, J., C. Mayer, and T. Sinai. 2013. "Superstar Cities." *American Economic Journal: Economic Policy*, vol. 5, no. 4 (November): 167–199.

Ilmanen, A. 2011. *Expected Returns: An Investor's Guide to Harvesting Market Rewards*. Chichester, UK: John Wiley & Sons.

Monnery, N. 2011. *Safe as Houses? A Historical Analysis of Property Prices*. London: London Publishing Partnership.

Nationwide. 2015. "UK House Prices Adjusted for Inflation" (www.nationwide.co.uk/about/house-price-index/download-data#xtab:uk-series).

Officer, L., and S. Williamson. 2015. "The Price of Gold, 1257–Present." Measuring Worth: www.measuringworth.com/gold.

Savills. 2015. "Market Survey: UK Agricultural Land 2015." Savills Rural Research UK: www.savills.co.uk/research_articles/141557/186386-0.

Shiller, R. 2015a. *Irrational Exuberance: Revised and Expanded*. 3rd ed. Princeton, NJ: Princeton University Press.

———. 2015b. Online data: www.econ.yale.edu/~shiller/data.htm.

Sutton, A. 1979. *The Diamond Connection: A Manual for Investors*. JD Press.

US Department of Agriculture. 2015. "Farmland Value" (www.ers.usda.gov/topics/farm-economy/land-use,-land-value-tenure/farmland-value.aspx).

US Geological Survey. 2015. "Gemstones: Statistics and Information" (http://minerals.usgs.gov/minerals/pubs/commodity/gemstones/index.html).

Weeken, O. 2004. "Asset Pricing and the Housing Market. *Bank of England Quarterly Bulletin*, vol. 44, no. 1 (Spring): 32–41.

6. The Role of Stock Exchanges in Financial Globalization: A Historical Perspective

Larry Neal

Professor Emeritus of Economics, University of Illinois at Urbana-Champaign
Research Associate, NBER

The re-emergence of a global financial market since the final collapse of the Bretton Woods system in 1973 evokes many analogies with the emergence of the first global financial market that existed from 1871 to 1914. Especially noteworthy is the expansion and spread of organized stock exchanges worldwide since 1973. As with the first financial globalization, many different strategies for successful business models have emerged for the world's leading stock exchanges. Although the scale and scope of trading activities in today's world stock exchanges are unprecedented, the basic issues they confront are the same as those of their predecessors. Then as now, open access markets making public their "price discoveries" have to deal with banks making private arrangements in confidence for their clients. Resolving this implicit conflict of motives remains a challenge for financial systems today.

In the ongoing expansion of global financial markets, which started at the end of the Bretton Woods monetary regime in 1973 and accelerated after 1989, the number and variety of stock exchanges has continued to grow. In 2015, the World Federation of Exchanges listed 189 stock exchanges around the world—13 in the United States alone and 96 combined in Europe, Africa, and the Middle East.

The number of exchanges today is daunting, and their future evolution is still uncertain. Nevertheless, a similar expansion in the number and size of the world's stock exchanges occurred when the first global financial markets emerged from 1871 to 1914. On the eve of World War I, a UK expert counted 89 principal stock exchanges around the world, with over half in Europe (mainly western Europe) and the rest largely in areas of European settlement (Lowenfeld 1909). Together, those markets allowed some 20 million investors to trade holdings in over $160 billion (nominal value) of securities. A French authority on stock exchanges at the time estimated that UK investors held 24%, Americans 21%, French 18%, and Germans 16% of the world's stock of securities (Neymark 1916).

Comparing the role that stock exchanges play in the world economy now with their role a century ago is even more telling. **Table 6.1** shows that in terms of the size of marketable financial assets in their economies a century ago, the four leading countries were, in ascending order, the United States, Germany, France, and the United Kingdom. Securities listed on markets during that time, including both bonds (government and corporate) and equities, ranged from 233% to 454% of GDP for the United States and the United Kingdom, 373% for France, and 223% for Germany. Comparing the par value of just equities in corporations to GDP, however, brings the United States (174%) ahead of the United Kingdom (145%), while bond and bank finance were clearly far more important during that time than public equity for firms in France (68%) and Germany (29%).

Table 6.2 compares these same four economies in 2015, but capitalization-to-GDP ratios are reported differently: they are calculated using the market value of (just) equities in their leading stock exchange(s). The two major competing exchanges in the United States, the NYSE (New York Stock Exchange) and NASDAQ, dominate the world's stock exchanges. They also now include many foreign securities, as do the competing exchanges in London, Paris, and Frankfurt.

Nevertheless, the importance of equities quoted on each country's leading markets as compared to their respective GDPs is not that dissimilar from the relative importance of listed equities in those countries one century ago. The United States and United Kingdom still have the highest ratios of market capitalization of equities quoted on their exchanges to GDP, although the adoption of the American model of electronic exchanges by Euronext in Paris has raised France's ratio considerably. Meanwhile, the diversion of the German exchange toward its alternative business of automated clearing

Table 6.1. Stock Market Capitalization in London, Paris, Berlin, and New York on the Eve of World War I (USD millions)

(All at par)	London 1913	Paris 1912	Berlin 1910	New York 1914
Government securities	24,515	18,703	15,896	3,357
Corporate equities + bonds	29,007	16,836	10,462	82,436
Total (at par)	53,522	35,539	26,358	85,793
Securities/GDP	454%	373%	223%	233%
Equities/GDP	145%	68%	29%	174%

Source: Hannah (2015).

Table 6.2.   Equity Market Capitalization Compared to GDP, 2015 (USD millions)

		Market Cap	GDP (2014)	Cap/GDP
United States				
	NASDAQ	7,473,479.61		
	NYSE	19,351,558.28		
	Total	26,825,037.89	17,419,000.00	154%[a]
Deutsche Boerse		1,780,828.02	3,704,913.10	48%
Euronext[b]		3,549,142.29	2,571,970.84	138%
LSE		4,242,301.28	2,530,467.22	168%

Notes: Market cap is in USD millions on 31 July 2015; GDP is in PPP USD for 2014.
[a](Nasdaq+NYSE)/GDP
[b]Euronext is a pan-European exchange that operates four national regulated securities and derivatives markets in Amsterdam, Brussels, Lisbon, and Paris, as well as the UK-based regulated securities market, Euronext London. For the purposes of this table, it serves as the proxy for France.
Sources: World Federation of Exchanges (2015); OECD (2015).

services for banks, exchanges, and derivatives has actually decreased the relative importance of equities there. Other stock exchanges, including the London Stock Exchange (LSE), have also found that their revenue from equity trading has fallen sharply while their revenue from clearing derivatives and providing data and indices has risen to be their major source of income (Gapper 2016).

The current leading exchanges in the world—in the United States, Europe, Japan, and China—have all de-mutualized from their historic, old-boy, club-like forms of organization and converted to some form of corporate ownership and governance. Consequently, they all now seek ways to generate overall profits for the exchange and their shareholders, whether by creating new products or attracting new customers. Their customers increasingly consist of institutional managers of huge portfolios held on behalf of pension funds, insurance companies, state and local governments, and sovereign wealth funds as well as hedge fund investors.

Moreover, all of today's exchanges have taken their trading venues completely electronic, seeking profit in the volume of trades they can facilitate. These trades are done in milliseconds across many alternative venues for a wide variety of clients spread across the globe. This is the world vilified by Michael Lewis (2014) in his book, *Flash Boys: A Wall Street Revolt.*[1]

At its heart, *Flash Boys* is a story of the centuries-old conflict between bankers and investment management firms, on the one hand, and stock traders on the other, about the best way to serve their clients. Acting on behalf of clients who have entrusted their financial assets to them, banks and investment managers like to conceal their actions from the prying eyes of competitors or, possibly, government regulators.[2]

Before the advent of electronic trading platforms, banks would negotiate large-volume transactions with favored customers "upstairs" (off the floor of the exchange) to avoid disturbing the rest of the market. Now, banks create "dark pools" of electronic trading that are open only to their customers. Traders in open-access exchanges, however, necessarily deal with possible competitors in a transparent market. They need to reassure their clients (and themselves) that they have obtained the best price possible, whether as a buyer or as a seller, so that the commission they charge is worth the service they are providing their customers. "Price discovery" is the name of the game in stock markets, now as in centuries past. For a successful banker, by contrast, keeping a client's price point confidential may be essential to retain his or her business.

By August 2015, IEX ATS (the alternative trading system created by Lewis' hero, Brad Katsuyama, to foil front-running by high-frequency traders) had become the 4th largest "dark pool" in US equity trading. Unlike competing ATS companies that are owned and operated by major international banks (e.g., UBS, Credit Suisse, Deutsche Bank, Morgan Stanley, and Merrill Lynch), IEX is strictly "buy-side" and is owned by a collection of mutual and hedge funds, such as Greenlight Capital and Pershing Square.[3]

Given that in 2012 the NYSE became part of Intercontinental Exchange, Inc. (ICE), which owns and operates 23 regulated exchanges in the United States and abroad and is owned by 10 of the largest banks in the world, the

---

[1]Lewis' hero, a securities trader for the Royal Bank of Canada named Brad Katsuyama, found that high-frequency traders were "front-running" the orders he placed for clients. In his rebuttal, *Flash Boys: Not So Fast, An Insider's Perspective on High-Frequency Trading*, Peter Kovac (2014) pointed out that this was the result of computer technology on electronic trading platforms advancing much more rapidly for traders in stock exchanges than for traders within banks.

[2]Before the sub-prime crisis of 2008, it now appears that some banks even concealed their actions from themselves!

[3]As of 2 September 2016, IEX had transitioned from being an ATS to a registered national securities exchange. It is now called the "Exchange" by Investors' Exchange LLC (see www.iextrading.com).

separation of banks and markets into separate organizations has become a historical relic. Before 1973, the Anglo-American financial systems could be seen as largely market driven, while banks dominated the European Continental financial systems. That distinction has become increasingly irrelevant in the 21st century.

In well-functioning and effectively regulated financial systems, the two forms of financial intermediation—through networks of institutions or through markets—are complementary. But when technical innovations occur more rapidly in one forum than the other, they can become substitutes. This certainly happened in the mid-1970s when disintermediation of savings and loan banks in the United States followed the collapse of the Bretton Woods system in 1971–1973. Mutual funds investing in short-term government securities yielding high rates of interest at the time quickly attracted household savings out of US commercial banks and savings and loan institutions, which were limited by law from raising interest rates for depositors. The competitive race for finding a sustainable complementarity among banks, markets, and regulators continues to this day.

How Did the Separation of Banks, Markets, and Regulators Begin?

Even before the railroad age (starting in 1830) created large-scale demands for external finance, the military powers of Europe found that sovereign debt could be a bountiful source of war finance (Neal 1990, 2015). The massive issues of new British national debt to confront the French revolutionary armies after 1793 led to a huge expansion of business for the brokers and jobbers who made a living trading British national debt in the coffee houses around London's Exchange Alley and in the lobby of the Bank of England. Their business had grown steadily after the Glorious Revolution of 1688–1689 (Dickson 1967; Murphy 2009; Neal 1990).

By 1801, the traders felt the need to build and maintain their own space to conduct trading among themselves for their respective customers. The motivation of the 260 proprietors, who had raised £20,000 in 400 shares of £50 each in 1801 to build the new stock exchange in London—the London Stock Exchange—was clearly expressed later by their chairperson: It was to keep their doors "open to honourable men and closed shut for ever to notorious cheats."

The latter obviously included the merchant bank Boyd, Benfield & Co., which was then undergoing bankruptcy proceedings after having taken the largest part of the huge issue of government debt floated in 1796. Boyd,

Benfield & Co. was a recently established merchant bank with affiliates in Antwerp and Amsterdam, acquired while Walter Boyd had been active as a banker in Paris until he left in 1793. His failure recalled that of Mitford & Merttins, a major goldsmith bank that had administered many of the subscriptions opened for new projects during the South Sea Bubble of 1720. The proprietors of the New Stock Exchange were determined, therefore, to keep out such parvenus who parlayed foreigner's money into speculative positions on the future of "the funds," as the various forms of British national debt were termed.

The proprietors (owners) delegated to the trustees and managers of the LSE the management of the closely held corporation for their mutual profit as shareholders. The subscribers (operators) delegated their powers, in turn, to the Committee for General Purposes. Thereafter, the Committee for General Purposes was elected by the members of the previous year, and then that committee would determine who would be members for the following year, year by year.

From this initial separation of the rights and responsibilities of ownership from the rights and responsibilities of operation, the path dependency of the governance structure was set. It was always in the interest of the operators to limit membership to individuals they could trust to complete each transaction; while the interest of the owners was to increase membership as much as possible because the annual fee paid by each subscriber had to be kept at the traditional level of 10 guineas for full members and 5 guineas for their clerks—fees that remained at this level through 1860. An early lawsuit against the LSE had argued successfully that fees had long been established for access to the various coffee houses that had hosted exchange activity throughout the 18th century and should be maintained. As a result, the profitability of the LSE depended on increasing the number of members over time. The low fees also deterred any competing stock exchange from arising in London.

The corporate structure and the respective incentives for owners versus operators of the London Stock Exchange determined the responses to the challenges of technological progress and the spread of industrialization worldwide for the rest of the 19th century. Successive innovations to encourage an increase of members who could solicit business from an ever-wider range of customers for an ever-expanding list of securities allowed the LSE to become the leading market for global capital by 1914 (see **Figure 6.1**).

But first, the new governance structure had to establish its legitimacy. It took another 30 years to solidify the LSE's governance structure in the face of repeated shocks to the market for securities. In 1810, an attempt was made to form a rival stock exchange, an attempt that barely failed in Parliament. The

Figure 6.1.   Micro-Structure of the LSE, 1812–1876

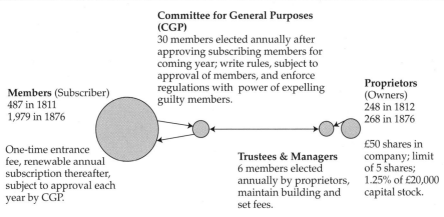

Source: Davis and Neal (2006).

challenge of a competitive exchange, however, motivated the Committee for General Purposes, representing the subscribers, to set out clearly in February 1812 the rules and regulations under which the exchange operated. These rules determined the structure of the LSE until 1876, when the need to build a much larger structure to accommodate the growing number of members led to an expansion of capital stock that was met by requiring new members to acquire shares as well as pay annual dues.

From the beginning, the LSE strictly prohibited members from being associated in any way with a bank. Even wives or family members of a member could not be employed in the management of a bank. Bankers were valued for their services in facilitating payments and attesting to the soundness of corporations wishing to list on the LSE, but they were kept at arms' length from negotiating actual transfers of securities on the exchange. The memory of the havoc created by bank failures during the South Sea Bubble and then Boyd, Benfield & Co. persisted until the Big Bang[4] of 1986.

Beyond excluding private bankers from the exchange, the members had to declare whether they were jobbers or brokers, which further segmented the personnel of the exchange. Jobbers essentially operated as "market makers," holding inventory in various securities and ready to buy or sell standard or odd lots of securities, making their money on the spread between bid and ask prices. They were typically the wealthier members of the exchange, and most were also proprietors who had put up capital for the initial building. Brokers,

---

[4]The "Big Bang" of 1986 refers to the expected increase in market activity after the LSE changed its rules as a result of the Thatcher government's deregulation of financial markets.

bringing in business from their network of customers, had to approach various jobbers to see what was the best price on offer for their principal, making their living from the commissions charged on each transaction.

Owners versus Operators

The most dramatic test of the LSE's initial governance structure came in 1822, and its resolution set the pattern for enlargement and innovation in the membership for decades to come. The issue dealt with the spate of defaulters among the younger, under-capitalized members of the LSE during the volatile period of 1819–1822. Many of these defaulters had laid off their risks with option contracts made with older, better-capitalized members but had then had defaulted. The Committee for General Purposes resolved to outlaw any future dealings in options among members of the exchange. Their main argument was that dealing in options put members in danger of violating Barnard's Law, effective since 1734, which set severe penalties for anyone dealing in options on long-term government debt. A vigorous battle ensued within the membership of subscribers for control of the committee at the next election.

Essentially, the battle pitched the older, better-established jobbers against the younger members, usually brokers. Abraham Montefiore, brother-in-law of Nathan Rothschild, was a leader of the "anti-optionist" or "constructionist" faction; while Jacob Ricardo, nephew of the deceased David Ricardo, was the outspoken leader of the "optionist" faction. Ricardo's arguments, reproduced in full in the minutes of the Committee for General Purposes, were obviously directed at the proprietors and their interests in maintaining a large membership of subscribers to the exchange. Ricardo argued that options were especially necessary for the younger members of the exchange and the less wealthy members during periods of price turbulence, such as had been experienced with the resumption of the gold standard (declared by Parliament in 1819 and taking full effect in 1821). Ricardo's argument was compelling, and the managers saw to it that Ricardo and his allies dominated the Committee for General Purposes elected in 1822. (Although 419 ballots were cast, all but 4 were declared ineligible by the scrutineers from the managers. Those 4 ballots determined that the new committee would have a majority of "optionists," headed by Jacob Ricardo.)

The compelling interest of the proprietors to maintain a substantial membership was even more clearly demonstrated shortly afterwards with the rise of interest in foreign securities, especially the bonds that were issued from 1822 on by the seceding colonies of the Spanish Empire in America. An entirely new group of traders arose who wished to trade in foreign securities—in both the bonds issued by the newly independent states of Spanish America and the shares in the newly privatized mines expropriated by the rebellious colonists. Again, the proprietors, with their eye on the revenues to be obtained from an expanding membership, were favorable to the requests of these traders for expanded and preferably separate facilities for carrying on this new trade. As a matter of principle, the strict constructionists raised the objection that the Deed of Settlement only referred to dealing in "British stocks," so they feared that dealing in foreign stocks would be illegal for the LSE. The "optionists," again with recourse to legal counsel, argued that while the deed mentioned British funds, it did not forbid dealing in foreign stocks.

Rather than resume warfare on this issue, the committee compromised by referring the matter to the trustees and managers, who responded quickly on behalf of the proprietors who saw an opportunity for increasing the profits of their closely held company. The proprietors rented an adjacent building, dedicated it to dealing in foreign stocks, and took responsibility for admitting the members to the foreign exchange but on the same terms as used by the Committee for General Purposes for admitting members to the London exchange. As a result, the proprietors were able to increase their revenues while maintaining the same restrictions on admissions to both exchanges. As long as the boom in foreign securities lasted (until the autumn of 1825), the representatives of the Foreign Stock Market found their membership increasing and consequently held fast to their determination for establishing independence from the Committee for General Purposes. By the election of 1823, the Foreign Stock Market had its own governance system, the Foreign Committee.

Faced with new securities devised by the London merchant banking houses eager to exploit the fabled (and much exaggerated) riches of Spanish America, the Foreign Committee proved to be the source of several innovations that were later incorporated into the rules and regulations of the LSE. For example, the first listing requirement formally stated by the governing committee of either exchange was passed by the Foreign Committee in April 1824. After a number of Latin American bonds had defaulted, the committee declared that it would not list any new bonds, stocks, or other securities issued by any foreign government that had defaulted on former loans until it had made some satisfactory arrangement with the holders of the former securities. The financial crisis of December 1825, created by the collapse of most Latin American securities, led to widespread bankruptcies among country banks and reduced the membership of the Foreign Stock Market. The few remaining members were absorbed into the LSE in 1832, well after the excitement in Latin American bonds and mining stocks had lapsed. Thereafter, any new securities to be listed on the foreign exchange also had to be approved beforehand by a standing committee of the London Stock Exchange.

London and the Provincial Exchanges

The formal markets for stocks and bonds in the United Kingdom were the LSE and the much smaller provincial stock exchanges. These markets were far from complete; Lavington (1921) estimated that, of the over 35,000 security issues in the United Kingdom, only 5,000 were officially quoted on any exchange; of those, "less than 400 have at any time a free market." For firms desirous of having their securities listed or quoted, access to the provincial markets was frequently easier than access to the LSE (Thomas 1973, p. 138).

The links among the provincial stock exchanges and between each provincial stock exchange and the LSE began in the 1830s. Brokers, whether in London or the provinces, merely acted as agents for their customers and filled their orders with jobbers in the primary market for the security in question. In the 1870s, however, to realize the possibilities of the expanding telegraph network in the British Isles and then with the European continent, eventually including the United States in 1866, the national network of agents was supplemented by the widespread innovation of shunting (arbitrage). A shunter bought securities for his own account in low-priced markets and sold them in high-priced ones. In the provinces, the shunter provided price information about securities that were primarily traded in other provincial markets and in London. By linking provincial investors to London jobbers, a shunter gave them access to the competitive facilities and to the breadth and depth of the main markets at near net prices.

London shunters, on the other hand, provided the city's brokers with supplies of "country" securities and with information about their prices in the major provincial stock exchanges. Thus, London investors had the opportunity to diversify into country issues that were not listed on the LSE. As a result of these inter-market links, for almost four decades the United Kingdom had a well-integrated capital market with London at the center, while joint-stock banks separately created an extensive network of branches.

Foreign Alternative Financial Systems

The successful example set by the United Kingdom's financial system, however, was not adopted by the competing industrial powers of the 19th century. Different legal and political environments in the United States, France, and Germany led each of them to create stock exchanges with different ways to perform essentially the same operations. Although the legal environment was broadly similar for the United Kingdom and the United States, for example, their different political structures led to differences in their organization of both banks and capital markets. Regional exchanges flourished in both countries, but in the United Kingdom they never competed with the central exchange in London for primacy. The continued expansion of the LSE membership, which peaked in 1907 at 5,473 members and 3,822 clerks, as well as the active role of shunters, ensured the dominance of the LSE.

In the United States, it took the Civil War (1861–1865) to establish permanently the preeminence of the New York Stock Exchange over the older exchanges of Philadelphia and Boston and the rising exchanges of Cincinnati and Chicago. Further, the NYSE fought a constant battle to establish and then maintain its primacy as the central marketplace in New York because its owners limited the number of trading positions, called "seats," to themselves, and each "seat" could act as either broker or jobber. New businesses that arose over the 19th century found their investors in the "curb" market just outside the NYSE building or, later, in the Consolidated Exchange that proved to be a strong competitor. (The New York Curb Exchange, organized out of the curb market in the early 1900s, later became the American Stock Exchange, which continues to exist as part of the NYSE under the name NYSE MKT LLC.)

By contrast, the LSE with its ever-expanding membership was able to encompass all the business in London and place the regional exchanges in a complementary, rather than competing, role throughout the 19th century. (The complementary role of the provincial exchanges was threatened, however, in 1912, when the members of the LSE both established minimum commissions and forbade jobbers to shunt business from other exchanges.) Banks and other financial institutions were expressly forbidden to participate in any of the UK exchanges, while on the US exchanges they were able to form partnerships with brokerage firms or buy seats directly until the regulatory reforms of the 1930s.

On the continent in the late 19th century, where the legal environment provided statutory monopolies for the central stock exchanges located in Paris and Berlin, the roles of the central exchanges were nevertheless different due to differences in the power of the central government. In Paris, a small group of *agents de change*, which became tightly organized over the century as a self-regulating *compagnie*, was able to call upon the enforcement powers of the central state from time to time to maintain its monopoly. The result was that the rules of the Paris Bourse remained essentially unchanged from the time of Napoleon until the breakup of its monopoly under pressure from the European Community in the late 1980s.

While the *agents de change* on the formal exchange were restricted by law to act only as brokers for securities that the government allowed to be listed for the general public, a complementary exchange (the Coulisse) immediately arose next to the Bourse. The Coulisse allowed both brokers and jobbers to act on behalf of investors in new securities, especially those marketed by joint-stock banks. By 1890, the Coulisse was known as the bankers' market and its trading volumes exceeded those on the formal market (known as the Parquet) in the 1890s. The role played by regional stock exchanges was minimal in France, however, because provincial business firms (even large-scale ones in coal and iron) relied mostly on local banks for their financing.

Exchanges in Germany in the 19th century also operated under statutory laws enforced by state authority. The fragmented political structure, however, meant that regional exchanges prospered before unification of the German Reich in 1871. Then, the Frankfurt exchange was displaced by Berlin as joint-stock banks moved their headquarters to the capital. Further, banks had always operated the Berlin exchange, their only restriction being to allow open access. Over time, however, different interest groups were able to change drastically both the rules of operation on the exchanges and the role they played in capital mobilization for the country. After 1898, when forward trading was outlawed, German banks moved much of their derivatives business to the more permissive exchanges in Amsterdam and London.

Conclusion

Since 1971, the progressive demutualization of membership for each exchange in the world and their adoption of corporate forms of governance, with banks taking major ownership stakes, recall the early days of conflict between owners and operators in the LSE. The initial separation of owners from operators in the case of London had the happy effect of promoting internal expansion and continued innovation in products and services for much of the 19th century, which augurs well for the improved efficiency and effectiveness of today's stock exchanges as they compete with each other in a global market.

When London's operators became the majority of the owners at the end of the 19th century, however, the LSE lost much of its dynamism because the members, mostly brokers, raised commissions and restricted the arbitraging activities of jobbers. Business increasingly went to regional exchanges in the United Kingdom and overseas to Europe and the United States. Competition among exchanges even in New York, as well as across the United States, however, led to the American financial system becoming the world's best-suited for financing the technology of the Second Industrial Revolution out of the chemical and auto industries, along with electricity and petroleum (Davis and Neal 2007).

Still, the links of personal exchanges needed to establish trust in the facilities for impersonal exchange—links that were so important for the historical development of stock exchanges—have yet to be re-created for modern information communications technology. The conflicting business models for banks and exchanges continue to be tested against advances in technology and regulators' concerns. Moreover, global competition needs to be sustained among both banks and exchanges if the benefits of finance for the global economy and its many participants are to continue.

Bibliography

Davis, Lance, and Larry Neal. 1998. "Micro Rules and Macro Outcomes: The Impact of Micro Structure on the Efficiency of Security Exchanges, London, New York, and Paris, 1800–1914." *American Economic Review*, vol. 88, no. 2 (May): 40–45.

———. 2006. "The Evolution of the Structure and Performance of the London Stock Exchange in the First Global Financial Market, 1812–1914." *European Review of Economic History*, vol. 10, no. 3 (December): 279–300.

———. 2007. "Why Did Finance Capitalism and the Second Industrial Revolution Arise in the 1890s?" In *Financing Innovation in the United States, 1870 to the Present*. Edited by Naomi Lamoreaux and Kenneth Sokoloff. Cambridge, MA: MIT Press.

Davis, Lance, Larry Neal, and Eugene N. White. 2003. "How it All Began: The Rise of Listing Requirements on the London, Berlin, Paris, and New York Stock Exchanges." *International Journal of Accounting*, vol. 38: 117–143.

Dickson, Peter. 1967. *The Financial Revolution in England: A Study in the Development of Public Credit, 1688-1756*. New York: St. Martin's Press.

Gapper, John. 2016. "The Death and Rebirth of the Stock Exchange." *Financial Times* (9 March): 13.

Gibson, George Rutledge. 1889. *The Stock Exchanges of London, Paris, and New York: A Comparison—Primary Source Edition*. New York: G.P. Putnam's Sons.

Gömmel, Rainer. 1992. "Entstehung und Entwicklung der Effektenbörse im 19. Jahrhundert bis 1914." In Hans Pohl, ed., *Deutsche Börsengeschichte*. Frankfurt am Main: Fritz Knapp Verlag.

Hannah, Leslie. 2015. "Unequal Fortunes, Unequal Firm Sizes, and Close Corporations in the Gilded Age." Paper presented at the Business History Conference, Miami, FL (24–27 June).

Hautcoeur, Pierre-Cyrille, ed. 2007. *Le marché financier français au XIXe siècle. Vol. 1. Le récit*. Paris: Publications de la Sorbonne.

Hautcoeur, Pierre-Cyrille, and Angelo Riva. 2012. "The Paris Financial Market in the Nineteenth Century: Complementarities and Competition in Microstructures." *Economic History Review,* vol. 65, no. 4 (November): 1326–1353.

Kovac, Peter. 2014. *Flash Boys: Not So Fast. An Insider's Perspective on High-Frequency Trading.* New York: Directissima Press.

Lavington, F. 1921. *The English Capital Market.* London: Methuen & Co.

Lewis, Michael. 2014. *Flash Boys: A Wall Street Revolt.* New York & London: W.W. Norton & Company.

Lowenfeld, Henry. 1909. *Investment, An Exact Science.* London: Financial Review of Reviews.

Michie, Ranald S. 1999. *The London Stock Exchange: A History.* Oxford, UK: Oxford University Press.

Murphy, Anne L. 2009. *The Origins of English Financial Markets: Investment and Speculation before the South Sea Bubble.* Cambridge, UK: Cambridge University Press.

Neal, Larry. 1990. *The Rise of Financial Capitalism: International Capital Markets in the Age of Reason.* New York: Cambridge University Press.

———. 2012a. "Rules Governing Exchanges: How They Were Shaped by, and Shaped, Global Financial Competition among Markets." In Gerald Caprio, ed., *Handbook of Key Global Financial Markets, Institutions, and Infrastructure.* Boston: Elsevier.

———. 2012b. *'I Am Not Master of Events': The Speculations of John Law and Lord Londonderry in the Mississippi and South Sea Bubbles.* New Haven, CT: Yale University Press.

———. 2015. *A Concise History of International Finance: From Babylon to Bernanke.* Cambridge, UK: Cambridge University Press.

Neymark, M.A. 1916. *La statistique internationale des valeurs mobilières.* Paris: Alcan.

Obstfeld, Maurice, and Alan M. Taylor. 2004. *Global Capital Markets: Integration, Crisis, and Growth.* Cambridge, UK: Cambridge University Press.

OECD. 2015. *Main Economic Indicators,* vol. 2015, no. 9. Paris: OECD Publishing (September).

Parker, William. *The Paris Bourse and French Finance,* New York: Columbia University, 1920.

Petram, Lodewijk. 2014. *The World's First Stock Exchange*. New York: Columbia University Press.

Schwartz, Robert. 1991. *Reshaping the Equity Markets*. New York: HarperBusiness.

Spray, David E., ed. 1964. *The Principal Stock Exchanges of the World: Their Operation, Structure and Development*. Washington, DC: International Economic Publishers.

Sylla, Richard. 2002. "Financial Systems and Economic Modernization." *Journal of Economic History*, vol. 62, no. 2 (June): 277–292.

Thomas, W.A. 1973. *The Provincial Stock Exchanges*. London: Frank Cass.

Vidal, Émile. 1910. *The History and Methods of the Paris Bourse*. Washington, DC: National Monetary Commission.

World Federation of Exchanges. 2015. "Monthly Reports" (www.world-exchanges.org/home/index.php/statistics).

7. Frictions: Lessons from the History of Financial Market Microstructure

Caroline Fohlin
Professor, Department of Economics, Emory University

The field of financial market microstructure analyzes how markets function at a fine level of detail—including how traders interact, how orders are placed and cleared, how information is relayed and priced, and how regulation and taxes affect market operations and costs. Microstructure theory shows that asymmetric information causes frictions that impede market quality, and the way markets organize and operate—along with outside factors that influence traders' decisions—affects how much friction exists. Add in uncertainty shocks that have occurred since markets developed over a century ago, and these frictions become even more difficult to manage. By using microstructure analysis to understand how past markets dealt with these shocks, we can learn lessons that inform current market behavior.

Introduction

The basic theory of microstructure pits traders and market makers against one another in strategic games in which players strive to maximize their profits. An extensive technical literature provides many variations and refinements of financial market microstructure analysis.[1]

Even in the most smoothly operating markets, investors and traders face a wide range of transaction costs. These costs vary depending on the nature of the securities traded, market organization, trading technology, and government regulation. Market microstructure influences a market's behavior under normal conditions and, perhaps more importantly, its response to unusual events. Today, unusual events—or uncertainty shocks—involve macro-level disruptions, such as the Greek debt and Eurozone crisis, as well as localized episodes, such as computer glitches. One hundred years ago, a global war threatened market quality, and financial panics destabilized markets to varying degrees every few years.

In this chapter, I offer ideas on what lessons we might glean from the history of financial markets, focusing on microstructure history. After an overview of historical market development, I lay out the major issues that pervade market microstructure analysis, regardless of the era. Then I present

---

[1]See the textbook by de Jong and Rindi (2009) for a compact survey.

highlights from the available historical microstructure analyses. Although the historical microstructure literature is currently limited, new work is underway to gather much more comprehensive data that will permit in-depth analysis. The most advanced of these new projects—largely due to data availability— concerns the NYSE (New York Stock Exchange), particularly in the three decades leading up to the crash of 1929. Where possible, this chapter also includes insights from other major markets of the pre-World War II era.[2]

Financial Market Microstructure

The key insight of microstructure theory is that asymmetric information causes frictions that impede market quality. The way markets organize and operate—along with outside factors that influence traders' decisions—affects how much friction exists. Thus, the study of microstructure is fundamentally the study of transaction costs—how they arise and why they vary—across securities and over time.

The overall cost of trading faced by a market participant incorporates a range of cost components: order processing costs; costs associated with inventory holding by market makers; and charges for accepting the risk of trading against insiders (i.e., adverse selection costs). Order processing costs remain largely fixed regardless of prices or trade size, but they also include any monopoly rents that market makers can capture. Thus, in monopolistic markets, order processing charges naturally exceed competitive rates; the effects may intensify for less frequently traded securities if few exchanges will trade them. Inventory holding costs compensate market makers for the risk of order imbalances, which vary significantly according to the volume, volatility, and liquidity of the market and of the particular security traded. Adverse selection costs come into play when salient information about a security is privately held; the market maker may experience losses once this information is revealed and the market price moves against him.[3]

Theory points us to a number of measures of market quality—most notably, its liquidity, which is the ease with which traders can transact. Market quality has numerous dimensions: transaction costs, speed of price discovery, price impact, and even volatility. And there are even more ways to measure it. First and foremost, microstructure studies analyze liquidity proxies, such as

---

[2]See Chapter 6 in this monograph for a broader survey of the development of exchanges in London, New York, Paris, and Berlin (Neal, forthcoming 2016).
[3]For theoretical treatments, see Glosten and Milgrom (1985) and Kyle (1985).

bid–ask spreads and price impact (i.e., how much prices change in response to trade).[4]

Key Issues Then and Now: Impediments to Market Quality. It is well known among financial industry professionals that market microstructure influences the functioning of markets. With such popular treatments as Michael Lewis' (2014) *Flash Boys*, the recent policy debates over "high frequency trading," and proposals for transaction taxes—as well as past and proposed future mergers among the world's major securities exchanges—the topic of market microstructure has come noticeably to the fore in the past decade.

Financial markets cope well with risk in situations where outcomes (returns) vary depending on the state of the world but market participants still have a good idea of the distribution of possible states and outcomes. Uncertainty arises when we do not even know the distribution of possible outcomes (returns), which can occur when a shock happens that affects the whole market or when a firm-specific problem arises that upsets a specific security. Uncertainty poses a major problem in operating financial markets because traders cannot accurately price assets with uncertain return distributions. Risk and uncertainty capture a whole range of problems that hinder markets from operating smoothly.

Markets have always had to manage a wide range of risks, some systematic and others idiosyncratic. Markets are generally ideally equipped to handle idiosyncratic risk. One of the main reasons for trading securities—and operating exchanges to do so—is to diversify investment portfolios to mitigate idiosyncratic risks, such as R&D investments and outcomes, new technology, and managerial or accounting differences.

Most issues that present risk also place outside investors at an informational disadvantage. Outsiders naturally learn salient information after insiders; moreover, in many cases even once outsiders have the information, they cannot evaluate it as precisely as insiders. This information asymmetry allows moral hazard to creep into markets and enables such misbehavior as front-running and insider trading. Whether committed by company insiders or by brokers and dealers, these actions hinder market quality by undermining trust—creating uncertainty—among uninformed investors. In extreme cases, uninformed participants will refuse to trade at all.

---

[4]More on these measures appears in the analysis section of this chapter. See Jones (2002) for a long-run view of spreads and broader trading costs for the largest traded stocks over the full 20th century.

Disruptions arise when uncertainty shocks, whether systematic or idiosyncratic, hit the market. How a market performs under these stress scenarios provides an important measure of market quality.

Market Fragmentation versus Market Power. Securities markets today operate like many other large-scale multinational businesses. They provide a particular set of services—price discovery and liquidity—and compete in a global marketplace for those services. The industrial organization of exchange services—the number and market power of producers—affects the production of their key output (information, or prices). As in many industries with network externalities, the trading industry faces a trade-off between the efficiency of consolidation and the costs of diminishing competition. Consolidation brings together more traders and potentially improves informational efficiency and speed of price discovery, but eliminating competition can give market makers monopoly power and raise costs.

Securities markets compete on price, as well as quality, and the price is the cost of trading, such as the bid–ask spread. The minimum spread, in turn, depends on the minimum tick size—the smallest amount by which prices may change—because it sets a lower bound on the bid–ask spread. Reducing the minimum tick size in the major markets (e.g., the NYSE's reduction from eighths to sixteenths to decimals in the late 20th century) can significantly narrow spreads.[5] Because competition can reduce spreads only so much, the tightening of quoted spreads moves the profit search to execution and raises issues of order priority and front-running.

Competition in the securities exchange business may therefore reduce the monopoly rents incorporated into order processing costs but, at the same time, increase trading costs associated with fragmentation of information and order flow—the inventory holding and adverse selection components. For this reason, market competition historically has waxed and waned because of the urge to consolidate information and order flow: Consolidation creates market power, which then induces new entrants to appear and undercut the monopolist. One can observe this pattern over recent decades, whereby formal markets have consolidated into giant, global marketplaces and continue to do so—exemplified by the 2016 plan to merge Deutsche Börse and the London Stock Exchange. At the same time, however, a spate of alternative trading systems—primarily start-up, electronic markets—has pulled a substantial share of trading out of the traditional exchanges.

These industry-level developments, along with a string of computer-related shutdowns, have spawned much public debate over the costs and

---

[5]See Chordia (2012).

benefits of multiple market places and national regulation of exchanges—promoting "best execution."[6] Today, the big markets worry about unregulated alternative trading systems, dark pools, and high-frequency traders; a century ago, they worried about bucket shops and regional exchanges as well as such upstart competitors as the Consolidated Exchange that operated almost next door to the NYSE.[7]

A Brief History of Financial Market Development

Most securities markets evolved out of markets that traded in either commodities or commercial paper; as a result, the originators tended to be merchants of some sort. Exchanges moved into securities trading as such instruments became more prevalent. Government debt made up the bulk of trading in most early securities markets, including the NYSE, which was founded in its rudimentary form in 1792 primarily to trade the new US government debt.

The earliest securities exchanges appeared atomistically and on a small scale, often constituting little more than organized groups of several brokers meeting in a particular spot on a regular basis. Markets appeared in all sorts of locations, with many of the earliest co-locating with other markets and fairs in which interested traders gathered in one location. Slow and costly transportation and information technology limited the scale and scope of these early markets and tended to locate them in such historically important trading locations as Antwerp, Amsterdam, Genoa, and London. In the United States, the earliest markets appeared in Boston, Philadelphia, and New York.[8]

Early markets in securities operated inside other businesses (such as coffee houses), in designated street locations—including under the famous Buttonwood tree on Wall Street—or, in some cases, in their own purpose-built meeting spaces, such as those in Antwerp (dating to the 16th century) and Amsterdam (created in 1602 by the Dutch East India Company). As the availability of government and corporate securities grew, stock exchanges gradually developed into formal organizations with rules and regulations and with their own buildings.

---

[6]See the *Wall Street Journal* article by Jonathan Macey and David Swensen, "The Cure for Stock-Market Fragmentation: More Exchanges" (31 May 2015): www.wsj.com/articles/the-cure-for-stock-market-fragmentation-more-exchanges-1433109068.

[7]On current competition, particularly vis à vis dark pools, see the article by Annabelle Ju in *Bloomberg*, which quotes Intercontinental Exchange (ICE) CEO Jeff Sprecher saying, "It'd be great if I could own the entire market. We can't. We won't. We never will. And what we do try to do is come up with solutions for our customers for the parts of the market where we do things well" (5 February 2015): www.bloomberg.com/news/articles/2015-02-05/a-top-dark-pool-rival-concedes-they-have-role-in-stock-markets.

[8]See Rousseau (2009) for a study of the Boston Stock Exchange in the mid-19th century.

With few securities to trade and few participants, the earliest exchanges wielded monopoly power over trading in their markets. As the number and scale of corporate firms expanded, however, the number of tradable securities increased and the population of traders and investors grew in step. Still, the number of traders, number of actively traded securities, and volume of trade typically remained very small until the late 19th century and, in many cases, well into the 20th.

Call Auction versus Continuous Trading. The small scale of trading required trading methods to match; as a result, early exchanges generally organized trading with call auctions. These call auctions used open outcry methods to collect bids to buy and offers to sell, one issue at a time, until the best price could be reached to clear the market as completely as possible. By gathering all participants interested in the same assets into the same location simultaneously, an auction incorporates all information available at a given point in time into transaction prices. The alternative, continuous trading with a specialist market maker, tends to fragment information over time because of the random arrival of buyers and sellers and their associated knowledge or assessment of asset values. Call auctions, therefore, allowed the most-efficient aggregation of information from the relatively small number of participants in those early markets.

By the latter part of the 19th century, some markets evolved into a continuous trading system because increasingly lengthy lists of stocks took too long to complete in a call auction. The NYSE, for example, moved to continuous trading in 1872 by using specialists at fixed trading posts.[9] Still, many markets—even such large and active ones as in Berlin—maintained the call auction format well into the 20th century.

Trading Technology and Speed. Securities market operations hinge on the aggregation of information, and therefore the technologies for moving people and transmitting information play the most dramatic role in both the informational and cost efficiency of financial markets. Each development in communications technology sped up the transmission of information and reduced latency, transaction time, and related transaction costs.[10] Communications technology also broadened the availability of information, eventually carrying news directly into individual businesses and homes.

Until the mid-19th century, market information moved via ships, horses, semaphore, and even birds. These rudimentary technologies kept markets

---

[9]See Davis and Neal (1998), where they compare organization and rules in London, New York, and Paris prior to 1914.
[10]See Hoag (2006).

confined primarily to those physically present in the given market location. Only those whose expected profits could overcome high costs, including time delay, would profit from engaging in markets; thus, markets remained small throughout their early history.

The invention of the telegraph in 1844 set off a boom in information technology over the second half of the 19th century. Telegraph communications spread throughout all major markets, and the opening of the trans-Atlantic cable in 1866 dramatically reduced the time and cost of trading between the key markets in London and New York.[11] The ticker, invented the next year, using dedicated telegraph connections, transmitted prices to those with ticker access in close to real time and revolutionized stock market communications. Still, individual investors could only access quotes by traveling to a broker's office, which added to the costs faced by those investors and thus continued to constrain participation in markets.

Telephone technology, first installed on the NYSE floor in 1878, also depended on networks of adopters to become useful and profitable. The ability to communicate orally sped communication times significantly and thus facilitated the adoption of the technology by a wider network of users, including those in individual homes. The number of telephones in place increased rapidly in the early 20th century, and the quality of the services improved as well over the late 19th and early 20th centuries. Telephones connected more and more distant locations and spread to ever-increasing numbers of people over time. Long-distance telephone technology developed in the early 20th century and expanded significantly around WWI, allowing the first call from New York to San Francisco in 1914.[12]

Computerization in the 1960s set off another round of reorganization of trading practices, while the internet and related technology fundamentally reshaped the trading industry and brought a wave of high speed trading in the early 21st century.

We now see debates over whether current trading methods produce transactions at too high a speed to allow accurate information and keep markets stable and liquid.[13]

On the occasion of the purchase of the NYSE by the Intercontinental Exchange (ICE), the *New York Times* quoted ICE CEO, Jeff Sprecher, who

---

[11]The NYSE website offers a compact timeline of technology introductions and other types of events at https://web.archive.org/web/20100501152051/http://www.nyse.com/about/history/timeline_technology.html.

[12]See the article "Across the Continent by Telephone" in *Scientific American* (6 February 1915): https://books.google.com/books?id=HcsxAQAAMAAJ&pg=PA129#v=onepage&q&f=false.

[13]See, for example, Farmer and Skouras (2012).

said, "New, electronic trading systems have greatly reduced the cost of buying and selling stocks, thus saving mutual funds—and, by extension, ordinary investors—countless millions. But they have also helped usher in a period of hair-raising volatility."[14]

What We've Learned from Historical Analysis So Far

Financial historians have worked hard in recent years to unearth and catalog a trove of new data on financial markets and related institutions. Microstructure studies, in particular, require high frequency data on individual securities, which has been lacking until very recently.[15]

New studies are tackling questions about market microstructure, many of which continue to interest today's market observers. To begin with, we now have a much clearer picture of how stock markets operated in the three decades prior to the Great Depression and subsequently during the onset of major federal regulation of the financial system. To be sure, much has changed over the intervening decades. Nonetheless, we can glean some useful lessons—or reminders of what we already know—from these past experiences.

Market Competition Is Good for Investors. Analysts today are well aware of the trade-offs inherent in market consolidation and market fragmentation, but the historical research so far is considerably less definite on the issue of market competition. Such historical research is underway; however, few studies have as yet considered the market microstructure effects of competition and cross listing of shares. The distant history of the NYSE paints a picture of centuries of attempts to monopolize the exchange business, starting with the initial 1792 Buttonwood Agreement signed by 24 brokers to create a trading cartel that set commissions and exclusive dealing in a prescribed list of securities.

Through the late 18th and the 19th centuries, minor competitors to the NYSE arose, and regional exchanges operated throughout the United States. But the first significant competitor came with the formation of the Consolidated Stock and Petroleum Exchange in 1885. Brown, Mulherin, and Weidenmier (2008) argued that competition from the Consolidated limited market power among NYSE market makers, as evidenced (in their view) by tighter spreads during the period of greatest competition, up to the

---

[14]Nathaniel Popper, "Buying the N.Y.S.E., in One Shot," *New York Times* (19 January 2013): www.nytimes.com/2013/01/20/business/jeffrey-sprechers-improbable-path-to-buying-the-nyse.html?_r=0.

[15]See Fohlin (2014) for details of the NYSE historical data-gathering initiative, funded by the US National Science Foundation.

early 1920s. Based on cross-sectional average spreads at the end of each year, NYSE spreads averaged about 10% narrower during this period.[16]

White (2013) takes a different approach and studies market shares of the NYSE and regional exchanges and argues that the NYSE declined in relative importance during the late 1920s (from roughly 90% to a nadir of about 70% around the time of the crash in 1929–30), because competitors to the dominant market (NYSE) could better accommodate the new technology firms entering the markets at the time. In other words, different markets serve different purposes and populations of companies and investors.

Other countries also supported multiple competing markets, sometimes as next-door neighbors—like the Consolidated in the United States—but more often in other cities—such as the regional exchanges in the United States. In England, Germany, and Italy, the dominant market operated as local monopolies, but other exchanges arose in regions with their own trading needs.

Fohlin and Gehrig (forthcoming 2016) take a more complex, higher frequency, and security-level view of competition. The basic idea is that although multiple marketplaces can fragment information and transfer power to informed insiders, such multiple market trading can also push investors to learn information, thereby raising the total level of information available on those securities that trade in more than one venue.

To examine the differences between dual- and single-traded firms in terms of transaction costs and liquidity, their study analyzes the impact of market competition on various measures of market quality. The analysis covers all stocks traded every trading day on the NYSE from 1905 through 1910 and thus permits unprecedented granularity in the analysis of historical market competition.[17]

First, preliminary results show that dual-traded stocks traded with lower spreads and also reacted less negatively to the severe liquidity freeze during the Panic of 1907. Second, the NYSE's May 1909 action, which

---

[16]However, using panel data on all NYSE stocks, Fohlin (2016a) reported that spreads increased substantially over the 1910s and 1920s due to changes in market composition. Thus, the finding in Brown et al. (2008) likely captures this effect and not necessarily the impact of competition.

[17]Although dual-traded stocks were larger and generally more liquid (higher volumes, lower spreads), the diff-in-diff procedure helps mitigate the selection bias by examining the differential impact of exogenous events. In Fohlin and Gehrig (forthcoming 2016), the authors are also investigating the closing of the NYSE "unlisted" department over the latter part of 1909 and early 1910. The exchange announced the impending closing in July 1909 but did not officially close the department until April 1910. All "unlisted" stocks had to either gain official listing or stop trading at the NYSE.

cleaved connections between NYSE members and the Consolidated, seems to have impacted all stocks. Even single-traded (NYSE-only) stocks had a significantly lower trading volume (a decrease of 75%) and larger spreads (3%) after the NYSE dictate relative to their dual-traded peers. Brokers without NYSE memberships, including those primarily associated with the Consolidated, would have previously transacted substantial amounts of business on the NYSE; however, the abrupt stop to these accounts clearly interfered with such trading. Dual-traded stocks' spreads actually declined about 40%, as did their trading volumes—albeit only by 16%. These preliminary results suggest the need for further investigation, but clearly the connections between the NYSE and the Consolidated played an important role in the operations of the NYSE.

Market Liquidity Reflects Information Flow. Recent research shows that stock exchanges of the early 20th century performed well, despite mostly looser regulation of markets, dealers, and corporations. The number of securities traded and their aggregate trading volume rose steadily over the early 20th century and grew rapidly during and after World War I. As new stocks representing smaller companies in new sectors were listed, average volume fell through the early 1920s but then grew rapidly later in the decade.[18] Similar patterns emerged in other advanced financial systems of the time, such as the United Kingdom, France, Germany, and even in the somewhat less-advanced Italy and Japan.[19]

In the decade prior to World War I, quoted spreads at the NYSE averaged about 2%. At the same time, however, the median spread was only 86 basis points and a quarter of trades took place with spreads less than 36 basis points. Volatility also remained low in the pre-WWI period and then climbed during the war and during the financial crisis of 1920–21 before dropping off a bit in the mid-1920s.[20] The new listings and exuberance of the later 1920s naturally led to growing volatility, with very high cost levels in late 1929. Spreads returned to pre-WWI levels during the Great Depression and continued to decline—with considerable variation—over the rest of the 20th century. From the 1960s through the early 1990s, Jones (2002) estimates that average proportional spreads ranged between 50 and 70 basis points for the large and generally liquid stocks of the DJIA. Yet broader averages show

---

[18]See Fohlin (2016a) for a comprehensive weekly picture of the NYSE up to 1929. Jones (2002) estimates various cost measures, including proportional spreads, for the narrower group of stocks used in the Dow Jones Industrial Average.

[19]See Fohlin (2012) on the development of financial systems during the pre-World War I period.

[20]This analysis uses the "quasi-volatility" measure calculated in Fohlin (2016a), which takes the difference between a day's high and low prices and divides by the closing price.

spreads still in the 1.5% range throughout the 1990s, with gradual declines toward 1% in the mid-1990s and significant declines to below 1% following the reduction in tick sizes to sixteenths in 1997 (and even lower, 0.58% on average, with decimalization in 2000–2001).[21]

Illiquidity increases broadly with macro shocks, such as war and general financial crises, and it also varies consistently with idiosyncratic risk (i.e., firm-level variation in quasi-volatility). Many new firms entered the market in the late 1910s and early 1920s, and their stock traded with greater price volatility and wider spreads. Those that had traded for many years, starting prior to the war, experienced little or no difference in their market quality measures during the immediate post-war period.

Although trading volume rises with growth of a market, volume alone does not always indicate market liquidity. In fact, burgeoning trading volume itself also created information gaps during the 1920s. Most especially at the end of the 1920s, in the heat of the bull market, capacity constraints began to widen spreads as market makers struggled to keep up with orders and make sense of the information they contained.[22]

Beyond the NYSE, a few studies have also analyzed various measures of spreads and trading costs. Gehrig and Fohlin (2006), for example, found remarkably low trading costs among a nearly comprehensive set of stocks trading in Berlin for four benchmark years (1880, 1890, 1900, and 1910). Burhop and Gelman (2011) have confirmed earlier findings using a sample of 27 frequently traded stocks over the period 1891 to 1912. New work on the relatively late appearing Stockholm Stock Exchange, starting in 1901, shows another story—an exchange with a low number of stocks, low liquidity, and high and fixed transaction costs.[23]

Opaqueness Damages Market Quality, Especially during Crises. Like markets today, markets in the past had to deal with episodes of crisis, formerly (and appropriately) known as panics. Panics arise and grow due to information problems. Historical analysis underscores the critical role of opaqueness in propagating crises. In particular, opaqueness about the companies whose stocks are being traded causes uncertainty among traders and an inability to assess news and price it appropriately. When corporate governance and accounting standards are lax, information is distributed more unevenly among traders and investors, and uncertainty problems become more likely.

---

[21]See Jones (2002) for the full 20th century, albeit for the narrow DJIA sample. For greater detail and broader impacts of the 1997 and 2000–2001 tick size reductions, see Chordia, Roll, and Subrahmanyam (2001) and Bessembinder (2003).
[22]Davis, Neal, and White (2007) and Fohlin (2016a).
[23]Kristian Rydqvist, personal communication.

Nowhere was this pattern more clearly apparent than in the Panic of 1907, a classic example of a rumor-led run on financial markets. In this case, rumors of bank and trust company insolvency caused heavy withdrawals of liquidity from money markets ("call money" or typically overnight loans used to finance stock market transactions). The liquidity freeze rapidly drove up spreads and other measures of illiquidity.[24] Notably, illiquidity had been rising ahead of the peak of the crisis and remained elevated well after the crisis had abated. Trading volume fell—another typical response to uncertainty—and remained low for many months following the crisis. Patterns of illiquidity varied significantly in cross section as well; more opaque stocks were harder hit, especially small companies and those in mining, where accounting and corporate governance standards lagged. Notably, illiquidity hit harder for stocks traded in the NYSE's "unlisted" department, where companies could trade without having to undergo the exchange's vetting process and meet reporting rules. Asset pricing analysis also demonstrates that the market priced illiquidity, producing a liquidity premium similar to today's markets.

This analysis demonstrates how critical transparency is to the proper functioning of markets and that liquidity offers a clear barometer of market health. Moreover, the 1907 panic offers evidence of how information problems help transmit illiquidity attacks throughout the financial system. The lesson here is to focus on maintaining market liquidity by encouraging transparency about the trading process and the quality of traded assets.

Uncertainty Shocks Destabilize Markets, and Interventions Can Restore Order. Sometimes, information is simply absent or too complex to understand immediately; in those cases, the market cannot achieve reasonable liquidity in short order. Under such conditions, market quality may be restored by taking a holiday because doing so provides traders the time they need to acquire and analyze information. Trading may halt for hours or for several days, in part or altogether, depending on the magnitude of the disruption, but suspensions always take place because of interference with information flows. Even in cases of what turn out to be relatively minor technical glitches—such as the July 2015 software problem at the NYSE—uncertainty allows misinformation to enter the market and hinders market quality.[25]

One of the greatest uncertainty shocks of the 20th century came in the summer of 1914, when Austria–Hungary invaded Serbia. When troops mobilized and it became clear that Germany and Russia were engaging for war,

---

[24]See Fohlin, Gehrig, and Haas (2016) for extensive analysis, including other market quality measures and spread decomposition.

[25]The NYSE website provides a rundown of market status, including even brief or partial halts to trading (which are fairly common). See www.nyse.com/market-status/history.

panic hit all of the markets, starting with Europe but quickly spreading to the NYSE. Volatility and spreads surged at the start of the war, and exchanges quickly shut down trading. The NYSE was the last major exchange to close and the first to reopen, on 12 December 1914. Other markets stayed shut or constrained in operations even longer.[26] During the closure, the US Treasury infused cash into the banking system via emergency currency under the renewed Aldrich–Vreeland Act.

The hiatus and accompanying liquidity infusions allowed markets to return almost to pre-disturbance condition spreads, and volatility had fallen significantly by the time of the reopening and continued to decline after the first few days of renewed trading.[27] Notably, when German U-boots sank the Lusitania in May 1915 and caused a brief wave of fear of US entry into the war, the NYSE reacted with a sharp spike in volatility and illiquidity. But once the brief uncertainty shock was resolved, markets returned quickly to normal levels, demonstrating once again the value of transparency and of the speedy resolution of uncertainty. The contrast between the NYSE's reactions to the Lusitania event, on the one hand, and to the initial outbreak of the war, on the other, provides a gauge of the magnitude of uncertainty shocks and how they may best be managed.

The historical record seems to show that quick resolution and restoration of transparency eliminate the need for, or at least shorten the time needed for, a trading holiday. In the more recent past, we have seen that during major uncertainty events—such as the May 2010 "flash crash," the 2008 Lehman Brothers bankruptcy, or the 11 September 2001 attacks—market interventions have improved quality.[28]

Conclusions

Today's financial markets operate with such speed and technological sophistication that it may be difficult to see how the experiences of history can provide much insight for modern finance. However, historical analyses of financial markets demonstrate that we can learn from the past. Historical microstructure studies, in particular, allow us to view many of the same processes and challenges that concern modern markets but in a slow, methodical way. The

---

[26]Notably, Silber (2007) finds that the "shadow" market (New Street Market) that opened up outside the NYSE during its early WWI closure operated with surprisingly good liquidity.
[27]See Fohlin (2016b).
[28]See Gehrig and Haas (2016) for a microstructure analysis of the impact of the Lehman bankruptcy. Although Pagano argued that short-sale bans harmed liquidity, the diff-in-diff analysis using ADRs of foreign stocks trading on the NYSE during foreign bans as per Appel and Fohlin (2010) showed that bans actually improved quality.

Bibliography

Allen, F., F. Capie, C. Fohlin, H. Miyajima, R. Sylla, Y. Yafeh, and G. Wood. 2010. "How Important Historically Were Financial Systems for Growth in the U.K., U.S., Germany, and Japan?" Working paper, University of Pennsylvania, Wharton School (http://fic.wharton.upenn.edu/fic/papers/10/10-27.pdf).

Appel, I., and C. Fohlin. 2010. "'Shooting the Messenger?' The Impact of Short Sale Bans in Times of Crisis." Working paper, Johns Hopkins University (http://papers.ssrn.com/sol3/papers.cfm?abstract_id=1595003).

Beber, A., and M. Pagano. 2013. "Short-Selling Bans Around the World: Evidence from the 2007–09 Crisis." *Journal of Finance*, vol. 68, no. 1 (February): 343–381.

Bessembinder, H. 2003. "Trade Execution Costs and Market Quality after Decimalization." *Journal of Financial and Quantitative Analysis*, vol. 38, no. 4 (December): 747–777.

Brown, W.O., J.H. Mulherin, and M.D. Weidenmier. 2008. "Competing with the New York Stock Exchange." *Quarterly Journal of Economics*, vol. 123, no. 4 (November): 1679–1719.

Burhop, C., and S. Gelman. 2011. "Liquidity Measures, Liquidity Drivers, and Expected Returns on an Early Call Auction Market." Working paper, Max Planck Institute (http://papers.ssrn.com/sol3/papers.cfm?abstract_id=1919522##).

Chordia, T. 2012. "Tick Size Regulation." Economic Impact Assessment EIA6, UK Government's Foresight Project, *The Future of Computer Trading in Financial Markets* (www.gov.uk/government/uploads/system/uploads/attachment_data/file/289035/12-1067-eia6-tick-size-regulation.pdf).

Chordia, T., R. Roll, and A. Subrahmanyam. 2001. "Market Liquidity and Trading Activity." *Journal of Finance*, vol. 56, no. 2 (April): 501–530.

Davis, L., and L. Neal. 1998. "Micro Rules and Macro Outcomes: The Impact of Micro Structure on the Efficiency of Security Exchanges, London, New York, and Paris, 1800–1914." *American Economic Review*, vol. 88, no. 2 (May): 40–45.

Davis, L., L. Neal, and E. White. 2007. "The Highest Price Ever: The Great NYSE Seat Sale of 1928–1929 and Capacity Constraints." *Journal of Economic History*, vol. 67, no. 3 (September): 705–739.

de Jong, F., and B. Rindi. 2009. *The Microstructure of Financial Markets.* Cambridge, UK: Cambridge University Press.

Farmer, J., and S. Skouras. 2012. "Review of the Benefits of a Continuous Market vs. Randomised Stop Auctions." Economic Impact Assessment EIA11, UK Government Office for Science (www.gov.uk/government/uploads/system/uploads/attachment_data/file/289050/12-1072-eia11-continuous-market-vs-randomised-stop-auctions.pdf).

Fohlin, C. 2002. "Regulation, Taxation, and the Development of the German Universal Banking System, 1884–1913." *European Review of Economic History,* vol. 6, no. 2 (August): 221–254.

———. 2012. *Mobilizing Money: How the World's Richest Nations Financed Industrial Growth.* New York: Cambridge University Press.

———. 2014. "A New Database of Transactions and Quotes in the NYSE, 1900–25 with Linkage to CRSP." Mimeo, Johns Hopkins University.

———. 2016a. "Transforming the NYSE: Crisis and Expansion during the Great War and Its Aftermath." Mimeo, Emory University.

———. 2016b. "Complex News and Investor Uncertainty: The NYSE Reaction to the Global Crisis of 1914." Mimeo, Emory University.

Fohlin, C., T. Gehrig, and M. Haas. 2016. "Rumors and Runs in Opaque Markets: Evidence from the Panic of 1907." DP10497, Centre for Economic Policy Research, London.

Fohlin, C., and T. Gehrig. Forthcoming 2016. "Stock Exchange Competition and Market Liquidity: New Evidence from the Height of the NYSE-Consolidated Rivalry." Mimeo, Emory University and University of Vienna.

Frydman, C., E. Hilt, and L.Y. Zhou. 2015. "Economic Effects of Runs on Early 'Shadow Banks': Trust Companies and the Impact of the Panic of 1907." *Journal of Political Economy,* vol. 123, no. 4 (August): 902–940.

Gehrig, T., and C. Fohlin. 2006. "Trading Costs in Early Securities Markets: The Case of the Berlin Stock Exchange 1880–1910." *Review of Finance,* vol. 10, no. 4: 585–610.

Gehrig, T., and M. Haas. 2016. "Anomalous Trading Prior to Lehman Brothers Failure." Finance Working Paper No. 424/2014, European Corporate Governance Institute (March): http://papers.ssrn.com/sol3/papers.cfm?abstract_id=2408489.

Glosten, L., and P. Milgrom. 1985. "Bid, Ask and Transaction Prices in a Specialist Market with Heterogeneously Informed Traders." *Journal of Financial Economics*, vol. 14, no. 1 (March): 71–100.

Gorton, G., and A. Metrick. 2012. "Securitized Banking and the Run on Repo." *Journal of Financial Economics*, vol. 104, no. 3 (June): 425–451.

Hoag, C. 2006. "The Atlantic Telegraph Cable and Capital Market Information Flows." *Journal of Economic History*, vol. 66, no. 2 (June): 342–353.

Hochfelder, D. 2012. *The Telegraph in America, 1832–1920*. Baltimore: Johns Hopkins University Press.

Huang, R., and H. Stoll. 1997. "The Components of the Bid-Ask Spread: A General Approach." *Review of Financial Studies*, vol. 10, no. 4 (Winter): 995–1034.

Jones, Charles M. 2002. "A Century of Stock Market Liquidity and Trading Costs." Working paper, Columbia University.

Kyle, A.S. 1985. "Continuous Auctions and Insider Trading." *Econometrica*, vol. 53, no. 6 (November): 1315–1335.

Lewis, Michael. 2014. *Flash Boys: A Wall Street Revolt*. New York & London: W.W. Norton & Company.

Neal, L. 2016. "The Role of Stock Exchanges in Financial Globalization." In *Financial Market History*. Edited by David Chambers and Elroy Dimson. Charlottesville, VA: CFA Institute Research Foundation.

Rousseau, Peter L. 2009. "Share Liquidity, Participation, and Growth of the Boston Market for Industrial Equities, 1854–1897." *Explorations in Economic History*, vol. 46, no. 2 (April): 203–219.

Rydqvist, K. 2016. Personal communication (Stockholm Stock Exchange History).

Silber, W.L. 2007. *When Washington Shut Down Wall Street: The Great Financial Crisis of 1914 and the Origins of America's Monetary Supremacy*. Princeton, NJ: Princeton University Press.

White, Eugene N. 2013. "Competition among the Exchanges before the SEC: Was the NYSE a Natural Hegemon?" *Financial History Review*, vol. 20, no. 1:29–48.

8. Initial Public Offerings: A Historical Overview

Carsten Burhop
Professor, Department of Constitutional, Social, and Economic History, University of Vienna

David Chambers
Reader and Academic Director, Newton Centre for Endowment Asset Management, Cambridge Judge Business School, University of Cambridge

Research into firms going public in the modern period has uncovered three stylized facts: the IPO cycle, IPO underpricing, and long-run IPO underperformance. These findings are based largely on US IPO data from the 1960s onward. However, IPO markets have existed for as long as stock markets themselves and were more developed in other countries than the United States the further back in time one goes. Financial market historians, therefore, have an important role to play in asking whether these stylized facts are robust over time or, alternatively, the result of modern capital market development.

Introduction

IPO (initial public offering) markets have existed as long as stock markets themselves and are integral to their historical development. They provide entrepreneurs with the opportunity to raise financing either for the firm or for themselves and investors with the opportunity to invest in new firms. Whether today or a century ago, entrepreneurs looking to take their firm public are concerned with the same three questions: 1) How soon can the firm go public? 2) What price will we get for our shares? 3) How will the shares perform after the IPO? An enormous body of modern finance literature deals with the answers to each of these questions.[1] The resulting wealth of empirical evidence has given rise to the following stylized facts, each of which corresponds to one of the previous three questions: 1) IPOs tend to exhibit substantial fluctuations in activity over time (there is an IPO cycle); 2) IPOs are, on average, underpriced and rise in price in initial trading; and 3) IPOs tend to perform poorly over the long run.

---

[1]Jenkinson and Ljungqvist (2001), Ritter and Welch (2002), and Ljungqvist (2007) provide excellent summaries of this literature.

However, all three stylized facts are based almost entirely on IPO data in the United States from the 1960s onward. Financial historians, therefore, have an important role to play in documenting early IPO markets and in asking whether these stylized facts are robust over time or, alternatively, modern-day phenomena. Before we address these stylized facts, we must first discuss issues that arise when compiling historical IPO data.

Historical IPO Data

The primary focus of historical IPO studies has been on listings of equity securities, typically ordinary shares (common stock). This is to ensure comparability with IPOs that today are characterized by firms selling equity. At the same time, it should be recognized that in the 19th century, many firms listed their bonds before their equity. Such leading investment banks of the day as Rothschild and Barings first cut their teeth underwriting new listings of sovereign bonds in London in the 1820s (Flandreau and Flores 2009). In the second half of the 19th century, they were joined by J.P. Morgan, Kuhn, Loeb & Company, and other investment banks in adding railroad bonds and then other corporate bonds to their underwriting business. One study of the cross-listing of US railroad securities on the London Stock Exchange (LSE) found that long-dated bonds were far more popular than common stocks in the period between 1870 and 1913 (Chambers, Sarkissian, and Schill 2016). In such markets as the United Kingdom and the United States, even as investor interest switched toward stocks in the early decades of the 20th century, a large number of IPOs involved selling preference shares (or preferred stocks) that were often bundled with ordinary shares—sometimes with voting rights attached. However, from the 1930s onward, the institutional investor appetite for equity surged and thus common stock IPOs became dominant.

One of the main challenges in constructing historical IPO datasets is to identify an IPO event. Starting with a definition, an IPO is the first occasion when any security issued by a firm is traded on a stock exchange, and it is accompanied by the sale of securities, either existing securities sold by insiders or new securities issued by the firm. Identifying whether an IPO has occurred can then be done in two stages. First, there should be a notification in a newspaper of an issue and listing on a stock exchange, or, even better, a prospectus giving details on the new issue. Second, we need to cross-check the issue details with either a stock exchange handbook, stock exchange listing files, or stock exchange price lists in order to distinguish between an IPO and a seasoned equity offering (SEO).[2] It is extremely useful if a prospectus

---

[2]An SEO is an offering of additional shares by a company that has previously offered its shares in an IPO.

exists, because this will indicate what information was disclosed to investors at the time of the IPO. Such information will help when modeling IPO underpricing over time by controlling for changes in firm characteristics and other particulars. In some cases, care must be taken when extracting data from other sources—such as handbooks, listing files, and sponsoring bank or broker files—not to include variables that were unknown to investors at the time of the IPO.

It is also worth being clear about what does not constitute an IPO. The above definition of an IPO does not include so-called "introductions"— that is, the conversion from unlisted to listed status of a firm with a sufficiently broad pre-IPO shareholder base without any actual sale of securities.[3] Typically, IPO datasets also exclude the following: closed-end funds (CEFs); "penny" stock IPOs, defined as those with a very low offer price; and government privatizations. CEFs neither involve raising new finance nor represent an "exit" event; they are nonetheless of interest because the size of their premia in initial trading to their underlying NAVs can be indicators of investor sentiment; see, for example, De Long and Shleifer (1991). Penny stocks tend to be excluded because they are highly speculative and are neither a reliable indicator of underpricing nor of corporate financing trends. Privatizations represent a minute proportion of the total IPO population and tend to be substantially underpriced to ensure that investors take up the shares.

Transfers of firms from a junior market and issues by firms already quoted on another exchange, either domestic or foreign, are also excluded. In contrast, a firm that simultaneously lists and issues securities on more than one market is counted as an IPO. This type of IPO was quite common a century ago. In addition to a main stock exchange located in their respective financial capitals, the United States, the United Kingdom, Germany, and France, for example, had a number of provincial or regional stock exchanges providing opportunities for firms to list their securities. Hence, stock exchanges in Chicago, Birmingham, Frankfurt, and Lille rivalled those of New York, London, Berlin, and Paris, respectively, in the late 19th and early 20th centuries.

Historians have been busy in this field in recent years. Hence, datasets have now been compiled for the United Kingdom, Germany, Belgium, the Netherlands, and Italy, focusing on the main stock exchanges and extending back to at least the beginning of the last century. **Table 8.1** summarizes the simple count of IPOs in each of these markets since 1900. In the United

---

[3]Introductions are less interesting because one of the reasons for analyzing IPOs is to estimate at what price and how much finance is raised via going public. They are, of course, relevant from the point of view of ascertaining the growth in the size and trading liquidity of stock markets.

Table 8.1. Number of IPOs by Decade since 1900

Year	UK	US	Germany	Rest of Europe
1900s	486	–	223	528
1910s	445	–	95	453
1920s	662	297	241	682
1930s	397	105	1	131
1940s	269	141	3	105
1950s	348	447	38	178
1960s	548	2,661	26	122
1970s	267	1,640	34	78
1980s	762	4,866	141	225
1990s	641	5,202	352	241
2000s	1,175	2,065	504	233
Total	6,000	17,424	1,658	2,976

Sources: UK data from Burhop, Chambers, and Cheffins (2014) for 1900–1913; Chambers (2010) for 1919–1939; Chambers and Dimson (2009) for 1940–1996; Paleari, Piazzalunga, Signori, Trabucchi, and Vismara (2014) for 1996–2014. US data from Simon (1989) for 1926–1940; Gompers and Lerner (2003) for 1940–1959; Jay Ritter for 1960–1979 and Jay Ritter's website (https://site.warrington.ufl.edu/ritter/files/2016/03/Initial-Public-Offerings-Updated-Statistics-2016-03-08.pdf) for 1980–2015. Germany data are from Burhop, Chambers, and Cheffins (2016) for 1900–1939 and from Deutsches Aktieninstitut (2013) for 1948 onward. For rest of Europe, data for Belgium are from SCOB database, Bourse de Bruxelles, Cours authentique, courtesy of Frans Buelens; for Italy, from Cattaneo, Meoli, and Vismara (2015); and for the Netherlands, from De Jong and Legierse (2014).

States, IPOs have only been traced back to 1926, and it has been difficult to identify IPO events in New York and in other US regional markets before that date. Over the whole period since 1900, the United States has unsurprisingly seen the most firms go public, followed by the United Kingdom and Germany. Whilst US activity is concentrated in the period from the 1960s onward, markets across Europe were much more important before then.

IPO Cycle

The IPO cycle refers to the tendency of IPOs to cluster together in time and to go through so-called "hot" and "cold" periods. In a hot market, many firms go public, whereas in a cold market, few or no firms do so. What explains the cycle? As might be expected, IPO activity tends to follow the economic and business cycle. When the economy is doing better (worse), capital expenditure needs increase (decrease); hence, more (fewer) firms demand equity financing and go public, other things being equal. Yet, the variation in activity is far greater than can be explained by the business cycle alone, so additional explanations for this hot and cold market phenomenon are required. Lowry (2003) analyzed US IPOs from 1960 to 1996 and identified investor sentiment and information asymmetry between IPO firms and investors as also being important. She found that, first, more IPOs occur when investors feel optimistic about stock market prospects; and second, because hot markets in IPOs tend to involve firms in new industries with high levels of information asymmetry, the first few firms going public are difficult for investors to understand and value. However, once these firms have gone public, investors learn and it becomes easier for other firms to follow suit.

Figure 8.1 shows IPO activity in the United Kingdom, the United States, and Germany for 1900-2013. We plotted the number of IPOs in a given year expressed as a percentage of the annual average number of IPOs over three periods, 1900–1949, 1950–1979, and 1980–2013. A figure above 100% means that IPO volume in that year exceeded the period average. The choice of sub-periods is designed to reflect the structural shifts in IPO markets across time and, in particular, the surge in IPO activity in the United States and the United Kingdom after 1980.

Several conclusions can be drawn from the information presented in Figure 8.1. First, it is clear that the IPO cycle existed across the whole of the 20th century. Several hot markets are recognizable: 1910–1911, 1928–1929, 1970–1972, the mid-1980s, and 1999–2000. Second, although there are idiosyncratic episodes, such as that in Germany in 1923, in general, hot markets across these three countries occurred around the same time. Third, Figure 8.1 shows that the scale of the most recent IPO bubble, the dot-com bubble of 1999–2000, does not appear to be an outsized event when compared to earlier IPO bubbles. Relative to the size of the market at the time, the bubble in rubber stocks on the London market in 1910–1911, the hot market in Berlin in 1923 and the surge of IPOs in London and New York in the late 1920s were all as big an event as the explosion in internet stocks at the end of the 20th century.

Figure 8.1.   IPO Activity in the United Kingdom, the United States, and Germany, 1900–2013

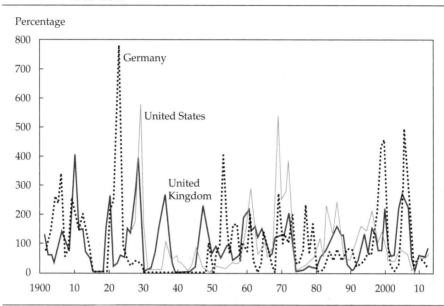

Notes: For each of the United Kingdom, the United States, and Germany, we display the number of IPOs in each year as a percentage of the long-run average annual number of IPOs for the sub-periods 1900–1949, 1950–1979, and 1980–2013.
Source: See Table 8.1.

IPO Underpricing

Underpricing is typically defined as the first-day return, or the change from the initial offer price published in the prospectus to the closing price recorded on the first day of trading.[4] A standard assumption is that an issuing firm seeks to maximize the gross proceeds of its IPO, subject to meeting such stock exchange listing requirements as the establishment of a liquid market in the shares. Evidence on the existence of positive initial returns, on average, began to emerge from the 1960s onward in the United States and the United Kingdom. Among a total of 52 empirical studies, IPOs were found to be underpriced on average in all cases, and all but eight countries displayed double digit (as a percentage) underpricing.[5] However, only one of these studies started before the early 1970s. The question that naturally arises is whether we observe underpricing if we go back further in time.

---

[4]In the case of call-auction markets, such as that in Berlin, only one price per day is quoted.
[5]See Jay Ritter's website: https://site.warrington.ufl.edu/ritter/files/2016/05/Int2016.pdf.

Large initial returns of IPOs on the LSE were highlighted by the *Economist* on 27 July 1929 at the height of the bull market. For example, a few months earlier, Ford Motor Company offered shares in its European subsidiary to London investors and an 87% first-day return was recorded. Despite such occurrences, comprehensive evidence on IPOs for the United Kingdom and Germany strongly suggests that underpricing was, on average, modest early in the 20th century and before.

When analyzing how underpricing has changed over time, there are several factors that need to be taken into account: changes in the risk characteristics of IPOs, shifts in the regulatory framework, and the involvement of reputable underwriters. Other things being equal, younger and smaller firms are riskier and investors will need to price-protect themselves against the possibility of an IPO turning out to be a "lemon" by demanding a reduction in the offer price, which leads to greater underpricing.[6] In contrast, tougher IPO regulation would be expected to reduce underpricing because investors would have less need to price-protect themselves by demanding a lower offer price. Analogously, stronger protection of minority investors should have better equipped shareholders to resist "bad" management, again minimizing the need for price protection. In addition, the involvement of reputable banks and brokers in IPO underwriting should help reduce underpricing, consistent with the idea that such underwriters are willing to certify the quality of the firm going public.[7]

One very long-run study examined UK IPO underpricing over the course of the 20th century, whilst controlling for changes in the risk characteristics, regulation, and underwriting of IPOs (Chambers and Dimson 2009).[8] Importantly, the main method of selling IPOs remained unchanged at least until the "Big Bang" in 1986.[9] This method was the fixed price offer, whereby the issuing firm and its sponsors set the offer price and make no adjustment to balance demand and supply once marketing of the issue begins. The study concluded that, after controlling for firms going public becoming larger

---

[6]Beatty and Ritter (1986) argue that underpricing should increase the ex ante uncertainty of the firm's value where investor heterogeneity exists. Ritter (1984) and Loughran and Ritter (1995) highlight changes in firm risk as one explanation for shifts in underpricing over time.
[7]For recent studies of the role of underwriters in US IPOs, see Carter, Dark, and Singh (1998) and Loughran and Ritter (1995). For historical studies of underwriting on UK IPOs in the 20th century and German IPOs pre-1914, see Chambers (2009) and Lehmann (2014) respectively.
[8]This study also controls for other important time-varying firm characteristics, such as the proportion of the firm sold at IPO. The expectation is that managers will care more about underpricing, the greater the proportion of the firm being sold. See Habib and Ljungqvist (2001).
[9]"Big Bang" is the name given to the deregulation of the London Stock Exchange. Subsequent to this date, the fixed price offer method gave way to the book building method.

and older, regulation becoming tougher and firms being much more likely to retain the services of a prestigious underwriter, underpricing surprisingly increased in the latter half of the 20th century compared with the first half.

Two reasons may explain this rise in underpricing of UK IPOs in the second half of the 20th century. First, the consolidation of the more than 20 domestic stock exchanges that existed before World War II into a single market in London subsequently led to the demise of competition for IPOs, and may have resulted in an increase in underpricing. A Birmingham firm going public in 1900 had a choice of listing either on its local stock exchange with a local underwriter or on the LSE with a London underwriter. As Frederick Lavington (1921) argued, high levels of trust existed between local investors, firms, and underwriters in provincial stock markets in the early 20th century. The implication was that local trust served to limit the need of investors to price-protect themselves and kept underpricing down, both in provincial markets and, thanks to the competition, in London. Second, the increased importance of reputable investment banks as well as institutional investors in, respectively, selling and buying IPOs from the mid-20th century onward may have resulted in their extracting higher initial returns for themselves (Chambers 2009). In contrast, the IPO underwriting market was extremely fragmented in the first half of the last century, with the leading investment banks noticeable by their absence.

Underpricing has continued to rise in the United Kingdom over the last three decades as it has elsewhere, reinforced by the general shift to the method of selling IPOs with which investors are familiar today, known as "book building." The proponents of the book building method of taking firms public believe that this level of underpricing is a good thing and necessary to pay smart investors for their information production. According to Benveniste and Spindt (1989), underpricing is necessarily higher under book building than the fixed price offer to entice knowledgeable investors to share their private information and set the final offer price more accurately. However, others argue that, in reality, investors do relatively little in terms of information production at the time of the IPO (Jenkinson and Jones 2009). The implication is that irrespective of the choice of IPO method, a substantial portion of underpricing today, as in the recent past, represents rents extracted from issuers by underwriting investment banks and their closest investment management clients.

The overall implication of the long-run UK evidence is that the levels of IPO underpricing witnessed over the last 50 to 60 years are a direct result of the manner in which modern IPO markets have evolved—namely, the greater role played by investment banks in taking firms public, the rise of institutional investors, and the reduced competition among domestic stock exchanges. The only other market where such evidence has been uncovered is Germany. In Berlin, IPO underpricing averaged around 3% from 1870 to 1913 (Burhop 2011; Lehmann 2014) compared to close to 10% over the period from the 1970s to the mid-1990s (Ljungqvist 1997) and then reached a substantially higher level during the late 1990s. Further research is needed on underpricing in early IPO markets.

Long-Run IPO Performance

Both investors and entrepreneurs also care about the performance of IPOs in the aftermarket. The cross-country evidence on IPOs in the final decades of the 20th century typically reports underperformance relative to the over-all market over the subsequent three to five years. Jenkinson and Ljungqvist (2001, Table 2.2, p. 55) summarized the results of empirical studies of long-run performance in 19 countries where all but 5 of them reported negative market-adjusted long-run returns.

One of the studies included a seminal paper by Loughran and Ritter (1995) claiming that there was a "new issues puzzle." According to the authors, the puzzle arose from the fact that even though US IPOs, on aver-age, underperformed the market in the three to five years following a listing through the 1970s, 1980s, and early 1990s, investors appeared unable to curb their appetite for investing in such deals. A subsequent study over the same time period challenged this claim, arguing that there was no such puzzle once firm characteristics were properly controlled for (Brav and Gompers 1997). Because IPOs are typically small-growth firms, their performance needs to be compared against seasoned firms that are also small-growth firms, not the overall market. When benchmarked in this way, IPOs did not appear to have underperformed.

An important out-of-sample study was subsequently able to adjudicate between these two competing views. Gompers and Lerner (2003) constructed a sample of US IPOs that covered the period from the early 1930s to the early 1970s. They concluded that US IPOs also did not, on average, underper-form once correctly matched with seasoned firms on size and growth/value. In other words, any underperformance versus the overall market is not an exclusively "IPO effect." However, this may have been of little consolation to investors who were aiming to do at least as well as the market. A more recent study of the long-run market-adjusted performance of German IPOs between 1870 and 1910 concluded that although IPO performance was very poor in the 1870s, a substantial improvement was seen in the subsequent three decades after regulatory improvements were made and IPOs performed in line with the market (Burhop, Chambers, and Cheffins 2016).

As with underpricing, long-run performance in earlier periods of history needs more research. The challenge in estimating IPO returns over the long run lies in accurately tracking what happens to firms that delist or disappear from stock exchange price lists. Mergers are particularly problematic when one does not know the terms on which recently listed firms were acquired by another firm. This becomes of a challenge as we go further back in time. Given such challenges, historians have undertaken the less onerous task of examining IPO survival rates. Although survival ignores the upside delivered by IPO winners, it serves to focus attention on the downside risks of IPO investing.

The survival rate is defined as the proportion of IPOs in a given year that survived as public companies until their fifth (or tenth) anniversary; correspondingly, failure is defined as a delisting resulting from the disappearance or liquidation of the firms in question where shareholders receive no consideration. IPOs that subsequently disappear because of a merger with another firm and where the shareholders receive value for their shares are not regarded as having failed. To date, IPO survival studies have been undertaken in the United States, the United Kingdom, Germany, and Italy. **Table 8.2** summarizes the findings of each of these studies.

Table 8.2. Summary of IPO Survival Studies

Study	Market	Period	Finding
Simon (1989)	US	1926–1940	Regional SE IPO survival improved post-1933 SEC Act from 67% to 88%, but NYSE IPO survival was unchanged at 90%.
Burhop et al. (2014)	UK	1900–1913	IPO survival on the more strictly regulated main market (98%) exceeded that on the junior market (81%) of the LSE.
Chambers (2010)	UK	1919–1939	IPO survival on the LSE was 80% 1919–1927, 64% in 1928–1929, and 96% in the 1930s.
Cattaneo et al. (2015)	Italy	1861–2012	IPO survival rates were higher during periods of tighter regulation.
Burhop et al. (2016)	Germany	1870–1926	Following the introduction of stricter laws regulating IPOs in 1884 and 1896, survival rates improved from 60% in 1870–1883 to almost 100% in 1897–1913.

Note: All survival rates reported in the table are estimated over five years.
Sources: See Table 8.1.

All the studies look at the important relationship between regulation and survival and conclude that tighter regulation is positively associated with higher survival rates. Regulation can take the form of statutory legislation, as was the case in the United States in 1933 and Germany in 1884 and 1896 when important laws were passed strengthening the screening and disclosure surrounding firms going public. Alternatively, IPOs can be self-regulated by the listing stock exchange. Self-regulation worked in the case of the NYSE, where nine out of ten IPOs that were launched during the bull market of the late 1920s survived the following five years.

Yet, the NYSE's early example of successful self-regulation appears to be the exception. Self-regulation did not work in the case of Berlin prior to 1884. At that point and again in 1896, legislation was passed that considerably strengthened regulation, and virtually all subsequent IPOs survived. Similarly, London investors in junior market IPOs experienced very low survival rates both before the 1930s and especially in 1928–1929, when only three in five IPOs subsequently survived in the following five years. This poor performance forced the LSE to ratchet up its *de facto* listing requirements and raise the effective minimum size, age, and profitability levels required for firms going public. As a result, survival improved dramatically in the 1930s and thereafter, when virtually all firms going public on the LSE up to the late 1970s survived.

Having abolished its junior market just after World War II, the United Kingdom re-introduced it in the shape of the Unlisted Securities Market (USM) in 1980; its successor, the Alternative Investment Market (AIM), was established in 1995. The latter market has one important difference compared to the poorly performing junior market of the early 20th century. Firms going public on AIM are required to appoint a nominated adviser ("Nomad") from among a pre-screened group of London brokerages, which then takes responsibility for ensuring that there has been full disclosure to the market (Gerakos, Lang, and Maffett 2013, Appendix I). This innovation offers the promise of riskier ventures now safely going public on a junior or "on ramp" market, which is less tightly regulated than the main market, to the potential benefit of both investors and the broader economy. In this sense, the UK experience suggests that some institutional learning has perhaps taken place in regard to IPO markets. So far, however, the results have been disappointing. Relative to similar firms traded on more regulated markets, AIM companies seem more likely to fail and, partly due to a lack of "high flyers," have delivered sub-standard overall returns to investors (Gerakos, Lang, and Maffett 2013; Dimson and Marsh 2015).

Of course, we need to exercise an element of caution when drawing conclusions about the impact of tighter regulation on IPO survival in that we have no way of knowing the counterfactual. In other words, we can never know which firms would have gone public in the absence of regulation, what would have happened to them, and what would have been the impact on industrial performance and investor wealth.

Concluding Comments

Financial historians can help investors place three well-documented stylized facts about IPO markets into historical context and understand how robust they are as we travel back in time. The tendency of IPOs to cycle through hot and cold markets is present throughout the long run of the 20th century. IPO underpricing, on the other hand, based on UK evidence at least, may be a feature of the way in which capital markets have developed toward the end of the 20th century. Finally, the limited evidence that exists on long-run aftermarket performance points to investors being disappointed—although in the case of the United States, these IPOs may well not have performed any worse than seasoned firms with similar characteristics. IPO survival is somewhat easier to measure, and history suggests that, in general, survival has been relatively lower when regulation has been light or non-existent and only improved when steps were taken to improve disclosure, toughen listing requirements, and protect investors.

Bibliography

Alexander, Ljungqvist. 1997. "Pricing Initial Public Offerings: Further Evidence from Germany." *European Economic Review*, vol. 41, no. 7 (July): 1309–1320.

Beatty, Randolph, and Jay R. Ritter. 1986. "Investment Banking, Reputation, and the Underpricing of Initial Public Offerings." *Journal of Financial Economics*, vol. 15, nos. 1–2 (January/February): 213–232.

Benveniste, Lawrence M., and Paul A. Spindt. 1989. "How Investment Bankers Determine the Offer Price and Allocation of New Issues." *Journal of Financial Economics*, vol. 24, no. 2: 343–361.

Brav, Alan, and Paul Gompers. 1997. "Myth or Reality? The Long-Run Underperformance of IPOs: Evidence from Venture and Nonventure Capital-Backed Companies." *Journal of Finance*, vol. 52, no. 5 (December): 1791–1821.

Burhop, Carsten. 2011. "The Underpricing of Initial Public Offerings at the Berlin Stock Exchange, 1870–1896." *German Economic Review*, vol. 12, no. 1 (February): 11–32.

Burhop, Carsten, David Chambers, and Brian Cheffins. 2014. "Regulating IPOs: Evidence from Going Public in London, 1900–1913." *Explorations in Economic History*, vol. 51 (January): 60–76.

———. 2016. "The Rise and Fall of the German Stock Market, 1870–1938." Cambridge University Economic and Social History, working paper.

Carter, Richard B., Frederick H. Dark, and Ajai K. Singh. 1998. "Underwriter Reputation, Initial Returns, and the Long-Run Performance of IPO Stocks." *Journal of Finance*, vol. 53, no. 1 (February): 285–311.

Cattaneo, Mattia, Michele Meoli, and Silvio Vismara. 2015. "Financial Regulation and IPOs: Evidence from the History of the Italian Stock Market." *Journal of Corporate Finance*, vol. 31 (April): 116–131.

Chambers, David. 2009. "Gentlemanly Capitalism Revisited: A Case Study of the Underpricing of Initial Public Offerings on the London Stock Exchange 1946–86." *Economic History Review*, vol. 62, no. 1 (August): 31–56.

———. 2010. "Going Public in Interwar Britain." *Financial History Review*, vol. 17, no. 1 (April): 51–71.

Chambers, David, and Elroy Dimson. 2009. "IPO Underpricing over the Very Long Run." *Journal of Finance*, vol. 64, no. 3 (June): 1407–1443.

Chambers, David, Sergei Sarkissian, and Michael Schill. 2016. "Market and Regional Segmentation and Risk Premia in the First Era of Financial Globalization." Darden Business School Working Paper 2179088 (25 November): http://papers.ssrn.com/sol3/papers.cfm?abstract_id=2179088.

De Jong, Abe, and Wilco Legierse. 2014. "What Causes Hot IPO Markets? An Analysis of Initial Public Offerings in the Netherlands, 1876-2009." Rotterdam School of Management, working paper.

De Long, J. Bradford, and Andrei Shleifer. 1991. "The Stock Market Bubble of 1929: Evidence from Closed-End Funds." *Journal of Economic History*, vol. 51, no. 3 (September): 675–700.

Deutsches Aktieninstitut. 2013. *Factbook des Deutsche Aktieninstituts*, Deutsches Aktieninstitut, Frankfurt.

Dimson, Elroy, and Paul Marsh. 2015. *Numis Smaller Companies Index Annual Review*. London: Numis Securities (15 January).

Flandreau, Marc, and Juan Flores. 2009. "Bonds and Brands: Foundations of Sovereign Debt Markets, 1820–1830." *Journal of Economic History*, vol. 69, no. 3 (September): 646–684.

Gerakos, Joseph, Mark Lang, and Mark Maffett. 2013. "Post-Listing Performance and Private Sector Regulation: The Experience of London's Alternative Investment Market." *Journal of Accounting and Economics*, vol. 56, nos. 2–3, supplement 1 (December): 189–215.

Gompers, Paul, and Joshua Lerner. 2003. "The Really Long-Run Performance of Initial Public Offerings: The Pre-NASDAQ Evidence." *Journal of Finance*, vol. 58, no. 4 (August): 1355–1392.

Habib, Michael, and Alexander Ljungqvist. 2001. "Underpricing and Entrepreneurial Wealth Losses in IPOs: Theory and Evidence." *Review of Financial Studies*, vol. 14, no. 2: 433–458.

Jenkinson, Tim, and Howard Jones. 2009. "IPO Pricing and Allocation: A Survey of the Views of Institutional Investors." *Review of Financial Studies*, vol. 22, no. 4: 1477–1504.

Jenkinson, Tim, and Alexander Ljungqvist. 2001. *Going Public: The Theory and Evidence on How Companies Raise Equity Finance*. 2nd ed. New York: Oxford University Press.

Lavington, Frederick. 1921. *The English Capital Market*. London: Methuen & Co.

Lehmann, Sibylle. 2014. "Taking Firms to the Stock Market: IPOs and the Importance of Large Banks in Imperial Germany, 1896–1913." *Economic History Review*, vol. 67, no. 1 (February): 92–122.

Ljungqvist, Alexander. 2007. "IPO Underpricing." In *Handbook of Corporate Finance: Empirical Corporate Finance*, ed. B.E. Eckbo. Amsterdam: Elsevier.

Loughran, Tim, and Jay Ritter. 1995. "The New Issues Puzzle." *Journal of Finance*, vol. 50, no. 1 (March): 23–51.

Lowry, Michelle. 2003. "Why Does IPO Volume Fluctuate So Much?" *Journal of Financial Economics*, vol. 67, no. 1 (January): 3–40.

Paleari, S., D. Piazzalunga, A. Signori, F. Trabucchi, and S. Vismara. 2014. *Academic EurIPO Fact Book 2014*. CreateSpace Independent Publishing.

Ritter, Jay, and Ivo Welch. 2002. "A Review of IPO Activity, Pricing, and Allocations." *Journal of Finance*, vol. 57, no. 4 (August): 1795–1828.

Simon, Carol J. 1989. "The Effect of the 1933 Securities Act on Investor Information and the Performance of New Issues." *American Economic Review*, vo. 79, no. 3 (June): 295–318.

Part 3: Bubbles and Crises

9. Bubble Investing: Learning from History

William N. Goetzmann
Edwin J. Beinecke Professor of Finance and Management Studies and Director of the International Center for Finance, Yale School of Management

History is important to the study of financial bubbles precisely because they are extremely rare events, but history can be misleading. The rarity of bubbles in the historical record makes the sample size for inference small. Restricting attention to crashes that followed a large increase in market level makes negative historical outcomes salient. In this chapter, I examine the frequency of large, sudden increases in market value in a broad panel of world equity market data extending from the beginning of the 20th century. I find that the probability of a crash conditional on a boom is only slightly higher than the unconditional probability. The chances that a market gave back its gains following a doubling in value are about 10%. In simple terms, bubbles are booms that went bad. Not all booms are bad.

Introduction

The broad awareness of financial history seems to correlate with extreme market events. For example, the closest comparison to the dot-com bubble of the 1990s was the run-up in US stock prices in the 1920s. During the 2008 financial crisis, the financial press frequently referenced past bubbles—periods of market euphoria followed by sharp price declines. In this chapter, I argue that using past crashes in this way is misleading to both investors and policymakers. Particularly during periods of market booms, focusing attention on a few salient crashes in financial history ignores the base rate for bubbles. In simple terms, bubbles are booms that went bad but not all booms are bad.

To illustrate the latter point, I present empirical evidence drawn from more than a century of global stock market data. I define a bubble as a large price decline after a large price increase (i.e., a crash after a boom). I find that the frequency of bubbles is quite small. The unconditional frequency of bubbles in the data is 0.3% to 1.4%, depending on the definition of a bubble.

An earlier version of this chapter (NBER Working Paper 21693) can be found at www.nber. org/papers/w21693. The author thanks Elroy Dimson, Paul Marsh, and Mike Staunton for the generous use of the DMS database and Michele Fratianni for providing the data on the Casa di San Giorgio.

149

Not only are bubbles rare, but they also are conditional on a market boom (i.e., increasing by 100% in a one- to three-year period). Crashes that gave back prior gains happened only 10% of the time. Market prices were more likely to double again following a 100% price boom.

I first present evidence about bubbles (as well as the lack of them) in very early equity investments. Next, I describe the databases used in the study and then provide the empirical analysis. Finally, I discuss the implications of the results for investors and regulators.

Data on Markets and Bubbles

The first bubbles precede the development of organized stock exchanges. Stuart Jenks (2010) reports evidence of a bubble in speculative German mining shares, *kuxe*, at the end of the 15th century.[1] Fractional equity interest in individual silver mines in the Hartz mountain district was evidently freely traded, purchased on credit, and occasionally had option-like features. Transactions were settled at financial fairs during which share prices could fluctuate dramatically.

These German mining shares were famously condemned by Martin Luther, who said in 1554 after being offered four kuxen: *"Ich will kein Kuks haben! Es is Spielgeld und will nicht wuddeln das selbig Geld."* This (roughly) translates as the following: I want no shares! This is play [speculative] money, and I will not make this kind of money multiply.[2]

In 1502, on the eve of sailing on his final voyage, Christopher Columbus expressed a desire that his son use his inheritance to purchase shares in the Casa di San Giorgio in Genoa, which he observed would generate "6% interest and constitute a very safe investment."[3] The firm was a financial institution that owned and managed government contracts and ultimately became a bank. Its board regularly declared dividends, and these, as well as the shares themselves, were actively traded.[4]

Shares in Genoa's Casa di San Giorgio fluctuated considerably in the 16th century. **Figure 9.1** shows an index of share prices and yields for Casa di San Giorgio. The dramatic doubling of prices in 1602 looks like a bubble to the modern eye because yields declined from 3% to 1.5%. This bubble sustained itself for a long time: Prices did not drop back to their former level until 1683. Likewise, a peak in 1622 looks, *ex post*, like a bubble, although the fortunes of Genoa as a financial power in the early 17th century also fluctuated

---

[1]Jenks cites Werner (1936) and Laube (1974) for empirical price evidence.
[2]See Braudel (1972).
[3]See Harrisse (1888).
[4]See Fratianni (2006).

Figure 9.1. Casa di San Giorgio Share Prices and Yields

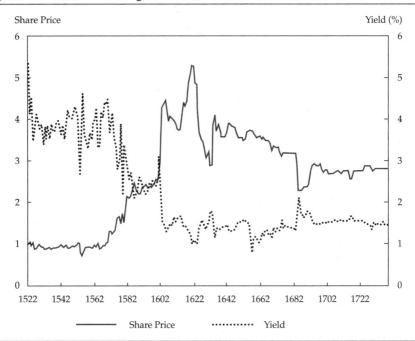

Source: Michele Fratianni.

considerably. The variation on both occasions might have been caused by rational speculation on events of the time. Nevertheless, they appear to fit a price-based definition of a bubble.

This bubble pattern, however, is not ubiquitous in the early history of equity shares. In Le Bris et al. (2014), there is no evidence of a bubble in the trading history of an even older corporation, the Bazacle Milling Company of Toulouse. Over an extended period—from the 1530s to 1946—stock prices for the Bazacle moved fairly closely with dividends.

The first discussions in England of a stock market bubble centered on the speculation in shares for start-up companies during the 1690s. Macleod (1986) argues that intellectual property rights were more likely the excuse for stock market speculation rather than the basis for real valuation in this first English market bubble.

The first great stock market bubble began in France, with the creation of the Mississippi Company by John Law. The Mississippi Company was an ingenious financial innovation that merged a bank empowered to issue currency with companies chartered for overseas trade. The price of shares grew by more than 10 times during 1719 and 1720. The Mississippi Bubble burst in the spring of 1720 when shares were made exchangeable with paper currency at a fixed rate, which resulted in a massive government commitment to propping up share prices by printing money.[5]

The Mississippi Bubble was followed shortly by the South Sea Bubble in London and a smaller but significant bubble for shares in the Netherlands. The British and Dutch bubbles subsequently burst in late 1720, and by the end of the year, the boom in stock market speculation was effectively over.

In a 2013 paper with Rik Frehen and K. Geert Rouwenhorst, I worked to understand the basis for this remarkable sequence of international stock bubbles from 1719–1720.[6] We found empirical and archival evidence that regulatory enforcement following the Bubble Act in London triggered a crash in the prices of insurance company stocks. This crash ultimately spread to the large trading companies and banks in the United Kingdom, and then it went overseas to the Dutch West Indies Company and a number of recently launched companies in the Netherlands.

Figure 9.2 illustrates the parallel growth in share prices for selected companies in London and Amsterdam during this period. The three London companies are Royal Exchange Assurance, London Assurance, and the South Sea Company. The two Dutch companies are the Dutch West Indies Company and Stad Rotterdam, an insurance company whose successor firm still exists today. The figure shows the scale of the London and Amsterdam bubbles. The South Sea Company rose by a factor of 7.5 over the year leading to the eponymous "South Sea Bubble." The two marine insurance companies grew by multiples of more than 10 and 13. Only the Dutch West Indies Company grew at a comparable scale in Amsterdam by a factor of 7. Stad Rotterdam did not quite double before declining in price.

Figure 9.2 also shows how interconnected the Dutch and British bubbles were. Although they rose at different times in the year 1720, the crash in the prices of the London insurance firms and the Dutch West Indies Company occurred at about the same time (a few days lag is consistent with travel times between the two financial centers).

In the United Kingdom, the Bubble Act curtailed the issuance and trading of unauthorized company shares and set back the development of an equity market as a vehicle for a financing enterprise. In the Netherlands, there was no such governmental response; nevertheless, initial public offerings stopped and a cultural re-examination of stock market speculation occurred. Stock schemes were ridiculed, and speculators were caricatured. One curious legacy

---

[5]See Murphy (1997) and Velde (2009).
[6]See Frehen, Goetzmann, and Rouwenhorst (2013b).

Figure 9.2 Stock Prices in London and Amsterdam, 1720

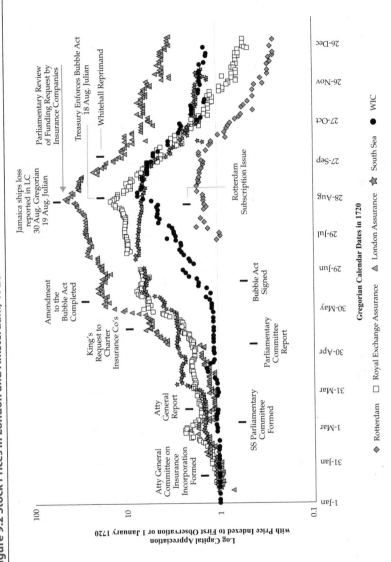

Source: International Center for Finance, Yale School of Management (http://som.yale.edu/faculty-research/our-centers-initiatives/international-center-finance/data/historical-southseasbubble).

of the 1720 international stock market bubble was a lavishly illustrated volume, *Het Groote Tafereel Der Dwaasheid* (*The Great Mirror of Folly*), which was printed just months after the crisis and included satirical poems, prints, plays, and engravings specifically intended to preserve the memory of the folly of speculation during the crisis.

Bubbles make interesting stories. Charles Mackay's classic book, *Memoires of Extraordinary Popular Delusions and the Madness of Crowds,* was first published in 1841 and is still in print. Using illustrations redrawn from *The Great Mirror of Folly,* Mackay poked fun at both the South Sea Bubble and the Mississippi Company, including them along with chapters on alchemy, fortune-telling, and "magnetizers." Mackay regarded stock speculation as a "madness which infected the people of England."

In Frehen, Goetzmann, and Rouwenhorst (2013b), cross-sectional evidence from the 1720 bubble indicates that the stock boom in 1720 was founded on economic fundamentals, including the economic potential of trans-Atlantic trade, innovations in maritime insurance, and the potential of the publicly traded corporation itself as a vehicle for enterprise. Likewise, Nicholas (2008) used cross-sectional evidence for companies with patents in the 1920s to show that, *ex post*, firms with valuable patents rose relatively more. In seeking to understand the economics underlying the causes of bubbles, Pástor and Veronesi (2009) built a model of technological innovation and tested it on cross-sectional historical data from the 19th century railroad boom in the United States. Perez (2009) explores the relationship between technological innovation and financial innovation in five major bubbles that occurred in the 19th, 20th, and 21st centuries. In each of these cases, evidence suggests that there was at least some method to the madness of the investors. Although potentially overly optimistic about valuations for new technology companies, investors in these bubbles identified, *ex ante,* the potential transformative value of innovations.

Analysis

Data. This brings us to the empirical analysis of market booms and busts. Dimson, Marsh, and Staunton (DMS) constructed an annual database of equity returns for 21 of the world's stock markets by collecting stock and dividend data beginning in 1900 and extending through 2014.[7] I used their total real return on equity indices, denominated in dollars, as the market

---

[7]The DMS database is distributed by Morningstar. More-detailed information is found in their annual global investment return yearbooks. For example, see Dimson, Marsh, and Staunton (2014).

measures for these countries. I augmented these with the annualized dollar-denominated stock market indices used in Jorion and Goetzmann (JG 1999). For countries in the DMS database, I dropped the JG indices, resulting in 20 remaining JG indices.

The JG indices were taken mostly from contemporaneous sources that sought to track indices in real time. The League of Nations (LofN) maintained indices for several countries beginning in 1919, and these were continued by the United Nations (UN). I collected these indices in a "follow forward" manner from the published periodicals and linked them to International Finance Corporation (IFC) indices available in the 1990s. The advantage of augmenting the DMS series is that the JG database contains a number of markets that failed or disappeared during the 20th century because of wars, revolutions, and other reasons.

Reliance on LofN and UN sources means that I did not control the manner in which the indices were created and thus cannot be sure that the capital appreciation returns calculated were actually obtainable. On the positive side, the JG indices derive from documentary data widely available in libraries through much of the 20th century. Hence, the frequency of past bubbles since at least 1920 has been available for establishing a "base rate" for price run-ups and crashes and their coincidence in time.

I included two additional series constructed for the International Center for Finance (ICF) at the Yale School of Management—the Saint-Petersburg (SPB) Exchange and the Shanghai Stock Exchange (SSE). Both are dollar-denominated, total return indices. Finally, I augmented both the JG and ICF series with Financial Times Stock Exchange (FTSE) dollar-denominated price appreciation series available in the Morningstar EnCorr database. I did not use the IFC or FTSE indices to add additional markets (although these could provide an even broader set of indices) because I wanted to avoid survival-conditioning bias. Taking markets that exist today and tracing them back may result in a series that is mean-reverting or displays more complex time-series behavior associated with recent growth (see Goetzmann and Jorion 1999), which could then bias the analysis of stock market performance conditional on a boom.

Table 9.1 lists the markets in this study and calculates summary statistics for the DMS and the JG/ICF databases. Note that the JG/ICF series are discontinuous and start and stop at various intervals. They are generally considered emerging markets and have a strong representation of countries in South America, Central America, and Eastern European countries. The JG/ICF series are more volatile by far, with an average standard deviation of 50% per year. Still, their average annual returns for years there are data is no

Table 9.1. Summary Statistics for Global Markets

Country	Source	Period	Mean	SD	Max	Min	Country	Source	Period	Mean	SD	Max	Min
Australia	DMS	1900–2014	0.13	0.24	1.07	−0.53	India	JG&FTSE	1940–2014	0.07	0.28	1.01	−0.65
Austria	DMS	1900–2014	0.09	0.39	2.00	−0.69	Pakistan	JG&FTSE	1961–2014	0.08	0.34	1.22	−0.75
Belgium	DMS	1900–2014	0.09	0.26	1.28	−0.50	Philippines	JG&FTSE	1955–2014	0.13	0.87	6.21	−0.63
Canada	DMS	1900–2014	0.11	0.20	0.72	−0.46	Argentina	JG&FTSE	1948–2014	0.19	0.92	4.55	−0.86
Denmark	DMS	1900–2014	0.11	0.24	1.06	−0.50	Brazil	JG&FTSE	1952–2014	0.19	0.60	2.32	−0.69
Finland	DMS	1900–2014	0.13	0.34	1.28	−0.72	Chile	JG&FTSE	1928–2014	0.12	0.39	1.18	−0.53
France	DMS	1900–2014	0.10	0.29	1.07	−0.73	Colombia	JG&FTSE	1937–2014	0.08	0.39	1.88	−0.55
Germany	DMS	1900–2014	0.18	0.80	7.00	−0.79	Mexico	JG&FTSE	1935–2014	0.14	0.37	1.15	−0.79
Ireland	DMS	1900–2014	0.10	0.26	1.10	−0.67	Peru	JG&FTSE	1942–1977, 1989–2014	0.11	0.44	2.23	−0.71
Italy	DMS	1900–2014	0.10	0.34	1.52	−0.62	Uruguay	JG&FTSE	1937–1943	0.10	0.21	0.32	−0.26

(continued)

Table 9.1. Summary Statistics for Global Markets (continued)

Country	Source	Period	Mean	SD	Max	Min	Country	Source	Period	Mean	SD	Max	Min
Japan	DMS	1900–2014	0.13	0.33	1.32	−0.92	Venezuela	JG&FTSE	1938–2007	0.08	0.55	3.90	−0.76
Netherlands	DMS	1900–2014	0.11	0.25	1.30	−0.63	Czech	JG&FTSE	1920–1944, 1995–2014	0.08	0.36	1.13	−1.00
New Zealand	DMS	1900–2014	0.12	0.26	1.40	−0.50	Greece	JG&FTSE	1930–1939, 1998–2014	0.14	0.60	2.74	−0.67
Norway	DMS	1900–2014	0.12	0.32	1.84	−0.63	Hungary	JG&FTSE	1926–1940, 1995–2014	0.10	0.44	1.05	−1.00
Portugal	DMS	1900–2014	0.14	0.44	2.05	−0.74	Poland	JG&FTSE	1922–1938, 1993–2014	0.24	1.25	7.45	−1.00
South Africa	DMS	1900–2014	0.13	0.30	1.86	−0.43	Romania	JG&FTSE	1938–1940, 2006–2014	−0.08	0.43	0.54	−1.00
Spain	DMS	1900–2014	0.10	0.28	1.51	−0.50	Egypt	JG&FTSE	1938–1961, 1995–2014	0.17	0.48	1.54	−0.54
Sweden	DMS	1900–2014	0.12	0.25	0.72	−0.54	Israel	JG&FTSE	1951–2014	0.13	0.35	0.86	−0.70

(continued)

Table 9.1. Summary Statistics for Global Markets (continued)

Country	Source	Period	Mean	SD	Max	Min
Switzerland	DMS	1900–2014	0.10	0.21	1.04	−0.35
United Kingdom	DMS	1900–2014	0.11	0.24	1.12	−0.50
United States	DMS	1900–2014	0.13	0.20	0.63	−0.44
		Average	0.12	0.31	1.57	−0.59
		Median	0.11	0.26	1.28	−0.54
		SD	0.02	0.13	1.31	0.14
		Min	0.09	0.20	0.63	−0.92
		Max	0.18	0.80	7.00	−0.35

Country	Source	Period	Mean	SD	Max	Min
China	ICF&FTSE	1900–1940, 1994–2014	0.04	0.31	1.20	−1.00
Russia	ICF & IFC	1900–1913, 1998–2014	0.17	0.67	2.85	−1.00
		Average	0.11	0.51	2.27	−0.76
		Median	0.11	0.43	1.38	−0.73
		SD	0.07	0.25	1.91	0.20
		Min	−0.08	0.21	0.32	−1.00
		Max	0.24	1.25	7.45	−0.26

Note: "SD" = standard deviation.

Sources: (1) Total return indices for stock markets in 21 countries over the period 1900 to 2014, converted to US dollars, provided by Dimson, Marsh, and Staunton (2014) via Morningstar. (2) Real capital appreciation indices for 18 countries from 1919 onward used in Jorion and Goetzmann (1999) and available on the website of the ICF. It is constructed from indices reported in League of Nations and United Nations periodicals, augmented with published IFC data. (3) Total return indices in US dollars for Russia and China from the International Center for Finance (ICF) at the Yale School of Management, constructed from official publications and/or newspaper sources. JG and ICF indices are augmented for recent years by the FTSE and IFC country dollar-denominated stock market appreciation indices as available via Morningstar.

higher than the DMS series. For series known to have been expropriated, a minus 100% return is included.

Booms and Crashes For the purposes of this analysis, a bubble is defined as a boom followed by a crash. A boom is a large, rapid increase in stock prices. A crash is a large, rapid decline in market prices. What is large? What is rapid? **Table 9.2** defines booms in two ways: (1) a single year in which a market value (or cumulative return) increased by at least 100%, and (2) a period of three years over which the market increased by 100%. This second definition is chosen so as to include the famous US bubbles of the 1920s and 1990s. Table 9.2 defines a bubble in two ways: (1) a drop of at least 50% in the following year, and (2) a drop of at least 50% over the next five years. There are other ways to use price dynamics to define a bubble. For example, a high price–earnings ratio is a common metric invoked as a bubble indicator. Long-term data for dividends are not available for most of the markets examined here. However, most people would agree that a doubling in market prices followed by a halving in value is a significant reversal. Further absent are details about economic fundamentals. Thus, this study can be interpreted as focusing on one common notion of a bubble, but not the only one.

Table 9.2 reports results for each of the two bubble definitions. Panel A shows the unconditional counts of market-years and the frequency of doubling and halving. Column 1 of Panel A, for example, shows that there are 3,387 market-years in the database, 72 of which were returns over 100% and 84 of which were returns under 50%. Moving to column 2, the market-year count declines to 3,308, reflecting the requirement of a prior year return.[8] Two percent of these market years (i.e., years with an existing prior year) were returns in excess of 100%.

In the "counts (frequencies) of doubling" row, Panel A of Table 9.2 follows the 72 market years that had 100% or better growth in a calendar year. The conditional frequency of doubling in the subsequent year is 8.33%, which is much higher than the population fraction in the row above. This is not surprising given that a doubling is more likely in volatile markets. Likewise, the probability of halving is 4.17%, which is about twice the unconditional probability. In the following year, 6 of the 72 "doubling" markets more than doubled again, and 3 of the 72 declined by a half or more, essentially giving back the prior year's gains. **Table 9.3** identifies these reversal events: Argentina in 1976–1977, Austria in 1923–1924, and Poland in 1993–1994.

---

[8]That is, conditional upon the existence of a return in a prior year, what is the frequency of doubling or halving? This excludes, for example, the first year in a series and a year following a resumption of market data after a break.

Table 9.2. What Happened When a Stock Market Doubled or Halved in Value

Panel A. 100% Real One-Year Price Increase

	T = 0 Count	T + 1 Count	T + 1 Conditional Frequency	T + 1 Unconditional Frequency	T + 5 Count	T + 5 Conditional Frequency	T + 5 Unconditional Frequency
Market-year counts (frequencies)	3,387	3,308		100%	3,122	—	
Double in value		68	—	2.06%	803	—	25.72%
Halve in value		73	—	2.21%	197	—	6.31%
Years with a 100% real price increase	72	72		2.13%	72		2.13%
Counts (frequencies) of doubling		6	8.33%	0.18%	19	26.39%	0.56%
Counts (frequencies) of halving		3	4.17%	0.09%	11	15.28%	0.32%
Years with subsequent 50% decline	84	76		2.48%	75		2.21%
Counts (frequencies) of doubling		10	13.16%	0.30%	27	36.00%	0.80%
Counts (frequencies) of halving		5	6.58%	0.15%	7	9.33%	0.21%

(continued)

Table 9.2. What Happened When a Stock Market Doubled or Halved in Value (continued)

Panel B. 100% Real Three-Year Price Increase

	T = 0 Count	T + 1 Count	T + 1 Conditional Frequency	T + 1 Unconditional Frequency	T + 5 Count	T + 5 Conditional Frequency	T + 5 Unconditional Frequency
Counts (frequencies)	3,271	3,186		100%	3,200	—	—
Double again in value		70	—	2.20%	788	—	25.90%
Halve in value		74	—	2.32%	192	—	6.31%
Three-year periods with a 100% increase	460	460		14.06%	451		13.79%
Counts (frequencies) of doubling		17	3.70%	0.52%	98	21.73%	3.00%
Counts (frequencies) of subsequent halving		21	4.57%	0.64%	47	10.42%	1.44%
Three-year periods with a –50% decline	203	178		6.21%	179		5.47%
Counts (frequencies) of doubling		15	8.43%	0.46%	85	47.49%	2.60%
Counts (frequencies) of subsequent halving		6	3.37%	0.18%	14	7.82%	0.43%

Notes: A boom is either (1) a return of more than 100% to a stock market index within a single year, defined according to availability in real- or dollar-valued and total or capital appreciation only; or (2) a return of more than 100% to a stock market index within a three-year calendar period, defined according to availability in real- or dollar-valued and total or capital appreciation only. A bubble is a boom followed by a bust, defined as either (1) more than a 50% decline in index value in the following year; or (2) more than a 50% decline over the following five years. The conditional bubble frequency is the percentage of booms followed by a bust. A crash is similarly defined as a decline in real- or dollar-valued and total or capital appreciation of a market index within a one-year or a three-year calendar period. Missing observations caused by interruptions of the market are deleted from frequency calculation. Data sources are reported in Table 9.1.

Table 9.3. Markets That Doubled in Value in Dollar (or Real) Terms in a Calendar Year

Country	Year	-1	0	1	2	3	4	5
Germany	1949	0.12	1	1.01	2.35	3.52	4.43	8.08
Peru	1989	0.31	1	0.77	1.61	3.54	4.43	6.41
Portugal	1985	0.38	1	3.05	8.82	6.24	8.04	6.09
Chile	1986	0.47	1	1.25	1.53	2.22	2.67	5.49
Peru	1991	0.48	1	2.20	2.75	3.98	4.85	4.72
Germany	1951	0.43	1	1.49	1.88	3.43	4.01	3.77
Brazil	1991	0.37	1	1.05	1.84	3.02	2.38	3.28
Austria	1985	0.33	1	1.22	1.21	1.30	2.90	3.28
Colombia	2004	0.44	1	2.02	2.24	2.53	1.83	3.23
United Kingdom	1975	0.47	1	0.86	1.48	1.76	2.14	3.08
Russia	1999	0.26	1	0.68	1.05	1.45	2.54	2.91
Pakistan	2002	0.45	1	1.31	1.42	2.23	2.19	2.90
Egypt	2004	0.46	1	2.54	2.92	4.53	2.09	2.77
Peru	1992	0.46	1	1.25	1.81	2.21	2.15	2.53
Colombia	2005	0.49	1	1.11	1.25	0.90	1.59	2.24
Italy	1985	0.42	1	1.71	1.45	1.64	2.35	2.18
Brazil	1969	0.30	1	1.79	3.45	1.84	1.94	2.15
Chile	1977	0.49	1	1.96	3.59	6.84	4.22	2.15
Brazil	2003	0.49	1	1.30	1.96	2.75	4.82	2.04
Italy	1933	0.46	1	1.26	1.33	1.19	1.35	1.34
Belgium	1940	0.44	1	1.77	1.92	1.75	1.36	1.33
Hungary	1996	0.49	1	1.95	1.77	1.96	1.42	1.28
Japan	1972	0.46	1	0.84	0.73	0.85	1.08	1.28
Portugal	1942	0.45	1	0.94	1.15	1.30	1.43	1.20
Egypt	2005	0.39	1	1.15	1.78	0.82	1.09	1.19
Ireland	1977	0.48	1	1.55	1.55	1.68	1.41	1.16
New Zealand	1933	0.42	1	1.15	1.19	1.18	1.24	1.09
India	2009	0.50	1	1.19	0.74	0.92	0.87	1.06
South Africa	1979	0.49	1	1.56	1.22	1.50	1.51	1.02
Austria	1989	0.45	1	1.13	0.94	0.75	0.99	1.00
Norway	1979	0.35	1	0.81	0.69	0.49	0.88	0.96
Mexico	1991	0.46	1	1.23	1.82	1.08	0.79	0.93
Argentina	1991	0.20	1	0.61	0.95	0.71	0.78	0.91
Argentina	1978	0.38	1	3.51	3.12	1.43	0.55	0.79
Portugal	1980	0.37	1	0.64	0.39	0.29	0.30	0.78
Austria	1946	0.49	1	1.12	0.53	0.53	0.44	0.75
Finland	1999	0.44	1	0.85	0.56	0.44	0.58	0.67
Netherlands	1940	0.43	1	0.72	0.80	0.97	0.73	0.67

(continued)

Table 9.3. Markets That Doubled in Value in Dollar (or Real) Terms in a Calendar Year (continued)

Country	Year	-1	0	1	2	3	4	5	Country	Year	-1	0	1	2	3	4	5
Portugal	1986	0.33	1	2.90	2.05	2.64	2.00	1.92	Austria	1923	0.40	1	0.48	0.36	0.48	0.60	0.63
Spain	1986	0.40	1	1.38	1.63	1.88	1.67	1.89	Russia	2009	0.49	1	1.23	0.97	1.08	1.11	0.59
Japan	1952	0.43	1	1.00	1.01	1.47	2.06	1.87	Venezuela	1996	0.44	1	1.27	0.60	0.61	0.62	0.56
Argentina	1976	0.18	1	0.48	1.28	4.48	3.98	1.82	Portugal	1987	0.35	1	0.71	0.91	0.69	0.66	0.54
Australia	1933	0.48	1	1.15	1.41	1.60	1.98	1.77	Italy	1944	0.40	1	0.53	0.49	0.42	0.47	0.52
Germany	1985	0.44	1	1.37	1.09	1.27	1.82	1.75	Brazil	2009	0.45	1	1.04	0.78	0.75	0.61	0.51
Finland	1933	0.45	1	1.12	1.26	1.84	1.85	1.75	New Zealand	1986	0.47	1	0.64	0.57	0.63	0.40	0.48
Germany	1923	0.23	1	1.09	0.71	1.69	1.57	1.74	Norway	1973	0.44	1	0.60	0.51	0.58	0.45	0.48
Chile	1991	0.49	1	1.18	1.55	2.19	2.05	1.71	Poland	1993	0.12	1	0.45	0.43	0.67	0.51	0.47
Colombia	1991	0.35	1	1.22	1.61	2.11	1.51	1.61	Venezuela	1990	0.20	1	1.34	0.59	0.69	0.58	0.44
South Africa	1933	0.35	1	1.31	1.52	1.94	1.62	1.58	Philippines	1993	0.45	1	0.92	0.81	0.94	0.35	0.39
Switzerland	1985	0.49	1	1.39	1.29	1.35	1.61	1.57	Germany	1926	0.42	1	0.93	1.03	0.78	0.57	0.36
Denmark	1972	0.48	1	1.12	1.03	1.33	1.48	1.54	Chile	1933	0.46	1	0.98	0.46	0.44	0.44	0.33
Czech	1922	0.47	1	1.17	1.03	0.98	1.05	1.52	France	1941	0.48	1	0.57	0.99	1.14	1.06	0.28
China	2003	.45	1	0.91	1.02	1.97	3.18	1.50	Poland	1927	0.47	1	0.88	0.57	0.39	0.21	0.20
Greece	1933	0.27	1	1.17	1.18	1.20	1.49	1.39	Argentina	1979	0.28	1	0.89	0.41	0.16	0.23	0.18
Philippines	1986	0.14	1	1.37	1.64	1.88	1.35	1.38	Germany	1940	0.49	1	1.15	1.07	0.88	0.75	0.16

Notes: This table reports the cumulated dollar-valued capital appreciation return to markets following a calendar year in which the dollar-valued index level at least doubled. Subsequent event-years in which the index value doubled again are highlighted in green. Subsequent event years in which the index gave back all or more of its one-year gain at some point in the next five years are highlighted in pink. Values are sorted on event-year five cumulative capital appreciation returns.

Table 9.2 shows that bubbles may take some time to deflate. Counts and frequencies at the five-year horizon are reported in the T + 5 columns. On the one hand, Panel A of Table 9.2 shows that after five years, 15.28% of the boom markets had crashed to less than half their levels at T=0. On the other hand, 26.39% of the markets had at least doubled in value again. After a stock market boom of at least 100% in a single year, the frequency of doubling in the next five years was significantly greater than the frequency of halving.

Note that the frequency of crashing at the five-year horizon is significantly higher for booming markets than the unconditional frequency, while the frequency of doubling after five years is about the same. Thus, a boom *does* increase the probability of a crash, but the crash probability is low. Panel A of Table 9.2 shows that a rapid boom is not a strong indicator of a bust; probabilities move from 2% to 4% at the one-year horizon (T + 1) and from 6% to 15% at the five-year horizon (T + 5). The significance of this shift depends, of course, on investor risk aversion. From a historical perspective, it is important to recognize that the overwhelming proportion of booms that doubled market values in a single calendar year were not followed by a crash that gave back these gains.

Table 9.2 also includes results for markets that halved in value in a single year. These are similar to the doubling market results. Subsequent tail events (doubling or halving) at the one-year and five-year horizons are higher than the unconditional probabilities of these events.

Doubling in a single year may be too restrictive as a definition of a boom. For example, the dot-com bubble of the 1990s evolved over several years. Panel B of Table 9.2 reports results for the second definition of a boom—one that doubles market value over a three-year horizon. This definition is chosen so that it includes the US booms of 1928 and 1999, and it also includes booms in the United States in 1935, 1945, 1956, and 1997. This broader definition of a boom generates 460 events of a doubling over three years—roughly 14% of the overlapping three-year return periods in the data. In the context of global equity markets, the 1928 and 1999 three-year bubbles, although not common, were not that unusual. After a three-year run-up, markets subsequently halved in the following year 4.57% of the time. This is about twice the unconditional probability of a one-year halving event, but it is still rare. At the five-year horizon, the probability of the market value declining by a half after five years is 10.42%, which is higher than the unconditional probability of 6.31% but not dramatically so.

It is important to note that the frequencies in Table 9.2 are conditional on data existing in subsequent years after the event of interest. That is why the table includes markets known to have closed after wars and revolutions; −99%

returns were assigned to them. A robustness test that assigns a –100% return to *all* missing observations (not reported) increases the frequency of halving for both conditional and unconditional distributions, but it does not affect the basic result that conditioning of a boom has a relatively minor effect.

Past studies of the mean reversion of stock markets suggest that what goes up must come down; a large boom should increase the probability of a future decline. However, focusing on the rejection of the null of no association between past and future multi-year market returns can be misleading for economic decision making. The fact that probabilities of a decline increase from 6% to 10% following a three-year boom may not be as relevant to investor choice as the fact that the chance of doubling in value is twice the chance of halving in value over that same horizon.

Conclusion

The most important thing a financial historian can tell investors about bubbles is that they are rare. Indeed, any discussion of bubbles quickly turns to history because recent evidence is lacking. Most models and analysis of stock market bubbles focus on a few well-known instances. Gathering data about the world's stock markets helps to fill in this lack of empirical evidence. The DMS and JG/ICF data provide some insight into the rarity of bubbles, showing that the overwhelming proportion of price increases in global markets were not followed by crashes.

Investor decision making under uncertainty involves a consideration of the probabilities of future outcomes and attitudes about these outcomes. The bubbles that did not burst are just as important for investors to know about as the bubbles that did burst. Placing a large weight on avoiding a bubble, or misunderstanding the frequency of a crash following a boom, is dangerous for the long-term investor because it forgoes the equity risk premium. If investors in the shares of the Casa di San Giorgio had sold out in 1603, for example, they would have missed a 20-year boom in prices and would have had to wait 80 years to be proven right.

For regulators, the evidence raises the question of whether deflating a bubble is the right course of action. If a bubble is associated with investment in new technologies with high economic potential as well as high economic uncertainty, it forces a choice between guarding against a financial crisis versus allowing productive investment.

This chapter presents a preliminary examination of bubbles in stock markets around the world over the last 115 years. Although economists often focus on a few representative and memorable bubbles, the analysis presented here suggests there are dozens more we should investigate. The list in Table

Bibliography

Braudel, Fernand. 1972. *Civilization and Capitalism, 15th–18th Century, vol. 2: The Wheels of Commerce*. First published in France under the title *Les Jeux de L'echange* (Paris: Librairie Armand Colin). Translation from the French by Siân Reynolds. First California paperback printing, Berkeley and Los Angeles, CA: University of California Press (1992).

Cameron, Rondo. 1978. "Reviews of Books." Book review of *The Cambridge Economic History of Europe, Volume V: The Economic Organization of Early Modern Europe*. Edited by E.E. Rich and C.H. Wilson. *Journal of Economic History*, vol. 38, no.3 (September): 810–812.

Dimson, Elroy, Paul Marsh, and Mike Staunton. 2014. *Global Investment Returns Yearbook 2014*. Zurich: Credit Suisse Research Institute.

Fratianni, Michele. 2006. "Government Debt, Reputation, and Creditors' Protections: The Tale of San Giorgio." *Review of Finance*, vol. 10, no. 4: 487–506.

Frehen, Rik G.P., William N. Goetzmann, and K. Geert Rouwenhorst. 2013a. "Finance in the Great Mirror of Folly." In *The Great Mirror of Folly: Finance, Culture, and the Crash of 1720*. Edited by William N. Goetzmann, Catherine Labio, K. Geert Rouwenhorst, and Timothy G. Young. New Haven: Yale University Press: 63–88.

———. 2013b. "New Evidence on the First Financial Bubble." *Journal of Financial Economics*, vol. 108, no. 3 (June): 585–607.

Garber, Peter M. 1990. "Famous First Bubbles." *Journal of Economic Perspectives*, vol. 4, no. 2 (Spring): 35–54.

Goetzmann, William N., and Roger G. Ibbotson. 2006. *The Equity Risk Premium: Essays and Explorations*. New York: Oxford University Press.

Goetzmann, William N., and Philippe Jorion. 1999. "Re-Emerging Markets." *Journal of Financial and Quantitative Analysis*, vol. 34, no. 1 (March): 1–32.

Goetzmann, William N., Lingfeng Li, and K. Geert Rouwenhorst. 2005. "Long-Term Global Market Correlations." *Journal of Business*, vol. 78, no. 1 (January): 1–38.

Harrisse, Henry. 1888. "Christopher Columbus and the Bank of Saint George (Ufficio di San Giorgio in Genoa): Two Letters Addressed to Samuel L.M.

Barlow, Esquire." Private print. London: Chiswick Press, C. Wittingham and Company.

Jenks, Stuart. 2010. "The First Bubble: Silver Mining in the Saxon Erzgebirge, c. 1470–1540" (http://marienbergminerals.com/wp-content/uploads/2015/10/The_first_bubble.pdf).

Jorion, Philippe, and William N. Goetzmann. 1999. "Global Stock Markets in the Twentieth Century." *Journal of Finance*, vol. 54, no. 3 (June): 953–980.

Laube, Adolf. 1974. "Studien über den erzgebirgischen Silberbergbau von 1470 bis 1546. *Forschungen zur mittelalterlichen Geschichte*, vol. 22, Berlin (Ost): Akademie-Verlag.

Le Bris, D.L., W.N. Goetzmann, and S. Pouget. 2014. "Testing Asset Pricing Theory on Six Hundred Years of Stock Returns: Prices and Dividends for the Bazacle Company from 1372 to 1946" (No. w20199). National Bureau of Economic Research.

Macleod, Christine. 1986. "The 1690s Patents Boom: Invention or Stock Jobbing?" *Economic History Review*, vol. 39, no. 4 (November): 549–571.

Murphy, Antoin E. 1997. *John Law: Economic Theorist and Policy-Maker*. New York: Oxford University Press.

Nicholas, Tom. 2008. "Does Innovation Cause Stock Market Runups? Evidence from the Great Crash." *American Economic Review*, vol. 98, no. 4 (September): 1370–1396.

Pástor, L., and P. Veronesi. 2009. "Technological Revolutions and Stock Prices." *American Economic Review*, vol. 99, no. 4 (September): 1451–1483.

Perez, Carlota. 2009. "The Double Bubble at the Turn of the Century: Technological Roots and Structural Implications." *Cambridge Journal of Economics*, vol. 33, no. 4: 779–805.

Velde, François R. 2009. "Was John Law's System a Bubble? The Mississippi Bubble Revisited." In *The Origins and Development of Financial Markets and Institutions from the Seventeenth Century to the Present*. Edited by Jeremy Atack and Larry Neal. New York: Cambridge University Press: 99.

Werner, Theodor Gustav. 1936. "Das fremde Kapital im Annaberger Bergbau und Metallhandel des 16. Jahrhunderts mit Berücksichtigung der Kuxspekulation und der Verhältnisse in anderen erzgebirgischen Bergstädter." *Neues Archiv für Sächsische Geschichte*, vol. 57, no. 2: 113–179.

10. "The Fundamental Things Apply": How to Face Up to Asset Market Bubbles

Eugene N. White

Professor of Economics, Rutgers University
Research Associate, NBER

Driven by the belief that an industry or the economy has entered a new golden age, asset bubbles are a reoccurring but infrequent phenomenon. Although difficult to measure, good fundamentals help initiate bubbles, which are then inflated by "irrational exuberance." Investors may attempt to ride a bubble or short it, but central banks should remain focused on the whole economy.

This day and age we're living in

Gives cause for apprehension

With speed and new invention

And things like fourth dimension...

The fundamental things apply

As time goes by.

—Herman Hupfeld, "As Time Goes By" (1942)

Bubbles in asset markets are propelled by investors' belief that some industry or the economy in general has entered a new era of unparalleled expansion—an era in which fundamentals that previously dictated more limited growth do not apply. At their origin, bubbles may indeed begin as a result of some new technology or rise in productivity that drives up asset prices. But the suddenness and the speed of change can lead to "waves of optimistic . . . sentiment, which are unreasoning" (Keynes 1936), or "irrational exuberance" (Greenspan 1996). In these cases, investors push prices beyond what is revealed *ex post* to be their fundamental values. The popping of a bubble forces painful reallocations of portfolios and resources, which are often accompanied by demands for government intervention.

Bubbles represent both opportunities and perils, and this chapter introduces the issues raised by bubbles that investors must face. Four questions are addressed: (1) Do bubbles exist?[1] (2) Can a bubble be measured? (3) Should a bubble be popped? (4) Can an investor protect himself or herself?

The answers to the first two questions reveal the difficulty of differentiating a bubble from a justifiable boom in asset prices. In answer to the third question, experience has shown that central banks should not attempt to pop bubbles because of the potential collateral damage from causing monetary policy to deviate from its targets for price stability and growth. The answer to the fourth question is more complicated. Some investors have been willing to take a wild ride on a bubble or attempt to short it, but their success has depended on a superior assessment of the fundamentals compared to their peers. In the near future, bubbles and the opportunities to profit from them may be circumscribed by a new regime of financial repression designed to limit risk-taking.

Question 1: Do Bubbles Exist?

It may seem strange to begin by asking whether bubbles exist, but the answer is intimately tied to the other questions. Although there may be a broad consensus today that bubbles exist, there has always been an influential section of the economics profession that has argued they do not (Williams 1938; Cochrane 2013). For these economists, markets are fine-tuned processors of information with no significant asymmetries of information between investors, financial institutions and markets, and industry. To understand the issues at hand, it is useful to review the fundamentals of asset pricing. Although presented in terms of equities, the following applies to all assets.

Fundamental principles of finance require that the price of a stock at a point in time, P_t, equals the present discounted value of all expected future dividends, $D_{(t+i)}$:

$$P_t = \frac{D_{t+1}}{(1+r)^1} + \frac{D_{t+2}}{(1+r)^2} + \frac{D_{t+3}}{(1+r)^3} + \ldots, \tag{10.1}$$

where i = 1, 2, 3, and so on, and r is the discount rate that the market considers appropriate. The discount rate has two components: a risk-free rate (usually treated as the long-term government bond yield) and an equity premium. The obvious problem for pure fundamentals-based valuation is that future dividends are unknown; the best the market can do is to make use of all available information to price the equity correctly. If the market succeeds

---

[1]Identification of bubbles in data sets for 21 of the world's leading stock markets is provided in the chapter by Goetzmann (2016).

in this task, it is regarded as efficient and prices have been set according to available fundamentals.[2]

Occasionally, for simplicity (a back-of-the-envelope calculation), analysts assume that all future dividends are equal (allowing the subscripts to be dropped) and certain. In that case, Equation 10.1 becomes the following:

$$P = \frac{D}{r} \text{ or } r = \frac{D}{P}. \tag{10.2}$$

D/P is the dividend yield. If all earnings, E, are paid out as dividends, then the price-to-earnings ratio is obtained: $P = E/r$, or $P/E = 1/r$. If an acceptable return is 6% on stocks, then the P/E is 16.7.[3] To provide more realism but retain a tractable model, the Gordon growth model specifies that dividends grow at a constant rate, g, so Equation 10.1 becomes:

$$P = (1 + g) D/(r - g).$$
$$P = (1+g)\frac{D}{r-g}. \quad P = \frac{(1+g)D}{r-g}. \tag{10.3}$$

Although simplified, the price-to-dividend ratio, price-to-earnings ratio, and Gordon growth model form the primary components in almost any ordinary discussion of market fundamentals or bubbles. Any change in the level or growth rate of dividends, the payout ratio, or the equity premium will alter the fundamental price of equities. A bubble appears when the price no longer correctly reflects these fundamental factors. It should also be noted that during a typical bubble, period growth, g, is projected to be higher while risk, reflected in r, is viewed as having diminished. The resultant small value for $r - g$ makes the price highly sensitive to any reappraisal of growth or risk, increasing volatility.

Given this background, what P/E might be considered "normal" and what might suggest a bubble? A P/E of 100 for an equity should raise some eyebrows. It implies that investors are paying a price for which they would be compensated if all earnings in the future do not change, and they are all paid out as dividends for the next 100 years while being discounted at a zero rate of interest or required return.

It might seem easy to set out some redline P/E or P/D above which the presence of a bubble is indicated, but any attempt to do so would be beset

---

[2]For a brief introduction to the efficient markets hypothesis and bubbles, see Kabiri (2015, chapter 2).

[3]This analysis ignores inflation or, alternatively, gives the *real* return (that is, if the acceptable real return, the return adjusted for inflation, is 6%, then the P/E is 16.7).

with a variety of problems. The most obvious case is that of a new industry—today we think of biotech or the internet—that has very high growth, often reinvesting and not paying any dividends in the near future. Even a conservative investor might be willing to countenance a P/E for a high-tech firm that would not be acceptable for an established industry.[4]

Determining whether equities have departed from their fundamental values is further complicated by the question of what the appropriate equity premium should be. The risk-free rate is usually viewed as constant or close to constant, at least in real (inflation-adjusted) terms, but the equity premium may be subject to fluctuations depending on how investors perceive the riskiness of an industry or an economy. During a bubble, not only may future earnings and dividends be overestimated but the irrationally exuberant also may see the equity premium as shrinking.[5] Given that equities are long-lived assets, small changes in the equity premium can yield large movements in prices.

Traditionally, it has been difficult to explain why some investors became excessively optimistic or pessimistic, except to claim there was a "madness" about a crowd. One intuitive explanation for irrational exuberance is the "greater fool theory," where an investor buys an asset on the assumption that it can be sold later to a "greater fool" at a higher price. The difficulty has been to translate this behavior into a formal model that is empirically testable. Since the 1990s, the field of behavioral finance (Shiller 2003; Sewell 2010) has grown up, seeking to explain why some investors may make systematic errors that contradict assumptions of rationality. This literature focuses on why market participants over- and underreact to information, which can create herding behavior, noise trading, bubbles, and crashes.

Obviously, not all investors are prey to overestimating earnings and underestimating the equity premium. Some market participants often recognize that prices have departed from fundamentals, and they might be able to limit the irrationality of overly optimistic investors by short selling. With short selling, contrarian investors borrow shares and sell the borrowed shares at the bubble-inflated current prices, waiting for prices to fall and yield them a profit by buying the shares back at a lower price. Apart from the fact that

---

[4]For example, the peak 1929 P/E was 165 for Columbia Gramophone, 120 for National City Bank, and 73 for Radio Corporation of America—all high-tech companies that continued to prosper. However, the P/E was 129 for Goldman Sachs Trading Company and 153 for the Adams Express Company—both of which collapsed in the crash. For a detailed analysis of the 1929 US stock bubble with abundant data, see Wigmore (1985).

[5]One striking example of the belief in the disappearance of the equity premium is found in Glassman and Hassett (1999), who claimed during the dot-com boom that it would collapse to 0.5% and the DJIA would reach 36,000.

short sales are often limited by government regulation, it is difficult for bears in equity markets to borrow for the long run-up in the boom phase of an asset bubble and wait patiently for the collapse. The longer the asset boom, the greater the difficulty in making short-sale bets. The problem in short selling is even greater in real estate markets because it is not feasible to borrow a house to sell it and then promise to buy it back to repay a loan (Glaeser 2013). However, in the 2000s boom, contrarians were able to short bonds secured by real estate using credit default swaps, profiting while also possibly contributing to the demise of the bubble (Lewis 2010). What is striking in this episode and earlier ones is that close attention to detail—here, the long and complicated prospectuses for the bonds—can reveal the weak fundamentals underlying the bubble.

In general, the limited ability of contrarian investors to thwart the exuberance of other investors creates the necessary conditions for bubbles to arise, but whether prices depart significantly from fundamentals has long been debated. Modern evidence for the existence of bubbles was first provided by Robert J. Shiller (1981), who constructed a measure of stock price fundamentals based on actual future dividends for the US stock market (1871–1987). He concludes that stock prices varied far more than could be justified by dividends. A large literature responded to his boldly presented findings, concerned with whether he had constructed the fundamental measure correctly and whether the deviations from actual prices were statistically significant. Although one might be tempted to regard this controversy as a tempest in an academic teapot, the cost of a collapsing bubble (or as some might prefer, "sharp changes in market valuation") may be quite high.

Question 2: Can A Bubble Be Measured?

The diversity of opinion within the economics profession about the presence and magnitude of bubbles is striking. In the early 20th century, John Maynard Keynes (1936) had little faith that investors paid much attention to fundamentals. Keynes called market prices "the outcome of the mass psychology of a large number of ignorant individuals [that] is liable to change violently as the result of a sudden fluctuation of opinion." On the other side of the Atlantic, John Burr Williams (1938) of Harvard disparaged Keynes' view, likening it to "a ghost in a haunted house" and insisting that stocks represented "the present worth of all the dividends to be paid upon it." This great divide had changed little on the eve of the 1990s bull market. Robert Shiller (1990) contends that "prices change in substantial measure because the investing public *en masse* capriciously changes its mind." In diametric opposition, John Cochrane (1991) had little respect for those whom he believed saw bubbles everywhere, stating: "Is it variation in real investment opportunities not captured by current discount-rate models? Or is it 'fads'? I argue that residual discount-rate variation is small (in a precise sense), and tantalizingly suggestive of economic explanation. I argue that 'fads' are just a catchy name for the residual."

Although these divisions remain, the dot-com boom and bust and, even more so, the subprime real estate disaster have convinced a greater portion of the economics profession that bubbles exist. Yet, not all economists are satisfied. Cochrane (2013), for one, accuses Shiller of lacking any objective means to identify bubbles and only offering a subjective approach that could be simply characterized as "I know it when I see it."[6] However, the subjective approach has highlighted common distinctive features of bubbles, which many experts agree are important.

Seven common features of bubbles have been identified.[7] (1) Bubbles involve rapidly changing fundamentals that usually reflect new technologies that alter prospects for productivity and growth, which, in turn, lead to (2) a long, accumulating series of positive asset returns. (3) Although experienced and/or inside investors dominate the initial phase of an asset boom, there is later entry by new, inexperienced, and less-informed investors who may exhibit herd behavior or engage in "noise trading," driving the prices ever upwards. Given the new technology or changed fundamentals, there is a greater asymmetry of information between insiders and outsiders that may fuel the credulity of outsiders. Thus, the "greater fools" begin to drive prices. (4) Interest in the asset market instigates the development of new investment vehicles that facilitate the flow of funds to the market. (5) Credit for leveraged investment in the asset expands, although there is dispute over whether the flood of credit is driven by demand or supply. (6) Interest in the market generates increased supply of the asset of interest. In equity markets, new initial public offerings (IPOs) flood the market. (7) Bubbles may arise without government interference, but policy often plays a contributing role in altering the fundamentals, encouraging new investors, and easing credit.

Table 10.1 presents some famous bubbles that share these features, giving their dates and impetus. In the source note to this table, interested readers are directed to in-depth studies of each episode. The early history of bubbles is discussed in the essay by Goetzmann (2016) in this monograph.

---

[6]The phrase "I know it when I see it" was most famously used by Justice Potter Stewart in the 1964 case Jacobellis v. Ohio when he declined to offer a precise definition of when a movie was pornography. He opined, "I know it when I see it, and the motion picture involved in this case is not that."

[7]This modified list is partly derived from Kabiri (2015, p. 50).

Identification and measurement look for long, positive series of returns followed by huge, abrupt negative returns—the classic bubble pattern. Mishkin and White (2003) and White (2006) identify six long booms (three or more years of 10% returns) and 15 stock market crashes in the 20th century. But these two phenomena are matched in only three instances—1928–1929, 1985–1987, and 1995–2000—and can be considered stock market bubbles. Similarly, White (2014) finds three real estate bubbles: 1922–1925, 1984–1989, and 2001–2006. In a companion chapter in this volume, Goetzmann (2016) provides a similar metric for identifying bubbles, examining data for 21 of the world's most important stock markets.

Employing a statistical technique to find sharp turning points, Bordo and Landon-Lane (2013) examine 18 OECD countries for stock, real estate, and commodity booms. For the United States, they uncover four real estate booms and seven stock market booms, which, when combined with an abrupt collapse with no recovery, nearly match the events selected by previous studies. These analyses may identify bubbles, but they do not inform us about how much of the rise in asset prices may be accounted for by fundamental factors and how much by a bubble component.

Table 10.1. Selected Famous Bubbles

Bubble	Dates	Impetus
Tulip mania	1673	Tulip cultivation
Mississippi bubble	1718–1720	Government refinance
South Sea bubble	1720	Government refinance
British railroads	1840s	Railroad technology
US real estate	1923–1926	Postwar housing demand
US stock market	1928–1929	High-Tech innovations
US stock market	1985–1987	High-Tech innovations/disinflation
US real estate	1984–1989	Macroeconomic stabilization
Japanese Nikkei and stock market	1986–1991	Productivity growth
Internet (dot-com)	1998–2000	High-Tech innovations
Subprime real estate	2005–2008	Mortgage finance innovations

Sources: For tulip mania and the Mississippi and South Sea bubbles, see Neal (1990) and Garber (2000). For British railroads, see Campbell (2012). For the Japanese markets, see Stone and Ziemba (1993). For the US stock market and real estate bubbles, see Glaeser, Gyourko, and Saiz (2008) and White (1990, 2006, 2014).

Identification of the fundamentals driving a rapidly rising market and then causing it to collapse has proven to be notoriously difficult. A key problem has been the measurement of the new technology and other intangible assets of firms boosting their equity prices. For the bubble of the 1920s, Fisher (1930) provides anecdotal evidence and McGrattan and Prescott (2004) an indirect measure of this factor. Using an innovative, direct measure—the effect of patents on stock prices—Nicholas (2008) shows that valuable technological innovations contributed significantly to the run-up, though not to the crash.

The problem in constructing a model to separate out the fundamental and non-fundamental factors driving asset prices is that if fundamentals do not completely explain price movements, one cannot claim there is a bubble element because the model may be misspecified or some variable mismeasured or omitted (Hamilton and Whiteman 1985; Flood and Hodrick 1990). Likewise, models that show there is no bubble (typically miss the crash) and may be overfitted (Sirkin 1975; Donaldson and Kamstra 1996; McGrattan and Prescott 2004). To circumvent this problem, market anomalies, which arise because of different groups' perceptions of fundamentals, may provide the best means for judging the existence and size of a bubble.

Closed-end mutual funds offer a unique means to assess the size of a bubble. The fundamentals for these funds, the constituent stocks, are known and fixed, and it is straightforward to calculate their net asset values (NAVs). There should be no substantial deviation of the price of a closed-end mutual fund from its NAV because it is easy to replicate. However, de Long and Shleifer (1991) report that during the US stock market boom of the late 1920s, these funds exhibited substantial premiums over their NAVs for the years 1927–1929 on the order of 30%, which then disappeared after the crash. This evidence suggests that small investors, for whom there would have been some cost to duplicating the portfolio of one these funds, were willing to pay a very substantial premium.

Lenders receiving equities as collateral from leveraged investors may not have the same assessment of the market as borrowers. Rappoport and White (1993, 1994) point out that in the late 1920s market for brokers' loans, lenders raised margin requirements and interest premiums as stock prices increased. Margin requirements were unregulated in this era, and lenders increased them from 25 to 50% during the course of the boom, suggesting that they believed there was an increasing possibility that a huge market correction was about to occur—that is, the bubble would pop. Applying options pricing models to brokers' loans, Rappoport and White (1994) demonstrate that there was a surge in implied volatility for stocks that were collateral for the loans. Further, using brokers' loan information, they estimated a bubble component in stock prices that first appeared in the fourth quarter of 1927 in the DJIA (Dow Jones Industrial Average), reaching 63% of its value on the eve of the crash. Observing the richer late 20th century options markets, Bates (1991) finds that for the 1987 crash, out-of-the-money puts became unusually expensive in the year before the crash; an options model with a jump-diffusion process indicates that a crash was expected.

These studies of market anomalies provide empirical evidence for the magnitude of bubbles. However, precise estimates remain elusive, if only because there are no direct tests and each group of agents view the risk from a bubble differently. Thus, although an asset boom might tempt an investor to enter on the assumption that there will be "greater fools" willing to buy at a higher price, there is no simple means to assess the magnitude of a bubble or when it might collapse with the fools in flight.

Question 3: Should a Bubble Be Popped?

Should the government and, in particular, a central bank attempt to suppress or pop asset bubbles? Unfortunately, a survey of economists or policy makers on this subject would yield scant agreement, reflecting in no small part their views on the existence of bubbles and the ability to accurately measure them. The natural starting point for discussion here is the US stock market boom and bust of 1928–1929.

During the prosperous 1920s, the US Federal Reserve focused on price stability; however, when the stock market began to rise rapidly in 1928, the Fed became concerned that credit was being siphoned away from "productive" to "non-productive" uses (i.e., the stock market). Initially, Fed officials tried to talk down the market and dissuade banks from providing brokers' loans. Immune to these lectures, the stock market continued to rise, leading the Fed to raise interest rates during the summer of 1929. Unfortunately, because the economy was just slipping into recession, this tightening not only contributed to the collapse of the bubble in October 1929 but also to a sharp recession, the first phase of the Great Depression. In retrospect, a consensus emerged that the Fed had gravely erred by switching its attention from price stability and the real economy to equity markets (Friedman and Schwartz 1963; Bernanke 2013).

The policy lesson from this disaster was that the central bank should not attempt to deflate an asset bubble because it is difficult to get the timing of an intervention correct; moreover, any intervention could undermine the bank's statutory goals (in the United States) of price stability and full employment. The appropriate role for a central bank was seen as limited to containing a larger crisis when a bubble popped of its own accord. This response was exemplified by the October 1929 actions of the Federal Reserve Bank of New York, which fulfilled the classic role of a lender of last resort by flooding the market with liquidity, preventing the crash from spilling over into the banking sector. Unfortunately, the Federal Reserve Board regarded the New York Fed's actions as tantamount to bailing out speculators and reasserted a tight monetary policy. The board was concerned about speculation and inflation even as the economy continued to falter.

The failure of the Fed to appropriately act as a lender of last resort during the four banking panics of 1930–1933 helped send the economy and all asset prices into a downward spiral. From the 1929 peak to the 1932 trough, stock indices fell nearly 90% (White 2006). Up to this point, the federal government had left securities regulation to the states. Starting in 1933, the New Deal legislation imposed a regime on the markets that required increased disclosure and set rules for trading on the exchanges and imposed high margin requirements for margin loans, brokers' loans, and short sales. In this new environment, the equities markets became quiescent, trading volumes collapsed, IPOs were few, and the Dow Jones Industrials only returned to their 1929 peak in 1954.

The post-1929 US response to the stock market crash—consisting of repression of various financial activities and institutions—exemplifies post-bubble experiences where a crash spills over from the affected asset market to the financial sector and the economy in general. Although claiming to hold irrational exuberance in check, these regulations (usually suggested by special interests) are common to many post-crash environments, hindering financial development and economic growth. In the aftermath of the 17th century Dutch tulip mania, for example, futures markets were suppressed at the behest of interest groups angered that established markets had been bypassed (Garber 1989, 1990). Similarly, the costly collapse of the South Sea Bubble led to passage in the United Kingdom of the "Bubble Act" in 1720, which constrained the growth of the equities market by stipulating that a joint stock company could be incorporated only by royal charter or act of Parliament. In France, the failure of John Law's Mississippi Company scheme prevented the chartering of any new banks for much of the 18th century. These interventions were usually presumed to kill off any future bubbles. They may have delayed bubbles by imposing costs on the financial sector, but the evolution of institutions and markets allowed bubbles to re-emerge eventually.

After the imposition of the New Deal regulations, it was generally assumed that a bubble would never again afflict the US equities market. The 1987 crash was thus a huge surprise. Fortunately, then-chairman of the Fed, Alan Greenspan, was a keen student of Friedman and Schwartz (1963) and applied the lessons of 1929 (White 2000). No effort was made to restrain the buoyant stock market, but the central bank was there to act as a lender of last resort. Once again, the Fed provided liquidity to ensure that the shock of the crash was not transmitted to financial institutions. Although stunned, the economy did not fall into recession and growth returned. The market recovered to its pre-crash high by mid-1989.

Consequently, unlike the 1929 crash, there was little pressure for new regulations in the wake of the crash of 1987; only "circuit-breakers" were introduced to halt trading when prices fell "too much." Occurring during the gradual deregulation of financial markets and institutions in the 1980s, the apparent ability of the Fed to contain the fallout from the 1987 crash was taken as evidence by economists and policy makers that deregulation could continue apace. Even the dot-com crash of 2000 did not radically change this new consensus, although the market did not bounce back as quickly as it did after the 1987 crash. In 2000, both the DJIA and the S&P 500 indices fell more from peak to trough (e.g., 49% for the S&P 500 in 2000 versus 34% in 1987), and they took longer to recover. The NASDAQ plunged nearly as far as did all the indices in the Great Depression. There was a post-crash recession in 2001, but it was relatively mild (White 2006).

In the early 21st century, a few academics (Cecchetti, Genberg, Lipsky, and Wadhwani 2000) proposed implementing Taylor rules for the conduct of central bank monetary policy that would incorporate not only the standard inflation and output gap targets but also targets for asset bubbles.[8] However, central bankers, such as Ben Bernanke (2002), maintained that the difficulty of identifying and measuring bubbles was too great to permit an appropriately measured policy response and avoid the mistakes of the 1930s. After the 2008 crisis, Bernanke (2013) reaffirmed that monetary policy should not be used to manage an emerging bubble. It was too blunt an instrument, and the size of the correction needed to treat the bubble would have large and undesirable effects on the whole economy. In his view, monetary policy should focus on macroeconomic stability, while regulation and supervision should be used to handle any financial instability.

Bernanke's view guided the response to the damage inflicted by the 2008 real estate crash on the economy and resulted in the implementation of intense regulation and supervision under the rubric of macroprudential policy. The new US regime, shaped by the Dodd–Frank Act of 2010, resembles the response to other devastating crashes: the imposition of an array of new regulations aimed at limiting the ability of institutions to take leveraged risks.

---

[8]A Taylor rule sets a central bank's target interest rate based on how far inflation and output have deviated from their targets.

Like the New Deal legislation before it, the Dodd–Frank Act has little concern for the costs imposed on financing and growth. Similarly, in the United Kingdom, the Bank of England was granted discretionary authority in 2015 to limit home loans by setting loan-to-value and debt-to-income ratios (Bank of England 2015). The focus of concern by the Bank of England and the government was on financial stability with less consideration for growth. In the European Union, authority for such rules remains with national authorities, although the European Systemic Risk Board may make recommendations (de Grauwe 2012). If the experience of past centuries is a guide, these powers can restrict the ability of existing financial institutions and markets to abet bubbles but not to prohibit their formation.

Question 4: How Can An Investor Protect Herself/Himself?

Bubbles present both a danger and an opportunity for the investor. The danger arises because one may be easily swept away with the herd. The less one knows about the underlying fundamentals of an asset—especially its long-run supply elasticity—the more dangerous it is to follow the crowd and anticipate "greater fools." However, opportunity arises because an investor may have better information, enabling him or her to ride the bubble up and exit before it collapses, although this is always fraught with the risk of a delayed departure.

Bubbles are dangerous for the individual and the economy as a whole because market prices of assets no longer reflect their fundamental values and thus distort the decisions of households, businesses, and the government sector. Households will consume more and borrow more under the bubble-induced illusion that they are wealthier. Similarly, firms whose market value is inflated by an asset bubble relative to their book value (Tobin's q) will be induced to expand and invest more, increasing borrowing or issuing more equity. If the asset boom pumps up the value of government-run pension funds, governments may expand benefits and be induced to shift into bubble-inflated assets.

When the bubble collapses, the perceived excess wealth evaporates. Pension benefits may be cut and taxes and contributions raised. Households and firms will also cut back on consumption and investment. Romer (1990) documents this effect for the collapse of the 1929 stock market bubble, where there was a notable drop in the purchase of consumer durables. This additional shock added a further downward impulse to an economy already in recession. Problems of a collapsing bubble are amplified if the owners of the boom assets are highly leveraged. The importance of this factor is laid bare by a simple comparison of the dot-com crash of 2000 and the subprime bust of 2008. Estimates of the initial wealth losses were of the same magnitude but had very different effects. In the case of the former, boom stocks were largely held by relatively unleveraged households and investors. The precipitous drop of the NASDAQ shares produced a large wealth shock, but it modestly contributed to the brief 2001 recession. In contrast, in 2007–2009, many of the subprime assets were held by leveraged financial institutions, which threatened their solvency and led to a credit contraction that propelled the US economy into the Great Recession.

Although it might be tempting to studiously avoid any asset with strongly rising prices, one would then miss out on opportunities that arise from strong fundamentals. One of the earliest examples of a successful investor riding a bubble was C. Hoare & Co. during the South Sea Bubble (Temin and Voth 2004). This English private bank did not apparently have inside information from the South Sea scheme or the activities of customers. Still, it behaved as though it knew the stock would soon be overvalued and therefore increased borrowing costs for speculating customers while making strategic purchases and sales on its own account. The ability to ride a bubble up depends on the sustainability of demand, which, in turn, depends on whether the herd of optimistic investors, the "greater fools," continues to invest, noting the risk of abruptly changing sentiment.

Sustainability also depends critically on the supply of the asset. It has been argued that investors fail to correctly anticipate how supply will respond to asset prices that rocket upwards. As in other bubbles, the South Sea Bubble engendered a rush of IPOs until halted by the Bubble Act of 1720. Hoare's survival and success during the South Sea Bubble reflected its refusal to leverage its investments while keeping an eye on the "greater fools" at large in British society.

Nearly three centuries later during the dot-com boom, hedge funds chose to ride the bubble, heavily investing in technology stocks as the market began to heat up, much like Hoare's bank. Generally, they appear to have skillfully anticipated the price peaks of individual stocks and sold their holdings. This awareness of exuberant investor sentiment did not, however, translate into taking short positions to correct the mispricing of the market. Hedge funds were deterred by the risks of engaging in such an attack, thereby permitting the mispricing to continue and the bubble to grow (Brunnermeier and Nagel 2004). Instead, the final flood of dot-com IPOs may have been the force that brought about the collapse, similar to what happened after new stock issues during the South Sea Bubble.

Conclusion

For the present, central banks will not attempt to use monetary policy to pop incipient bubbles. Instead, a new worldwide regime of intense regulation, echoing the policies of the 1930s, will seek to restrain investors, homeowners, and financial institutions from pushing up asset prices and taking on excessive risks. Yet history suggests that, in the longer run, bubbles will eventually re-emerge, probably in markets not anticipated by regulators. In general, the characteristics of a bubble described in this chapter should be a warning sign for any concerned investor that asset prices are moving ahead of fundamentals. Although sophisticated investors will seek to ride these bubbles, it remains difficult to determine with any precision how much asset prices may rise or when they may collapse. Moreover, investing during a bubble depends on gaining cautionary insights to avoid being overwhelmed by irrational exuberance.

Bibliography

Bank of England. 2015. "The PRA's Intended Implementation Approach to FPC Directions on Loan to Value and Debt to Income Ratio Limits." Bank of England Prudential Regulation Authority (www.bankofengland.co.uk/pra/Documents/publications/cp/2015/prahousingtoolsstatement0715.pdf).

Bates, David S. 1991. "The Crash of '87: Was It Expected?" *Journal of Finance*, vol. 46, no. 3 (July): 1009–1044.

Bernanke, Ben S. 2002. "Deflation: Making Sure 'It' Doesn't Happen Here." Remarks before the National Economists' Club, Washington, DC (November).

———. 2013. *The Federal Reserve and the Financial Crisis*. Princeton, NJ: Princeton University Press.

Bordo, Michael D., and John Landon-Lane. 2013. "Does Expansionary Monetary Policy Cause Asset Price Booms: Some Historical and Empirical Evidence." NBER Working Paper 19585 (October).

Brunnermeier, Markus K., and Stefan Nagel. 2004. "Hedge Funds and the Technology Bubble." *Journal of Finance*, vol. 59, no. 5 (October): 2013–2040.

Campbell, Gareth. 2012. "Myopic Rationality in a Mania." *Explorations in Economic History*, vol. 49, no. 1 (January): 75–91.

Cecchetti, Stephen, Hans Genberg, John Lipsky, and Sushil Wadhwani. 2000. "Prices, Asset. and Central Bank Policy." Geneva Report on the World Economy 2, CEPR and ICMB.

Cochrane, John H. 1991. "Volatility Tests and Efficient Markets: A Review Essay." *Journal of Monetary Economics*, vol. 27, no. 3 (June): 463–485.

———. 2013. "Three Nobel Lectures, and the Rhetoric of Finance." *The Grumpy Economist* (blog): http://johnhcochrane.blogspot.com/2013/12/three-nobel-lectures-and-rhetoric-of.html (17 December).

de Grauwe, Paul. 2012. *Economics of Monetary Union*. Oxford, England: Oxford University Press.

de Long, J. Bradford, and Andrei Shleifer. 1991. "The Stock Market Bubble of 1929: Evidence from Closed-End Mutual Funds." *Journal of Economic History*, vol. 51, no. 3 (September): 675–700.

Donaldson, R. Glen, and Mark Kamstra. 1996. "A New Dividend Forecasting Procedure That Rejects Bubbles in Asset Prices: The Case of 1929's Stock Crash." *Review of Financial Studies*, vol. 9, no. 2: 333–383.

Fisher, Irving. 1930. *The Stock Market Crash and After.* New York: Macmillan.

Flood, Robert P., and Robert Hodrick. 1990. "On Testing for Speculative Bubbles." *Journal of Economic Perspectives*, vol. 4, no. 2 (Spring): 85–101.

Friedman, Milton, and Anna J. Schwartz. 1963. *A Monetary History of the United States, 1867-1960.* Princeton, NJ: Princeton University Press.

Garber, Peter M. 1989. "Tulipmania." *Journal of Political Economy*, vol. 97, no. 3 (June): 535–560.

———. 1990. "Who Put the Mania in Tulipmania?" *In Crashes and Panics: The Lessons from History.* Edited by Eugene N. White. Homewood, IL: Dow Jones-Irwin: 3–32.

———. 2000. *Famous First Bubbles: The Fundamentals of Early Manias.* Cambridge, MA: MIT Press.

Glaeser, Edward L. 2013. "A Nation of Gamblers: Real Estate Speculation and American History." NBER Working Paper 18825 (February).

Glaeser, Edward L., Joseph Gyourko, and Albert Saiz. 2008. "Housing Supply and Housing Bubbles." *Journal of Urban Economics*, vol. 64, no. 2 (September): 198–217.

Glassman, James K., and Kevin A. Hassett. 1999. *Dow 36,000: The New Strategy for Profiting from the Coming Rise in the Stock Market.* New York: Random House.

Goetzmann, William N. 2016. "Bubble Investing: Learning from History." In *Financial Market History.* Edited by David Chambers and Elroy Dimson. Charlottesville, VA: CFA Institute Research Foundation.

Greenspan, Alan. 1996. "The Challenge of Central Banking in a Democratic Society." American Enterprise Institute (5 December).

Hamilton, James D., and Charles H. Whiteman. 1985. "The Observable Implications of Self-Fulfilling Expectations." *Journal of Monetary Economics*, vol. 16, no. 3:(November): 353–373.

Kabiri, Ali. 2015. *The Great Crash of 1929: A Reconciliation of Theory and Evidence.* Basingstoke, England: Palgrave Macmillan UK.

Keynes, John Maynard. 1936. *The General Theory of Employment, Interest and Money*. London: Macmillan.

Lewis, Michael. 2010. *The Big Short, Inside the Doomsday Machine*. New York: W.W. Norton & Co.

McGrattan, Ellen R., and Edward C. Prescott. 2004. "The 1929 Stock Market: Irving Fisher Was Right." *International Economic Review*, vol. 45, no. 4 (November): 991–1009.

Mishkin, Frederic S., and Eugene N. White. 2003. "U.S. Stock Market Crashes and Their Aftermath." In *Asset Price Bubbles: The Implications for Monetary, Regulatory, and International Policies*. Edited by William C. Hunter, George G. Kaufman, and Michael Pomerleano. Cambridge, MA: MIT Press: 53–80.

Neal, Larry D. 1990. "How the South Sea Bubble Was Blown Up and Burst: A New Look at Old Data." In *Crashes and Panics: The Lessons from History*. Edited by Eugene N. White. Homewood, IL: Dow Jones-Irwin: 33–56.

Nicholas, Tom. 2008. "Does Innovation Cause Stock Market Runups? Evidence from the Great Crash." *American Economic Review*, vol. 98, no. 4 (September): 1370–1396.

Rappoport, Peter, and Eugene N. White. 1993. "Was There a Bubble in the 1929 Stock Market?" *Journal of Economic History*, vol. 53, no. 3 (September): 549–574.

———. 1994. "Was the Crash of 1929 Expected?" *American Economic Review*, vol. 84, no. 1 (March): 272–281.

Romer, Christina. 1990. "The Great Crash and the Onset of the Great Depression." *Quarterly Journal of Economics*, vol. 105, no. 3 (August): 597–624.

Sewell, Martin. 2010. "Behavioural Finance." Working paper, University of Cambridge (www.behaviouralfinance.net/behavioural-finance.pdf).

Shiller, Robert J. 1981. "Do Stock Prices Move Too Much to Be Justified by Subsequent Movements in Dividends?" *American Economic Review*, vol. 71, no. 3: 421–436.

———. 1990. "Market Volatility and Investor Behavior." *American Economic Review*, vol. 80, no. 2 (May): 58–62.

———. 2003. "From Efficient Markets Theory to Behavioral Finance." *Journal of Economic Perspectives*, vol. 17, no. 1 (Winter): 83–104.

Sirkin, Gerald. 1975. "The Stock Market of 1929 Revisited: A Note." *Business History Review*, vol. 49, no. 2 (Summer): 223–231.

Stone, Douglas, and William T. Ziemba. 1993. "Land and Stock Prices in Japan." *Journal of Economic Perspectives*, vol. 7, no. 3 (Summer): 149–165.

Temin, Peter, and Hans-Joachim Voth. 2004. "Riding the South Sea Bubble." *American Economic Review*, vol. 94, no. 5 (December): 1654–1668.

White, Eugene N. 1990. "The Stock Market Boom and Crash of 1929 Revisited." *Journal of Economic Perspectives*, vol. 4, no. 2 (Spring): 67–83.

———. 2000. "Banking and Finance in the Twentieth Century." In *The Cambridge Economic History of the United States*. Edited by Stanley L. Engerma and Robert E. Gallman. Cambridge, England: Cambridge University Press: 743–802.

———. 2006. "Bubbles and Busts: The 1990s in the Mirror of the 1920s." In *The Global Economy in the 1990s: A Long-Run Perspective*. Edited by Paul W. Rhode and Gianni Toniolo. Cambridge, England: Cambridge University Press: 193–217.

———. 2014. "Lessons from the Great American Real Estate Boom and Bust of the 1920s." In *Housing and Mortgage Markets in Historical Perspective*. Edited by Eugene N. White, Kenneth Snowden, and Price Fishback. Chicago: Chicago University Press: 115–160.

Wigmore, Barrie A. 1985. *The Crash and Its Aftermath: A History of Securities Markets in the United States, 1929-1933*. Westport, CT: Greenwood Press.

Williams, John B. 1938. *The Theory of Investment Value*. Cambridge, MA: Harvard University Press.

11. Financial Crises

Charles Goodhart
Professor Emeritus, London School of Economics and Political Science

The economic history of the last three centuries has been speckled with finan-cial crises, most of them involving bank failures.[1] The effects of these crises on the real economy and on asset values in general have varied from extremely severe to relatively trivial. In numerous cases, an incipient crisis has been partly or completely averted by timely and effective central bank activity; however, these cases do not figure in the various lists of actual financial cri-ses compiled by economists. It is therefore important to study not only the factors that led to crises but also the factors that prevented them.

The Facts

We can learn as much from studying why financial crises did not occur as we can from studying why they did. Perhaps the most important recent case of an averted crisis was the potential default of Mexico, Argentina, and Brazil in 1981–1982. If that situation had not been defused, it could have resulted in the insolvency of almost all the major city center banks in the United States and some in Europe. It was potentially the most acute financial crisis in the post-WWII era prior to the global financial crisis in 2007–2009, and yet it is almost always excluded from listings of actual crises. There are numerous additional cases, some still undisclosed for confidentiality reasons, in which financial crises were prevented or moderated by official action.

In other instances, inaction or inappropriate action by the authorities led to the crisis becoming both more severe and longer lasting.[2] It is arguable that this was so in the United States in 1929–1933 and in Japan in 1991–1995. So, the scale of financial crises is not a straightforward datum but rather the outcome of a combination of an adverse shock interacting with the efforts (or lack thereof) of the authorities to offset that shock.

---

[1]For those wishing to pursue this subject more deeply, some excellent additional books to read include Aliber and Kindleberger (2015); Calomiris and Haber (2014); Grossman (2010); and Turner (2014).

[2]The absence of a central bank able to inject additional liquidity when the financial system became stressed was a major reason why the United States was prone to such crises (e.g., 1873, 1890, 1907) prior to the founding of the Federal Reserve System in 1913.

Although classifying financial crises is not an easy matter, there have been numerous attempts to do so. A recent working paper by Danielsson, Valenzuela, and Zer (2016) refers to the following:

> This paper is also part of the vast empirical literature that studies the determinants of crises. A prominent early example is Demirguc-Kunt and Detragia[c]he (1998), who consider the factors affecting the probability of banking crises for 65 countries for the period of 1980 to 1994. By constructing a data set of banking and currency crises, spanning 120 years, Bordo et al. (2001) document that capital controls affect the probability of a crisis. More recently, several authors have made use of the Reinhart and Rogoff (2009) database, including Reinhart and Rogoff (2011), who focus on banking crises and relevant variables affecting their likelihood. More recent studies along similar lines are Gourinchas and Obstfeld (2012); Jordá et al. (2010); Schularick and Taylor (2012).[3]

Having decided what set of outcomes counts as a financial crisis (i.e., *not* a set of original shocks because these cannot be assessed), it is then possible to present frequency distributions of their arrival. An example is found in Table 3.5 from Eichengreen and Bordo (2003), shown below as **Table 11.1**. Also see Figure 7 in Danielsson et al. (2016).

Table 11.1 shows that although there were plenty of other crises still continuing (e.g., relating to geopolitical events or to balance-of-payments crises), remarkably few banking and financial crises occurred between about 1937 and 1973. One of the central questions of any study of financial crises should

Table 11.1. Crisis Frequency

Year	Banking Crises	Currency Crises	Twin Crises	All Crises
1880–1913	2.30	1.23	1.38	4.90
1919–1939	4.84	4.30	4.03	13.17
1945–1971	0.00	6.85	0.19	7.04
1973–1997 (21 countries)	2.03	5.18	2.48	9.68
1973–1997 (56 countries)	2.29	7.48	2.38	12.15

Source: Eichengreen and Bordo (2003), Table 3.5.

---

[3]Jordá co-authored this 2010 paper with Schularick and Taylor. Also see Laeven and Valencia (2008).

be why there were so few during this period. What follows is a set of contributory factors:

1. Banks were repressed and forced to lend to their own governments, which were riskless. Banks emerged from WWII with portfolios full of safe, short-dated government debt, only slowly thereafter run down.

2. Competition among banks and between banks and other financial intermediaries was consciously restricted. Banks and other financial intermediaries were encouraged by the authorities to set cartelized margins/spreads that, more or less, guaranteed satisfactory and stable profitability.

3. Capital controls remained in place, so competition from abroad and large-scale international capital flows were largely restricted.

4. Memories of the Depression and prior bank failures remained fresh, so bank managers were risk averse.

5. Unexpected post-war inflation kept property and equity values rising, making private sector borrowers safer.

Although the absence of bank failures was a plus, the banks were repressed and largely treated as quasi-nationalized utilities. This meant that the services banks could provide to private sector clients—apart from some large, favored manufacturers and exporters—were limited.

Banks are risky and thus liable to default for two related reasons. First, their assets—their claims on bank borrowers (IOUs)—are (individually) riskier than the IOUs that they offer to depositors, which commit to repayment at par. Banks attempt to handle such credit and interest rate risk by diversification, skilled monitoring, and holding loss-bearing equity capital. Second, the duration and maturity of their assets is typically much longer than that of their liabilities, where their deposits are generally repayable on demand (sight deposits) or at short notice (e.g., seven-day time deposits). So, banks undertake maturity mismatch. They try to cope with adverse cash flows by holding reserves of cash at the central bank; by holding additional, easily saleable, liquid assets; by arranging lines of credit with other banks; and by limiting the overall extent of maturity mismatch.

Although one of the classic economic models of bank runs attributes them to adverse cash flows that are essentially random (see Diamond and Dybvig 1983), this is virtually *never* the case in reality. Instead, some shock makes depositors and/or other short-term creditors—in wholesale repo and interbank markets—concerned that the market value of their bank's asset portfolios has fallen relative to its capacity, via its equity, to absorb such a loss. Withdrawing and switching deposits to another institution are almost costless, and depositors get paid out in full sequentially as they come forward. As a result, until the bank is forced to close and gets forced into bankruptcy, once a run on a bank starts it is rational to join it. Even a slight concern about bank solvency can, and does, promote liquidity problems for a bank. Serious bank liquidity problems rarely happen without there being a solvency worry in the background.

Causes of Crises

Bank failures and defaults occur when a bank runs out of the cash reserves necessary to meet a continuing adverse cash flow (i.e., when it becomes illiquid). The number of instances when a bank shuts its doors because its auditors or management team confess to a shortage of capital (relative to regulatory requirements) is vanishingly small. In a developing crisis, the overriding need is for liquidity. That means that as a crisis develops, the affected banks are likely to sell whatever they can even at depressed values (i.e., fire sales).

Thus, the failure of one bank can adversely affect the strength of associated banks through a variety of channels. First, and simplest, the failing bank may owe money to other banks, such as through the interbank market, which will no longer be repaid in full or at the time due. This interaction has been intensively modelled (see Allen and Gale 2004a, 2004b), but empirical research has generally found such direct linkages to be of second-order importance (see Upper and Worms 2004; Upper 2006). That being said, a key reason for the rescue of Continental Illinois National Bank and Trust Company in 1984 was that it held sufficiently sizeable interbank deposits from some 40 or so small, corresponding, mostly midwestern US national banks whose own position would be put at risk if Continental Illinois closed. The FDIC's intervention reflected the growing concern that some banks are "too big to fail."

The second reason why one bank's failure may endanger other banks is that the fire sale of assets by the first failing bank prior to failure and the subsequent sales by the liquidator after failure can reduce the current market value of similar assets held by other banks. When mark-to-market valuation is used, such a fall in asset values reduces the accounting estimates of both profits and equity in other banks holding similar assets.

The third reason, which builds on the first two, is that the failure of bank X is an extraordinarily bad signal for creditors of banks W, Y, and Z, which are thought, rightly or wrongly, to have similar asset structures to (or be owed money by) bank X. In most other sectors of the economy, the failure of firm B *benefits*, on balance, similar firms A, C, and D via a reduction in competition and overcapacity. The reverse is true in banking, where contagion trumps competition. When a bank fails, the immediate response is to explore which other bank is next in line to come under pressure. If the UK bank Northern Rock collapses, for example, can Bradford and Bingley and Alliance and Leicester be far behind? The answer was no: All of these banks had to be rescued in quick succession.

A particular problem with the current proposal of a "bail-in"—forcing a bank's creditors to bear some of the burden by having part of the debt they are owed written off—is that it will involve a hurried audit of the scale of loss that such creditors will have to meet.[4] For obvious reasons of self-protection, the auditor involved will want to give a conservative (i.e., low) valuation. And, of course, the audit will be even more difficult to conduct in the middle of a crisis, with all that implies for immediately current market valuations. The resultant bad signal for other banks in a bail-in system is, therefore, likely to be considerably worse than in a bail-out system (when the government can take a longer view). So, the new bail-in approach to resolution may lead to enhanced contagion.

Indeed, one of regulators' shortcomings is that they tend to focus on the conditions in *individual* banks (microprudential) rather than on the conditions of the banking (or financial) *system* as a whole (macroprudential). Microprudential regulation tends to provide incentives to banks to hold broadly similar portfolios, usually in line with the portfolios adopted by the most admired and leading banks. Although this protects each bank from idiosyncratic shocks, however, the system as a whole may be more at risk to total failure from a sizeable common shock. This latter concern suggests that some proposed structural changes, such as breaking up big banks, would be unavailing in the face of a common shock unless steps were simultaneously taken to enhance diversity of asset portfolios and business models.

This analysis allows us to assess under what circumstances financial (banking) crises are going to be more, or less, severe. When a loss of value is idiosyncratically confined to a single bank and is widely recognized to be so, contagion is highly unlikely. Thus, fraud—such as that which sunk Barings (committed by Nicholas Leeson) or damaged Société Générale (committed by Jérôme Kerviel)—will generally not be systemic. Operational risk will be systemic only if the failing found in one bank is thought to be widely spread and applicable to other banks. If a bank has adopted an individual business policy that focuses on unusual investments and/or clients (e.g., BCCI and

---

[4]In a "bail in," fixed-interest creditors are required to make good prior losses and rebuild the required equity buffer through hair-cuts and transfer of their claims from fixed interest to equity status in strict reverse order of seniority.

Johnson Matthey), then its failure will not cast suspicion on other banks; it will be regarded as *sui generis*.

In contrast, crises are likely to be more severe and contagious when there is a common shock to an asset class that is widely held by banks. This shock is likely to be more severe if it punctuates a prior boom in such asset values, leading to a widespread reassessment of appropriate valuations, and if banks were heavily involved in lending to that asset class or lending based on such collateral. The shock will also be greater if some combination of generalized optimism, competition, and rivalry for market share had led banks to increase leverage and economize on holding liquid assets. Such behavior is much more probable when economic conditions seem sunny and warm. As Minsky (1982, 1986) pointed out, macroeconomic stability engenders financial instability.[5] The three most severe financial crises of the last century—the United States in 1929–1933, Japan in 1991–1999, and the global financial crisis of 2007–2009—all occurred after a particularly successful decade with strong growth and stable prices. The longer-term future seemed rosy.

Until World War II, banks did not invest heavily in household mortgages (except in a few cases, for example in Florida in the 1920s). Instead, they financed businesses and were heavily involved in lending to railroads and purchasing bonds and, in the United States, in making call loans to the equity market. Much wealth was tied up in agricultural land, and the banks lent directly to farmers against the collateral of land. Therefore, cyclical downturns in the valuations of foodstuffs, land, and equities (especially railroads) could weaken, providing a common shock to banks. This was especially so where banking was largely done on the basis of small unit banks, as in the United States, which were less diversified and had more concentrated asset portfolios.

In the 1970s and 1980s, the business model of banks altered and became *much* riskier. Large corporations began to finance themselves more through capital markets and less via banks. Banks, instead, based an ever-increasing share of their asset portfolios on urban property-related lending—both commercial real estate and household mortgages. This grew so fast that it exceeded the ability of banks to fund through deposit expansion (Schularick and Taylor 2012; Jordá, Schularick, and Taylor 2014). Banks funded this excess by increasing their reliance on non-deposit wholesale borrowing (e.g., from shadow banks), which was uninsured, and by continuing to run down their previously extensive holdings of government debt. From 1970 to 2005, government debt ratios generally declined and the bulk of such debt was

---

[5]See also Wray (2016).

absorbed at relatively low yields by long-term institutional funds, pension funds, and insurance companies.

During this time, maturity mismatch was increasing because mortgages and property lending have longer durations than business loans. Some attempt was made after 2000 to offload such lending to better-placed intermediaries by securitization, but all too often such securitized mortgages (mortgage-backed securities, MBS) were not distributed outside the banking sector; instead, they remained within it (e.g., Lehman Bros, UBS). At the same time, as duration mismatch was worsening, owned asset liquidity was declining rapidly. Government debt holdings were slashed, and cash and liquidity ratio requirements were sharply cut or abandoned. There was a false belief that funding liquidity—the ability to borrow cash through wholesale markets—was a sufficient and much cheaper source of liquidity than holding liquid assets on the bank's own book. Once a common shock led to a general concern about many banks' valuation and solvency, these wholesale markets dried up and the crisis unfolded.

The global financial crisis (2007–2009) was a joint liquidity *and* solvency crisis, as is true of most financial crises. Indeed, it is arguable that the insufficiency of liquidity was much more to blame for the crisis than the insufficiency of bank capital (although with European banks often having a leverage ratio of over 40, or even 50, to 1, the case is moot). The international regulatory committee, the Basel Committee on Banking Supervision (BCBS), tried to outline a common position on liquidity requirements for international banks (Goodhart 2011), but the central bank governors did not have the stomach to push it through, having been exhausted by the struggle to agree on a common capital ratio (Basel I).

After most severe financial cycles, efforts are taken to ensure that such a damaging event does not happen again; however, these efforts can amplify the financial cycle. For example, resulting legislation has included the prohibition of joint stock companies after the South Sea bubble, the Glass–Steagall Act after 1929–1933, and the Dodd–Frank Act and Vickers Report after 2007–2009. The regulations keep financial intermediaries from doing what they find most efficient and effective, because if the intermediaries would voluntarily behave in this way, the regulation would not be needed. In particular, the requirement to raise equity ratios quickly and dramatically (Bank of England governor Mark Carney talks about a factor of 10 times) with no strong direction, in the EU at least, on *how* this was to have been achieved was partly responsible for the deleveraging and slow growth of both bank lending and deposits since 2009. We can assume that as our economies recover and normality returns, such impediments to banking and financial intermediation will slowly but surely get removed, perhaps just in time for the next financial crisis.

There was a fairly common view that the links between investment and commercial banking contributed to the 1929–1933 disaster. In this view, the Glass–Steagall Act (1933) requiring their separation strengthened the system, and its erosion and eventual repeal in the 1990s was instrumental in setting the scene for the global financial crisis. However, there is little to no evidence for any of these claims (see Calomiris and Haber 2014, especially footnote 82, p. 191; Kroszner and Rajan 1994; McDonald 2015).

Macroeconomic Effects of Crises

Financial crises occur when a financial intermediary, usually a bank, fails, which results in a scramble for liquidity. This happened in the case of John Law's Mississippi Company, the South Sea Company, Overend Gurney, Knickerbocker Trust Company, Creditanstalt, and Lehman Brothers. The list goes on and could be extended to other banks and other countries. No equivalent list of nonfinancial company failures sparking panics, crises, and generalized downturns exists.

Cyclical downturns connected with, and reinforced by, a financial crisis tend to be more severe and last much longer than normal recessions (Jordá, Schularick, and Taylor 2014; Reinhart and Rogoff 2009). Why is this? We all need to make payments to get resources to consume and/or to produce. Our own IOUs are not generally acceptable, because the ordinary agent may default either strategically or under *force majeure*. So, we have to rely on our access to the more acceptable IOUs of others—in most cases, banks (see Minsky 1982) but also, of course, the IOUs of the government and of the central bank.

If our access to acceptable IOUs and thus our ability to make payments for everything suddenly appears at risk, then our livelihood is also at risk. As a result, we stop making deferrable payments, hoard such acceptable IOUs as we can get, and sell less liquid assets to gain access to more liquid assets. The financial panic transmutes into an economic collapse. During the two quarters following the failure of Lehman Brothers in September 2008 (2008 Q4 and 2009 Q1), the economic condition of the world declined more sharply than in any six month period in 1929–1933.

It is an extraordinary condemnation of the state of macroeconomics in 2007 that almost all the models then in use assumed that agents never defaulted, let alone banks. Without the possibility—indeed, a certain positive probability—of some default, there can be no money. In that view, everyone's IOU is perfectly acceptable ("money" being the IOU that is considered best).

There is no concept of liquidity, because none is needed, and there are no banks. In such models, a financial crisis was simply not possible.

Almost by definition a financial crisis is not predictable. If it had been predictable, agents would have taken defensive measures (e.g., selling the risky asset or holding sufficient reserves against it) that would have defused the crisis before it hit. As Avinash Persaud has noted (2015), crises do *not* so much occur from banks taking consciously risky positions as when banks find that some investment classes are actually much riskier than they had imagined or had been led to believe by the regulatory authorities. House mortgages and securitized mortgage-backed securities (MBS) in 2007–2009 are the most obvious examples.

Credit rating agencies are routinely condemned for having given ratings that were too optimistic on such securitized MBS. In practice, however, few of the senior tranches did default; the allocated default probabilities were not far off. Instead, problems arose when market values dropped precipitously in response to fire sales and panic. When such assets were held in banks' trading books, they had to be marked to market. As a result, the current, panic-related decline in value went directly into the profit and loss account and capital valuation. The use of mark-to-market valuations is inherently procyclical, leading to exaggerated estimates of profitability and capital strength in good times and exaggerated pessimism during bad times. At least now the regulatory authorities can use stress tests to attempt to mark all assets to their probable value during crises (i.e., mark-to-crisis) in a semi-consistent fashion.

Whereas the timing and triggers for a crisis are unpredictable, there are some warning signs. When everyone, perhaps especially taxi drivers, believes that the purchase of asset X is the royal road to riches, that is the moment to short it, if possible. If such assets are being purchased on the back of bank loans and the growth and/or level of bank credit is unusually high, that is a danger signal for a forthcoming financial crisis. When macroeconomic performance has been remarkably strong and stable, and everyone (perhaps especially politicians, central bankers, and economists) is extrapolating that strength for the indefinite future, remember that the trapdoor can open any time. In short, panics occur when greed has dominated fear.

On the one hand, it is difficult to be a successful contrarian. Contrarians oppose the momentum of thought as well as the momentum of markets, and they will be wrong more often than not.

On the other hand, the momentum or carry trader who reaches out for risky yield is going to make small positive returns most of the time, but he could face a huge loss if a crisis does ensue—rather like skiing on a pristine avalanche slope. Too many of us are overconfident in our ability to read the signs and do so safely.

Possible Cures for Crises?

More Capital and Liquidity? Financial crises are caused by an insufficiency of capital to absorb losses, thus causing fears of default. Once the resultant spate of withdrawals begins, there is an insufficiency of liquidity, causing the actual defaults to occur—similar to a self-fulfilling prophecy. So, if a crisis seems imminent or is in process, the obvious answer would seem to be to inject more capital and more liquidity into those financial intermediaries under pressure.

There are two problems with this approach. First, the private sector will not want to risk its money in such circumstances, so the rescue would have to come from the public sector (i.e., the taxpayer). Although this may often be the best possible use of taxpayer's money, it will be portrayed and appear as a transfer of funds from innocent, poor taxpayers to rich bankers, which is a political disaster for the policy maker.

Second, any form of insurance tempts the insured to take more risks. (Life insurance is a *possible* exception.) If those running out of liquidity, such as Northern Rock, are to be provided with the needed cash on easy terms by the central bank, will this not just encourage everyone else to skimp on (expensive) self-insurance by holding more low-yielding liquid assets in their portfolio—in short, moral hazard? If Dick Fuld had really believed that the US authorities would let Lehman default, he might have worked harder to prevent that from happening. Lehman's failure was so devastating in part because it was so unexpected, especially after the prior rescue of Bear Stearns.

The concern about moral hazard is valid, but the authorities' response to a potential crisis is likely to be slower and more grudging than what would have been desirable (with the benefit of hindsight). If the monetary authorities are led by those who fear moral hazard more (less) than contagion, crises are likely to be fewer (more frequent) but more (less) severe when they occur.

If one cannot rely on the authorities to inject extra capital and liquidity whenever a crisis is threatened because of political/moral hazard concerns, perhaps one can reduce the frequency and/or severity of crises happening at all by *requiring* banks to hold more equity (and/or other forms of loss-absorbing capital) at all times and more liquid assets. This is exactly what has been done with Basel III.

Although there is no doubt that banks held too little equity and too few liquid assets prior to 2007–2008, the transition to a banking system with more equity has been badly handled, at least in Europe. The benefit of additional equity largely accrues to existing bank debtholders, who are now safer, whereas the prior equity holders become diluted. The response to a request to bankers and their shareholders to achieve a higher capital ratio has been to delever and exit certain functions (e.g., market making), which, especially with the deleveraging, tends to slow down the recovery. Also, although the new system to bail-in creditors via more total loss absorbing capacity should work perfectly in the event of an idiosyncratic failure, it is far less sure that the new system could handle a severe common shock with a great potential for contagion any better than in the past (see Avgouleas and Goodhart 2015).

Finally, the toughened ratio controls will lower the return on equity in banking, although bank equity *may* (or may not) now be seen as somewhat safer and hence needing a lower return. The implications are that banks will lobby against and try to "optimize" (i.e., "game") such controls. As a result, financial intermediation will shift to other less regimented channels (e.g., via fintech), and banking growth, including monetary and loan expansion, will be more constrained by capital limitations.[6]

Structural Changes? Our own IOUs are not accepted in payment because we are prone to default for a variety of reasons. Thus, we have turned to using and accepting the IOUs of certain intermediaries (i.e., banks) as money. But banks can also be risky. When such risks coalesce, a panic and crisis can ensue.

Why not make banks riskless by allowing them to issue money only against absolutely safe assets (i.e., narrow banks)? The proposal is to separate money creation from (risky) credit creation. This was the principle behind Ricardo's proposals that led to the 1844 Bank Act, the 1933 Chicago Plan for banking reform, and many subsequent similar proposals (Lainà 2015).

A problem is that the credit-creating risky bank cannot be allowed to issue relatively short-dated IOUs (liabilities). If it could issue such short-dated liabilities, there would be huge pro-cyclical flows of funds between the narrow (safe, low-yielding) and the risky (but higher yielding) banks (see Goodhart 1995, chapter 2; Goodhart and Jensen 2015). So, the risky banks could be allowed to issue only long-dated debt (say, over three months) and equity. But that would make it risky for them to make short-term loans because they would then have a maturity mismatch. If banks issued long-term debt and short-term interest rates fell, they could be running at a cash loss. The risky banks would be most (least) profitable when the yield curve was downward

---

[6]It is important to note that quantitative easing has so massively expanded banks' cash reserve ratios that liquidity should not prove a constraint for the foreseeable future.

(upward) sloping in a boom (recession). With risky credit-creating banks able to advance credit only against the availability of long-dated liabilities, the availability of overdraft facilities, unused credit card finance, and short-dated lending would be put at risk. Essentially, we want banks not only to process our payments but also to provide us with additional funds to make necessary payments at times when we do not already have a sufficient credit balance at the bank. This latter function would be put at risk in a "narrow bank" system.

Note that the problem just described comes from the maturity mismatch that would occur in the risky banks if they lent short against long liabilities. In the 19th century, the prime defense against risk in banking was to avoid maturity mismatch.[7] A banker who has short-dated liabilities should balance these by holding short-dated assets (e.g., bills of exchange), and long-dated assets should be funded by long-dated (or at least sticky) liabilities.

It is this precept that has been increasingly abandoned in recent years (Goodhart and Perotti 2015). In particular, banks have become increasingly and heavily involved in long-term mortgage lending, so much so that they have had to call upon wholesale funding, rather than more inert, and insured deposits to finance their assets (Jordá, Schularick, and Taylor 2014; Schularick and Taylor 2012). Three periods of severe financial stress have occurred in the United Kingdom since World War II: 1973–1975, 1991–1992, and 2007–2009. All have involved a boom followed by a bust in property finance, largely financed by bank credit expansion. This has been the case in advanced economies more widely (Schularick and Taylor 2012).

Securitization of mortgage debt and on-sale distribution to better maturity-matched holders were a possible partial solution, but for a variety of reasons already noted, these actions largely failed in 2007–2009 and have been scaled back. An alternative approach would be to restrict maturity mismatch more directly (e.g., through some version of a net stable funding ratio). Of all the regulatory reforms proposed since the global financial crisis, this has been the slowest to progress. Indeed, there has been a marked disinclination

---

[7]In an April 1861 edition of the *Economist* article on "How to Read Joint Stock Bank Accounts," (6 April, pp. 366–367), Walter Bagehot warned against judging a bank primarily on the adequacy of its capital and reserves. Rather, "we should add together all the liabilities of the bank—its circulation, its drafts, and its deposits—see what the total is carefully; and then we should compare it with the amount of cash, loans to bill brokers, Government securities, and other immediately tangible and convertible assets which the bank has in hand. If the available money bears a good proportion to the possible claims, the bank is a good and secure bank." On the question of "the specific proportion between the cash reserve and the liabilities of the bank to the public," Bagehot refused to "lay down any technical or theoretical rule upon it." The cash ratio must be allowed "to vary in some degree with the nature of the bank's business."

to recognize the major role that the use of short-term bank funds to finance long-term property investment has played in enhancing the continuing fragility of our banking systems.

Instead, there has been a tendency to lay the blame for such fragility on the more exotic features of investment banking and try to shut them down or divorce such activities from more traditional retail banking. The Volcker Rule on proprietary trading in the United States, the Vickers ringfencing of UK retail banks, and the Liikanen Report in the EU are examples. They derive from a misreading of the underlying causes of the global financial crisis and hence will do little good; however, they will raise the costs and lessen the efficiency of the banking system.

Governance Changes? Decisions are taken by people and not by abstract impersonal institutions. If there is a belief that bankers, and perhaps financiers more widely, are intentionally taking on more risk than would be socially optimal, then we need to reconsider the incentive structure that encourages them to do so.

The incentive structure in the modern corporation, including that of banks, has become one that encourages both risk-taking and short-termism (Kay 2009; Smithers 2013). Management answers to shareholders and are usually large shareholders themselves, being rewarded with bonuses in the form of equity to align their incentives with that of shareholders. Shareholders have limited liability so are in the position of holding a call option on the firm. Particularly because shareholders can diversify much better than workers or even suppliers, they have a much higher risk appetite (and, in some cases, higher than socially optimal).

There also is a fiscal benefit in raising funds through debt rather than equity and a disincentive to ever reversing a debt overhang—a ratchet effect (Admati, DeMarzo, Hellwig, and Pfleiderer 2015). This is because much of the benefit of new equity issue goes to fixed-interest creditors, who are now safer, whereas the equity holders are diluted. This is a powerful influence that drives leverage upward.

Because CEOs have, in practice, a relatively short time in charge of the firm, their incentive is to increase leverage in pursuit of short-term equity gains, with little downside. The pension pot will still be massive and contractually fixed even if the bank tanks.

If there is a desire to control banks', and more broadly firms', risk-taking, this is perhaps the more fundamental place to start. Yet there has been very little appetite to do so. It would be desirable to remove the tax advantage of debt by giving equity an equivalent tax break (Mirrlees et al. 2011). But this is a complex issue and too much of a digression to discuss here.

Another issue is whether the provision of limited liability to *all* equityholders remains appropriate. In the early 19th century, most bankers had unlimited liability. When industry required large scale financing, banks had to become comparably larger. This growth required equity finance from outsiders, a requirement inconsistent with unlimited liability. But, even then, for many decades in the United States, bank equityholders had an extra contingent liability to make a further payment equal to the nominal value of their share (Bodenhorn 2015); still, the entire margin of safety led them to increase leverage.

Perhaps the extra contingent call on shareholders for funds in the event of distress (i.e., a bail-in via equity shareholders) could be scaled according to each shareholder's ability to influence the decisions taken by the bank. In that case, small shareholders would retain limited liability, large shareholders double liability, and a control shareholder unlimited liability. Equivalently, board members would have double liability, as would all bank employees earning over £1 million per year. The CEO would have unlimited liability.

As may be expected with such a radical idea, there has been no enthusiasm at all to reconsider such governance arrangements for banks.

Conclusions

Economic agents default on their promises to pay (IOUs) on a regular basis. As a result, our own IOUs are *not* acceptable in payment. Instead, we have turned to using the IOUs of more trustworthy institutions: banks. But banks themselves are not riskless because their own assets are not riskless. Banks' assets have a variety of risks derived from maturity mismatching and credit risk. Thus, occasionally banks themselves fail, and such failures may become contagious. When that happens, the perceived need for liquidity dramatically increases for all private sector agents, both bank and non-bank. This reaction can cause a sharp decline in demand. Such financial crises have been occasional but have a major influence on our economic development when they occur. It is remarkable that most macroeconomic models have abstracted entirely from these facts of life.

Can anyone forecast when such crises will hit? No, but we can discern when they may become more likely—for example, when there is an asset boom largely financed by bank credit expansion in a context of general macroeconomic over-optimism. Can we alter the structure of the banking and financial system to make such crises less frequent and less virulent? Perhaps to some extent, but the attempts to do so in the last few years have been largely misguided. First, they have underestimated the adverse transitional effect of increases in required capital ratios on deleveraging. Second, they have put the blame for the global financial crisis primarily on the culture and ethos of investment banking rather than on the long-standing nexus between property boom-and-bust cycles and banking conditions. A deeper and more critical look into the structure of housing finance is long overdue.

The achievement of a financial-crisis-free economy is chimerical. The degree of banking repression that occurred from the 1930s to the 1960s and that would again be required to make a narrow banking system operate successfully would deny the public financial services that they value and that could be accessed elsewhere in the absence of exchange controls. We should, instead, aim for a system that can tolerate and withstand crises, avoiding the macroeconomic consequences felt in 1929–1933 and again in 2008–2009.

I doubt that this can be done without public sector intervention and support at times of financial stress. But the public and the press responses to the bail-outs of banks, however objectively necessary and beneficial, were strongly adverse during the global financial crisis. So, the direction of travel in reform has been to shift the burden of financial failure onto other private sector shoulders. Perhaps this may work; perhaps not. We will see in due course.

References

Admati, A.R., P.M. DeMarzo, M.F. Hellwig, and P. Pfleiderer. 2015. "The Leverage Ratchet Effect." Stanford Graduate School of Business Working Paper 3029 (31 December).

Aliber, Robert Z., and Charles P. Kindleberger. 2015. *Manias, Panics, and Crashes: A History of Financial Crises.* 7th ed. UK: Palgrave Macmillan.

Allen, F., and D. Gale. 2004a. "Financial Intermediaries and Markets." *Econometrica*, vol. 72, no. 4 (July): 1023–1061.

———. 2004b. "'Financial Fragility, Liquidity, and Asset Prices." *Journal of the European Economic Association*, vol. 2, no. 6 (December): 1015–1048.

Avgouleas, E., and C. Goodhart. 2015. "Critical Reflections on Bank Bail-Ins." Journal of Financial Regulation (February): 1–27.

Bodenhorn, H. 2015. "Double Liability at Early American Banks." NBER Working Paper 21494 (August).

Bordo, M., B. Eichengreen, D. Klingebiel, M.S. Martinez-Peria, and A.K. Rose. 2001. "Is the Crisis Problem Growing More Severe?" *Economic Policy*, vol. 16, no. 32 (April): 51–82.

Calomiris, Charles W., and Stephen H. Haber. 2014. *Fragile by Design: The Political Origins of Banking Crises and Scarce Credit.* Princeton, NJ: Princeton University Press.

Danielsson, J., M. Valenzuela, and I. Zer. 2016. "Learning from History: Volatility and Financial Crises." Working paper (1 May): http://ssrn.com/abstract=2664275.

Demirgüç-Kunt, A., and E. Detragiache. 1998. "The Determinants of Banking Crises in Developing and Developed Countries." *IMF Staff Papers*, vol. 45, no. 1 (March): 81–109.

Diamond, D.W., and P.H. Dybvig. 1983. "Bank Runs, Deposit Insurance, and Liquidity." *Journal of Political Economy*, vol. 91, no. 3 (June): 401–419.

Eichengreen, B., and M. Bordo. 2003. "Crises Now and Then: What Lessons from the Last Era of Financial Globalization?" In *Monetary History, Exchange Rates and Financial Markets: Essays in Honour of Charles Goodhart*, vol. 2. Edited by P. Mizen. Cheltenham, UK: Edward Elgar.

Goodhart, C. 1995. *The Central Bank and the Financial System*. Cambridge, MA: MIT Press.

———. 2011. *The Basel Committee on Banking Supervision: A History of the Early Years, 1974–1997*. Cambridge, UK: Cambridge University Press.

Goodhart, C., and M. Jensen. 2015. "A Commentary on Patrizio Laina's 'Proposals for Full-Reserve Banking: A Historical Survey from David Ricardo to Martin Wolf'." *Economic Thought*, vol. 4, no. 2 (September): 20–31.

Goodhart, C., and E. Perotti. 2015. "Maturity Mismatch Stretching: Banking Has Taken a Wrong Turn." Centre for Economic Policy Research Policy Insight 81 (May): http://voxeu.org/print/58918.

Gourinchas, Pierre-Olivier, and Maurice Obstfeld. 2012. "Stories of the Twentieth Century for the Twenty-First." *American Economic Journal: Macroeconomics*, vol. 4, no. 1 (January): 226–265.

Grossman, Richard S. 2010. *Unsettled Account: The Evolution of Banking in the Industrialized World since 1800*. Princeton, NJ: Princeton University Press.

Jordá, O., M. Schularick, and A.M. Taylor. 2010. "Financial Crises, Credit Booms, and External Imbalances: 140 Years of Lessons." NBER Working Paper 16567 (December): www.nber.org/papers/w16567.

———. 2014. "Betting the House." CESifo Working Paper 5147 (December).

Kay, J. 2009. *The Long and the Short of It: Finance and Investment for Normally Intelligent People Who Aren't in the Industry*. London: The Erasmus Press Ltd.

Kroszner, R.S., and R. Rajan. 1994. "Is the Glass-Steagall Act Justified? A Study of the US Experience with Universal Banking before 1933." *American Economic Review*, vol. 84, no. 4: 810–832.

Kroszner, R.S., and P.E. Strahan. 1999. "What Drives Deregulation? Economics and Politics of the Relaxation of Bank Branching Restrictions." *Quarterly Journal of Economics*, vol. 114, no. 4: 1437–1467.

Laeven, L., and F. Valencia. 2008. "Systemic Banking Crises: A New Database." IMF Working Paper WP/08/224 (November): www.imf.org/external/pubs/ft/wp/2008/wp08224.pdf.

Lainà, P. 2015. "Proposals for Full-Reserve Banking: A Historical Survey from David Ricardo to Martin Wolf." *Economic Thought*, vol. 4, no. 2: 1–19.

McDonald, O. 2015. *Lehman Brothers: A Crisis of Value*. Manchester, UK: Manchester University Press.

Minsky, H.P. 1982. *Can "It" Happen Again? Essays on Instability and Finance.* Armonk, NY: M.E. Sharpe.

———. 1986. *Stabilizing an Unstable Economy.* New Haven, CT: Yale University Press.

Mirrlees, J., S. Adam, and T. Besley. R. Blundell, S. Bond, R. Chote, M. Gammie, P. Johnson, G. Myles, and J. Poterba. 2011. *Tax by Design.* Oxford, UK: Oxford University Press.

Persaud, A.D. 2015. "Reinventing Financial Regulation: A Blueprint for Overcoming Systemic Risk." VoxEU.org (20 November): http://voxeu.org/article/blueprint-overcoming-systemic-risk.

Reinhart, C.M., and K.S. Rogoff. 2009. *This Time Is Different: Eight Centuries of Financial Folly.* Princeton, NJ: Princeton University Press.

———. 2011. "From Financial Crash to Debt Crisis." *American Economic Review,* vol. 101 (August): 1676–1706.

Schularick, M., and A.M. Taylor. 2012. "Credit Booms Gone Bust: Monetary Policy, Leverage Cycles, and Financial Crises, 1870–2008." *American Economic Review,* vol. 102, no. 2 (April): 1029–1061.

Smithers, A. 2013. *The Road to Recovery: How and Why Economic Policy Must Change.* Chichester, UK: John Wiley & Sons.

Turner, John D. 2014. *Banking in Crisis: The Rise and Fall of British Banking Stability, 1800 to the Present.* Cambridge Studies in Economic History—Second Series. Cambridge, UK: Cambridge University Press.

Upper, C. 2006. "Contagion Due to Interbank Credit Exposures: What Do We Know, Why Do We Know It, and What Should We Know?" Mimeo, BIS.

Upper, C., and A. Worms. 2004. "Estimating Bilateral Exposures in the German Interbank Market: Is There a Danger of Contagion." *European Economic Review,* vol. 48, no. 4 (August): 827–849.

Wray, L.R. 2016. *Why Minsky Matters: An Introduction to the Work of a Maverick Economist.* Princeton, NJ: Princeton University Press.

Part 4. Financial Innovation

12. Structured Finance and the Origins of Mutual Funds in 18th-Century Netherlands[1]

K. Geert Rouwenhorst

Robert B. and Candice J. Haas Professor of Corporate Finance and Deputy Director of the International Center for Finance, Yale School of Management

Financiers in the 18th-century Netherlands produced a remarkable set of innovations that form the foundation of modern-day markets for mortgage-backed securities, pension funds, mutual funds, and depository receipts. Merchant bankers constructed claims and securities that repackaged existing financial instruments. These innovations mark the origins of structured finance. In designing these new financial instruments, merchant bankers appear to have understood many concepts used in modern finance, including the notion of diversification, value investing, the importance of collateral, investor preference for positive skewness, and agency conflicts associated with delegated money management. The question that emerges from this episode of history is why the ultimate adoption of these financial innovations has been relatively slow.

Introduction

Over the past two decades, mutual funds have become the primary investment for small investors. At the turn of the 21st century, the number of mutual funds in the United States exceeded the number of securities listed on the New York Stock Exchange.[2] Compared to direct investments in individual stocks and bonds, mutual funds offer the advantages of liquidity and diversification at a relatively low cost. Although the popularity of mutual funds is relatively recent, the origins of mutual funds date back to the early days of organized stock trading.

---

[1]Permission was granted to adapt and partially reprint Rouwenhorst (2005) in this chapter. In addition, this chapter incorporates material presented at the Financial Market History workshop, Cambridge, UK (23–24 July 2015), hosted by the Cambridge Judge Business School Newton Centre for Endowment Asset Management.

[2]The Investment Company Institute's (2016) *Investment Company Fact Book* reports more than 15,000 mutual funds in the United States in 2015, as compared to 2,400 firms listed on the NYSE.

The founding of the Foreign and Colonial Government Trust in 1868 marks the beginning of mutual funds in the Anglo-Saxon countries. By that time, however, investment trusts had existed in Holland for almost a century. In 1774, the Dutch merchant and broker Abraham van Ketwich invited subscriptions from investors to form a closed-end trust named *Eendragt Maakt Magt*—"Unity Creates Strength," which is the maxim of the Dutch Republic. The founding of the trust followed the financial crisis of 1772–1773, and Van Ketwich's aim was to provide small investors with limited means an opportunity to diversify. Risk spreading was achieved by investing in bonds from Austria, Denmark, Germany, Spain, Sweden, Russia, and a variety of colonial plantations in Central and South America.

The first mutual fund originated in a capital market that was in many ways well developed and transparent. More than 100 different securities were regularly traded on the Amsterdam exchange, and the prices of the most liquid securities were made available to the general public through broker sheets and, at the end of the century, a price courant.[3] The bulk of trade took place in bonds issued by the Dutch central and provincial governments and bonds issued by foreign governments that tapped the Dutch market. The governments of Austria, France, England, Russia, Sweden, and Spain all came to Amsterdam to take advantage of the relatively low interest rates. Equity shares were scarce among the listed securities, and the most liquid issues were the Dutch East India Company, the Dutch West India Company, the British East India Company, the Bank of England, and the South Sea Company. The other major category of securities consisted of plantation loans, or negotiaties,[4] as they were known in the Netherlands. Issued by merchant financiers, these bonds were collateralized by mortgages to planters in the Dutch West Indies colonies Berbice, Essequebo, and Suriname.

As merchants and brokers learned how to expand the range of investment opportunities to the general public during the 18th century, mutual funds gradually emerged. Securitization and stock substitution were the two principal innovations that were created during that period. Securitization uses the cash flows of illiquid claims as collateral for securities that can be traded in financial markets. In a stock substitution, existing securities are repackaged individually or as part of a portfolio—either in smaller denominations or at a lower cost than the underlying claims—to make them easier to trade.

---

[3]The courant was a biweekly publication that listed security prices as well as real estate transactions and announcements of dividends and security offerings. See Neal (1990).

[4]Riley (1980) points out that the term "negotiatie" has no direct counterpart in the modern English language. In 18th-century Holland, it applied to any investment undertaking organized and managed by a financial intermediary that sold shares to the general public.

Often, these innovations were designed to overcome barriers associated with investing abroad, such as foreign registration requirements and the costs of collecting interest or dividends, which prevented smaller investors from participating in securities markets. This broadening of the Dutch capital market eventually led to the forerunners of today's closed-end mutual funds and depository receipts.

Predecessors of Mutual Funds

Prior to the 18th century, a number of investment vehicles emerged that created a joint interest in a pool of financial and nonfinancial assets. Although these securities were not identical to modern mutual funds, they manifested some of the same characteristics. Their evolution sheds light on the first investment trusts to create tradable ownership of a financial securities portfolio. The first major type was a contract of survival. This type included life annuities and, in particular, tontines. The second type included plantation loans.

Contracts of Survival. In a tontine, a borrower promises to pay a group of individuals an annuity that will be divided among the surviving members. As group members die, the payout to the survivors increases. Many early tontines were organized by governments, but examples of private tontines are known to date back to the 17th century. Unlike public tontines, in which the payment promise was backed by the power of taxation, private tontines required some form of collateral to guarantee the periodic payments to participants. In a "capital tontine," participants' initial contributions were used to purchase financial securities. If the underlying portfolio consisted of bonds that paid interest at a fixed rate, then, barring default of the securities, the annual payments could be guaranteed. If the investment portfolio of a private tontine consisted of company shares, no fixed payments could be guaranteed; the participants could only hope that the company would maintain its dividend policy. Unlike most government tontines that promised an annuity but no repayment of principal, the collateral of a capital tontine would be divided among the remaining participants when a prespecified number of group members had died.

Private tontines resembled investment trusts in the joint ownership of financial securities. The difference from mutual funds becomes increasingly fine over time as private tontine societies invested in diversified portfolios. For example, a private tontine organized in The Hague in 1770 under the name *Uit Voorzorg* invested its initial contributions in a portfolio of securities that closely resembled the investments of *Eendragt Maakt Magt* and other

Figure 12.1.   Capital Tontine, 1687

Notes: Figure 12.1 shows a private capital tontine of 10,000 guilders on 20 lives, Amsterdam, 20 February 1687. It was a contract of survival divided into 20 portions on the lives of people born on or before 1 July 1657. The initial participants' contributions would be invested in bonds of the city of Amsterdam or the state of Holland and kept in a safe at the office of a notary public. The annual interest would be divided among the holders of contracts on the surviving nominees, who were often family members, until all but two nominees had died. At that time, the underlying bond portfolio would be split between the two remaining beneficiaries. The names of the subscribers and names and age of the nominees were printed on the back of the contract.

early mutual funds. However, shares in a private tontine were difficult to transfer because they were tied to the lives of its nominees. Moreover, the objective of tontines was income smoothing rather than providing diversification or portfolio management to its participants. According to the directors of *Uit Voorzorg*, the society intended to use its revenues "to pay its members an annual sum of money in the form of a pension."

Plantation Loans The second type of security that shares characteristics with mutual funds is the 18th-century plantation loan, which securitized mortgages to planters in the West Indies. The practice of transforming private loans into publicly traded securities was pioneered by the firm of Deutz & Co. as early as 1695. Johan Deutz was the factor of the Austrian emperor and advanced him loans requiring the revenues from his mercury mines as security. To finance the loans, the firm issued bonds in the Dutch capital market using these revenues as security.

In 1753, Deutz & Co. applied the same technique to mortgage loans to West Indies plantation owners. The firm played a dual role of financier and commission agent. Deutz arranged to issue bonds in the Dutch capital market and used the proceeds to provide mortgages to the plantation owners in Suriname. In return, the owners were obliged to ship their crops back to Deutz, who acted as their commission agent in the Netherlands. The proceeds from these sales as well as the real property of the plantations, including the equipment and the slaves, served as security for the interest and principal payments to the bondholders.

Similar loans soon followed from other firms to plantations in the Dutch colonies of Essequebo, Demerary, and Berbice, as well as to British plantations in the West Indies. Between 1753 and 1776, nearly 200 plantation loans were brought to market in Amsterdam and accounted for the majority of new security introductions during this period.

The plantation loans took many forms. Some were made to specific individual plantations or groups of plantations. Others indicated only the region where the capital would be employed, leaving merchant financiers considerable freedom in allocating the bond proceeds. The latter type of loan left investors holding a security that promised fixed payments from an unspecified portfolio of mortgages, apparently without any recourse to the merchant financiers. When many of the plantation loans defaulted at the end of the 18th century, investors were forced to convert their bonds into equity stakes in the plantations.

The plantation loans contained some elements of an investment trust, but their investments (mortgages to planters) were not securities in themselves. Furthermore, their primary purpose was not to provide diversification or portfolio services. Merchants used their reputation to mobilize capital on behalf of planters in return for the right to factor shipments of tobacco, cocoa, and coffee. By issuing the bonds, they could expand their business without tying up the firm's capital. Nevertheless, the plantation loans were an important innovation in their own right because they securitized the debt service of loans to planters. As such, they can be viewed as the forerunners of modern mortgage-backed securities. Many of the early mutual funds allocated a significant portion of their portfolios to plantation loans, closely linking their fortunes when continental European conflicts led to a reshuffling of colonial possessions near the end of the 18th century.

Figure 12.2. Plantation Loan, 1769

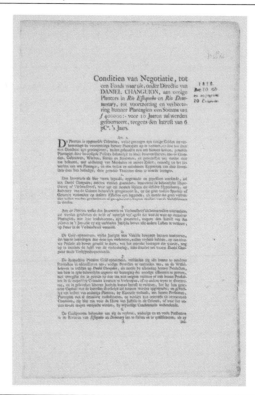

Notes: Preamble of a 1769 plantation loan of Daniel Changuion, one of the investments of *Eendragt Maakt Magt*: "Conditions of a negotiatie, for a fund, under the direction of Daniel Changuion, to furnish a sum of F. 400,000; to planters in *Rio Essequebo* and *Rio Demerary,* for continuation and improvement of their plantations at an annual interest rate of 6 percent.

"Article 1. The Planters in aforementioned colonies, which are inclined to draw moneys for improvement and continuation of their plantations, and have been approved by the director, are obliged at their own cost to have their plantations appraised by sworn appraisers, including the grounds, buildings, works, male and female slaves, and other belongings, but excluding furnishings and things that are unnecessary for cultivation."

The First Mutual Fund: *Eendragt Maakt Magt*

In July 1774, an Amsterdam broker by the name of Abraham van Ketwich invited subscriptions to a negotiatie named *Eendragt Maakt Magt*. The negotiatie would invest in bonds issued by foreign governments and banks and in plantation loans in the West Indies. Investors were promised a dividend of 4%, with adjustments depending on the annual investment income of the portfolio. The initial plan was to dissolve the negotiatie after 25 years, at which time the liquidation proceeds would be distributed among the remaining investors. Subscription was open to the public until all 2,000 shares were placed; thereafter, participation in the fund would be possible only by purchasing shares from existing shareholders in the open market. Investors chose to either receive shares registered in their name or purchase shares in bearer form (*in blanco*). The transfer of bearer shares was easier because it did not require registration with the issuer, but both types were freely tradable. Based on these characteristics, *Eendragt Maakt Magt* would most likely be classified today as a closed-end investment trust, which issues a fixed number of shares representing ownership of a portfolio of tradable securities. According to W.H. Berghuis (1967), it is considered the first "mutual fund."[5]

Much of what is known about *Eendragt Maakt Magt* is based on a manuscript copy of its "prospectus," drawn up by the notary public Paulus van Huntum, and an unissued copy of a share certificate. Both of these have survived in the municipal archives of the city of Amsterdam. The share certificate is essentially a printed version of the prospectus and contains 17 articles describing the details of portfolio formation, management fees, and payout policies.

Article I of the prospectus names Dirk Bas Backer and Frans Jacob Heshuysen as commissioners of the *negotiatie*; they were entrusted with the oversight of the fund's investment policies. The daily administration of the trust was assigned to the broker Abraham van Ketwich. In practice, the role of the commissioners was intended to be limited because the prospectus allowed little discretion regarding the investment policies. Article II specifically detailed 10 categories of potential investments—including Danish and Viennese banks, Danish Tolls and Holsteyn, Russia and Sweden, Brunswick and Mecklenburg, Postal services of Saxony and Peatlands of Brabant, and Spanish Canals Imperial and Taouste. About 30% of the portfolio would be invested in a variety of plantation loans to planters in the British colonies, Essequebo, and the Danish American Islands.

The organizers were sensitive to their fiduciary responsibilities to investors. The prospectus required Van Ketwich to provide an annual accounting to the commissioners and produce, upon request, full disclosure to all those interested parties to ensure "good and proper management at all times." For his services, the administrator would receive a commission of 0.5% at the founding of the trust, plus an annual compensation of 100 guilders per class. The physical securities that the trust invested in were stored at the office of Van Ketwich in an "iron chest with three differently working locks" to which the commissioners and the notary public kept the separate keys.

---

[5]A 1773 plan for a similar investment trust organized in Utrecht has survived, but it is not known whether it was ever successfully placed on the market.

Figure 12.3. *Eendragt Maakt Magt*

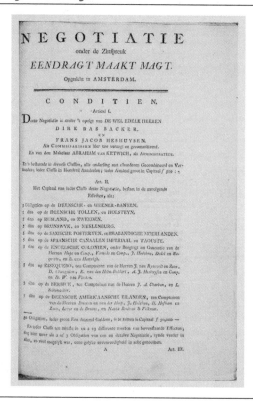

Note: The front page of the share certificate in *Eendragt Maak Magt* lists the bonds that the negotiatie would invest in.

In addition to specifying its investments, the prospectus required that the portfolio would be diversified at all times. The 2,000 shares of *Eendragt Maakt Magt* were subdivided into 20 "classes," and the capital of each class was to be invested in a portfolio of 50 bonds. Each class was to consist of at least 20 to 25 different securities, to contain no more than two or three of a particular security, and to "observe as much as possible an equal proportionality."

Despite this explicit diversification requirement, *Eendragt Maakt Magt* contained a curious and complicated lottery, which, from a diversification perspective, imposed "unnecessary" risk on its investors. The lottery worked as follows: Not all investment income from the underlying portfolio would be passed on to the fund investors as dividends; rather, a portion was to be used to retire shares by lot at a premium over the par value of the shares and also to increase dividends to some of the outstanding shares. The lottery introduced

Figure 12.4. Plantation Loan, 1768

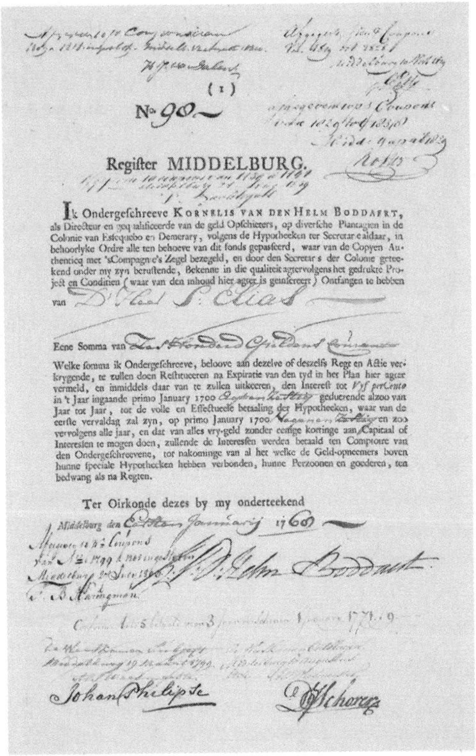
(1)

No 90

Regifter MIDDELBURG.

Ik Ondergefchreeve KORNELIS VAN DEN HELM BODDAERT, als Directeur en gequalificeerde van de geld Opfchieters, op diverfche Plantagien in de Colonie van Esfequebo en Demerary, volgens de Hypotheeken ter Secretarie aldaar, in behoorlyke Ordre alle ten behoeve van dit fonds gepasfeerd, waar van de Copyen Authenticq met 'sCompagnie's Zegel bezegeld, en door den Secretaris der Colonie geteekend onder my zyn beruftende, Bekenne in die qualiteit agtervolgens het gedrukte Project en Conditien (waar van den inhoud hier agter is geinfereert) Ontfangen te hebben van

Eene Somma van

Welke fomma ik Ondergefchreeve, beloove aan dezelve of deszelfs Regt en Actie verkrygende, te zullen doen Restitueeren na Expiratie van den tyd in het Plan hier agter vermeld, en inmiddels daar van te zullen uitkeeren, den Interest tot Vyf perCento in 't Jaar ingaande primo January 1700 geduerende alzoo van Jaar tot Jaar, tot de volle en Effectueele betaaling der Hypotheeken, waar van de eerste vervaldag zal zyn, op primo January 1700 en zoo vervolgens alle jaar, en dat van alles vry-geld zonder eenige kortinge aan Capitaal of Interesfen te mogen doen, zullende de Interesfen werden betaald ten Comptoire van den Ondergefchreevene, tot nakominge van al het welke de Geld-opneemers boven hunne fpeciale Hypotheeken hebben verbonden, hunne Perzoonen en goederen, ten bedwang als na Regten.

Ter Oirkonde dezes by my onderteekend

Middelburg den

Notes: Figure 12.4 shows a plantation bond issued by Kornelis Van Den Helm Boddaert on 1 January 1768. This bond was one of the securities *Eendragt Maakt Magt* invested in. The 20-year, 5% bond was secured by mortgages on plantations in the colonies of Essequebo and Demerary. To secure the payments to the bondholders, up to five-eighths of the appraised value of the plantations could be mortgaged. Plantations needed to be periodically reappraised. The mortgage arrangement with the plantation owners includes a variety of clauses to ensure repayment.

positive skewness to the returns of an otherwise diversified portfolio. Its elaborate structure suggests it was a deliberate attempt to increase the appeal of the trust to small investors.[6]

Although curious from a modern-day perspective, lotteries were a common element of 18th-century securities, and it is likely that Van Ketwich

[6]Barberis and Huang (2008) provide a theoretical framework that motivates the attractiveness of skewness in otherwise diversified portfolios.

modeled his investment trusts after other existing negotiaties.[7] The embedded lottery should not detract from the significance of *Eendragt Maakt Magt:* It offered investors an opportunity to participate in and trade a diversified portfolio of securities. Because the prospectus allowed little flexibility with respect to the fund's investment policies, it is unlikely that Van Ketwich aimed to attract investors by offering superior returns through professional portfolio management. *Eendragt Maakt Magt* simply repackaged existing securities that were already traded in the Amsterdam market. The negotiatie was likely aimed at smaller investors, who would be unable to achieve this level of diversification on their own account. The bonds in its portfolio had a face value of 1,000 guilders, and replication of the portfolio by purchasing these securities in the open market was only feasible for investors of considerable wealth. *Eendragt Maakt Magt* created an opportunity to obtain portfolio diversification in portions of 500 guilders.

Little direct evidence exists about what motivated Van Ketwich to organize the fund, but circumstantial evidence is consistent with the objective of diversification. Its inception follows the financial crisis of 1772–1773, which bankrupted British banks because of overextension of their position in the British East India Company. When the crisis spread to Amsterdam, several banking houses were pushed to the brink of default. Being a broker, Van Ketwich may have perceived a sentiment for diversified investments among his clientele. Subsequent negotiaties in which Van Ketwich was involved explicitly advertise the benefits of diversification to attract small investors. It is perhaps surprising that the portfolio did not include equity shares or domestic and British bonds, but these securities were in short supply while domestic interest-bearing securities were available in small denominations.

Subsequent Funds

The initial success of *Eendragt Maakt Magt* soon invited followers. In 1776, a consortium of Utrecht bankers founded the negotiatie *Voordeelig en Voorsigtig* (Profitable and Prudent). This time, Abraham van Ketwich did not act as an administrator, but he was most likely closely involved because the prospectus lists his office as a collection agency for periodic dividend payments. The

---

[7]For example, a negotiatie on loans to planters in Essequebo and Demerary introduced in 1772 by Karel van den Helm Boddaert and Adolf Jan van Heshuisen and Co. (family and business associate of the director of *Eendragt Maakt Magt*) contained an almost identical lottery provision. The mortgages of this negotiatie were projected to earn 8% per year, of which only 4% would initially be passed on to investors as dividends. The remainder of the investment income was used to retire shares at a premium over par and gradually increase the dividends on the remaining shares to 6% per year. The prospectus of this plantation security contains a detailed schedule of gradual capital repayment over a 25-year period.

prospectus of *Voordeelig and Voorsigtig* is accompanied by an appendix that explains the advantages of diversified investing using *Eendragt Maakt Magt* as an example.[8] The opening paragraph reads like it is taken directly from a modern textbook on portfolio theory. It states that it is undisputable that prudent investing requires the manager to do the following:

> spread as much as possible monies over good and solid securities. Because nothing is completely certain but subject to fluctuations, it is dangerous for people to allocate their capital to a single or a small number of securities. Not everyone has the opportunity to invest his money in a variety of securities . . . . For the sum of *525* guilders one can participate in this *negotiatie* . . ., which will be profitable with sufficient certainty. No one has reason to expect that all securities in this *negotiatie* will cease to pay off at the same time, and the entire capital be lost. If one had reason to fear such general bankruptcy, one never ought to invest any money.

The prospectus of *Voordeelig en Voorsigtig* closely followed the wording of *Eendragt Maakt Magt,* and its investment list mirrored its predecessor, including the diversification requirement. Forty percent of the portfolio was to be allocated to plantation loans, although these were not detailed by name. The most interesting difference is that shares of *Eendragt Maakt Magt* were listed among the potential investments of the fund. *Voordeelig and Voorsigtig* was a "fund of funds."

In 1779, Abraham van Ketwich introduced his second mutual fund named *Concordia Res Parvae Crescunt,* the Latin origin of *Eendragt Maakt Magt.*[9] Although Van Ketwich's second fund resembled his first in both name and structure, an important difference was that it offered more freedom in investment policy. The prospectus only states that the *negotiatie* would invest in "solid securities and those that based on decline in their price would merit speculation and could be purchased below their intrinsic values, . . . of which one has every reason to expect an important benefit"—a phrasing that suggests the *Concordia Res Parvae Crescunt* may be the grandfather of modern value funds.

---

[8]Koninklijke Bibliotheek, The Hague, catalogus Knuttel, no. 19132.

[9]"Concordia res parvae crescunt, discordia maximae dilabuntur" is attributed to the Roman historian Sallust, meaning "In harmony small things grow, dissension dissolves the greatest."

Figure 12.5. First Value Fund *Concordia Res Parvae Crescunt*

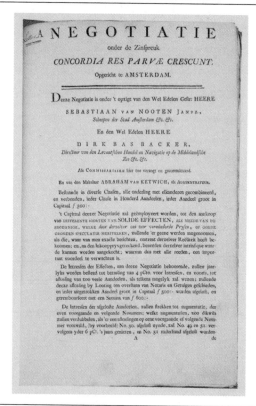

Notes: The first page of the share certificate in the negotiatie *Concordia Res Parvae Crescunt* states that the fund would invest in "solid securities and those that based on decline in their price would merit speculation and could be purchased below their intrinsic values, . . . of which one has every reason to expect an important benefit."

The Demise of the Early Mutual Funds

The fortunes of the early mutual funds were closely linked to the fortunes of their predominant investments: plantation loans in the West Indies. The outbreak of the Fourth English War in 1780 hampered colonial shipments to their Dutch commission agents, affecting the proceeds that were pledged as the security for holders of the plantation loans. For example, the price of Deutz's first plantation loan fell by 35–40% and bondholders were asked to accept interest rate reductions. In 1782, the decline in investment income forced Van Ketwich to suspend the redemption of shares in *Eendragt Maakt Magt* and lower dividend payments several years later.[10] By the end of the

[10]Berghuis (1967, pp. 62–68).

century, all three funds had disappeared from the official published price record of the Amsterdam stock exchange; transaction prices show up only at irregular private auctions by securities brokers. At the end of the scheduled life of *Eendragt Maakt Magt* in 1799, participants agreed to extend the negotiatie until the shares could be redeemed at par. In 1803, the management of the affairs of *Eendragt Maakt Magt* and *Concordia Res Parvae Crescunt* were taken over by the firm of Van Ketwich and Voomberg. By 1811, the share price of *Eendragt Maakt Magt* reached a low of 25% of its nominal value of 500 guilders, but it eventually recovered. This seems miraculous, but the fund actively repurchased shares in the open market when prices were depressed. In 1824, a liquidating dividend of 561 guilders was paid to the remaining participants. Final settlement of shares in *Concordia Res Parvae Crescunt* took substantially longer. After 114 years, it was officially dissolved in 1893. In 1894, a final distribution of 430.55 guilders per share of 500 guilders was paid, which was 87% of the original investment. Despite its misfortunes, or perhaps because of them, *Concordia Res Parvae Crescunt* is among the longest-lived mutual funds to ever have existed.[11]

Speculation on the Financial Fortunes of the United States

Despite the poor performance of the first investment trusts, there are also many success stories. During the 1780s and 1790s, more than 30 investment trusts emerged with the single objective to speculate on the future credit of the United States. Together with France and Spain, the Netherlands was one of the major financiers of the American Revolution. Between 1782 and 1791, an estimated 32 million guilders were raised in Amsterdam and Antwerp, much of which was spent to finance war supplies. These advances occurred following a period of steady deterioration in the credit of the United States. The war expenses, combined with a limited ability to raise revenues through taxation, had flooded the American market with paper currency that was issued by both the states and the Continental Congress. The currency was expected to be self-liquidating as it was used to settle future taxes, but currency issues had far outgrown the anticipated tax liabilities. The consequence was a steady depreciation of the value of the continental currency.

Currency, however, constituted only a fraction of the paper obligations in circulation. During the war, the quartermaster and commissary departments had issued certificates to private individuals in lieu of impressments of goods, and soldiers had been issued certificates for military pay. Combined with a

---

[11]The Foreign and Colonial Government Trust was founded in 1868 and reorganized a decade later to become the Foreign and Colonial Investment Trust. It still exists today and thus is the longest-lived mutual fund.

myriad of interest-bearing debt instruments issued by the federal government and the states, the economy was flooded with financial paper claims. To make matters worse, nobody knew the exact magnitude of the outstanding obligations or who was responsible for repayment. Some states retired obligations from the Congress, while other states argued that Congress was responsible and should assume part of the states' debts that were incurred through the war. In 1782, Congress sent commissioners to the states to inventory all outstanding obligations. If claims were stated in depreciated currency, they were to be translated into specie value; for the balance, "final settlement certificates" were issued. This process of "liquidation" established the outstanding balance of the government's obligations but did not solve the problem of how to pay for them. Investors were mixed about the prospects for full repayment. As a result, the market price of liquidated debt fluctuated between 15 and 40 cents on the dollar in 1788, depending on the location and type of the original claim.

In this same year, Amsterdam bankers Pieter Stadnitski and Hendrik van Vollenhoven organized a negotiatie that held US liquidated debt. The prospectus stated that the investment portfolio consisted of 6% liquidated debt with a face value of $840,000, which was acquired at 60 cents on the dollar. The negotiatie was planned for 25 years, and the prospectus called for a gradual redemption of shares over the life of the fund. Like in Van Ketwich's negotiaties, this was accomplished using a portion of the investment income to redeem shares at a premium while keeping the underlying collateral intact. But instead of increasing the dividends on unredeemed shares, the excess of investment income over promised dividends was used to accelerate the rate of share redemption over time at increasing premiums.

The fund's terms were certainly attractive relative to the promised returns on other forms of debt securities in the Amsterdam market and stalled subsequent US efforts to place new loans in the Netherlands. Why would investors pay 100% on the dollar for a new loan at 6% when similar claims could be purchased at a 40% discount through investment trusts? If the United States were to ultimately honor its obligations, new bonds would offer their promised 6% return while an investment in the negotiatie would yield between 8 and 14%, depending on the exact timing of redemption. No matter the course of events, Stadnitski and Van Vollenhoven were to be the major beneficiaries in this negotiatie. Although the prospectus called for a 1% annual management fee on the investment income of their portfolio, the bulk of their compensation was to be received up front. Shares in their investment trust were sold at a price that implicitly valued the liquidated debt of the United

States at 60% of its face value, but it is estimated that the debt had been purchased at around 42 cents on the dollar, an immediate return of almost 50%.

According to P.J. van Winter (1933), the negotiatie of Stadnitski and Van Vollenhoven was the first in a series of 29 trusts invested in US debt that were successfully placed in the Amsterdam market between 1787 and 1804.[12] Their success made them the dominant category of foreign investments listed in the Amsterdam Prijscourant (price list) during the early 1800s.

Depository Receipts

Closed-end mutual funds and plantation loans are examples of liquidity creation through asset substitution and securitization. The plantation loans created a tradable interest in portfolios of illiquid mortgages, and mutual funds made it possible for small investors to hold and trade diversified portfolios of securities. Although diversification was not the primary motive behind the funds invested in the US debt, the trusts provided domestic liquidity in foreign securities that were difficult to trade in Amsterdam because of the foreign registration requirements. It would take two more decades for the purest form of asset substitution, which was directly aimed at lowering the cost of foreign investing, to emerge.

In the 18th and 19th centuries, government borrowing often took place through a "book of public debt," a large ledger containing the names of investors. Investors would receive a receipt that could be presented at the treasury to collect periodic interest payments. Although foreign participation was not precluded per se, in practice it was limited to large investors and financial institutions that could overcome the registration requirements and difficulties associated with the collection of interest abroad.

By the end of the 18th century, Hope & Co. had become the principal banker raising money in Holland for the Russian czar. In addition to directly issuing bonds on behalf of the czar, the firm also helped to popularize a mechanism for small investors to participate in inscriptions in the Russian book of public debt. The Office of Administration of Hope, Van Ketwich, Voomberg, and Widow W. Borski, founded in 1824, took foreign inscriptions in its name and offered "certificates," or depository receipts, backed by these inscriptions to the Dutch public.[13] In return for a small fee, the firm would administer the collection of interest payments abroad,

---

[12]Van Winter (1933, appendix 4).

[13]This was certainly not the first office of administration. According to Bosch (1948), this particular firm emerged from the firm of N.&J.&R. Van Staphorst, Ketwich & Voomberg and W. Borski, which was formed in 1805. According to Riley (1980), Van Ketwich partnered in an administration office investing in French annuities as early as 1802.

Figure 12.6.   Inscription in the Russian Book of Public Debt, 1854

Note: The 1854 inscription is in the name of Amsterdam brokers Hope, Ketwich, Voomberg, and Wed. W. Borski.

Figure 12.7.   Dutch Depository Receipt, 1857

Note: The 1857 depository receipt issued by Hope and Co., Ketwich and Voomberg, and Wed. Borski in Amsterdam was backed by inscriptions in the Russian book of public debt.

which would be passed on to the certificate holders upon presentation of the coupons attached to the certificates. The added advantage of the depository receipts was that they were freely tradable in bearer form in Amsterdam, thereby circumventing the registration requirements of the original inscriptions. If desired, investors could always tender the depository certificates to the administration office in exchange for an original inscription in the foreign book of public debt. To further alleviate investor concerns, the certificates explicitly specified that the administrators would keep the original inscriptions in "an iron chest, with three different working keys, one of which would remain in the hands of a notary public."

Depository receipts were initially created to facilitate trade in foreign government debt, but their presence became widespread on the Amsterdam stock market in the second half of the 19th century. Their application economized on onerous registration requirements associated with the trading of US railroad stocks, which required transfer in the company books, and the collection of foreign dividends. In 1863, the firm of Boissevain and Teixeira de Mattos set up an Office of American Railroad Stocks to purchase shares in Illinois Central Railroad Company. The original shares were deposited with a notary public, against which the office issued "Certificates Illinois Central Railroad Company" in portions of one, five, or ten shares. The certificates were freely negotiable in bearer form, and they contained coupons for collecting the dividends that would accrue on the original shares. Transfer of certificate ownership did not require transfer in the company books in the United States, because the administration office remained the owner of record. However, investors retained the right to request that the original shares be placed in their names upon the tendering of the depository receipt. To accommodate foreign investors, some US companies managed a transfer book for their shares in London but never in Amsterdam, probably because of the widespread use of depository receipts. When JPMorgan introduced the American Depository Receipt (ADR) on the UK retailer Selfridge's in the United States in 1927, the bank was able to build on more than a century of European experience.

Nineteenth-Century Mutual Funds

The first documented investment trust outside of the Netherlands is the Foreign and Colonial Government Trust, founded in 1868 in London. Like *Eendragt Maakt Magt*, it invested in foreign government bonds.[14] According to its prospectus, the goal was to provide "the investor of moderate means

---

[14]See Chambers and Esteves (2014).

Figure 12.8.   Depository Receipt on US Railroad in Amsterdam, 1854

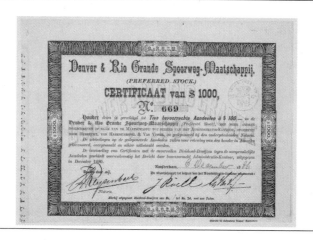

the same advantages as the large capitalist, in diminishing the risk of investing in foreign and colonial government stocks, by spreading the investment over a number of different stocks." It was modeled after the Dutch trusts in the sense that investment income was projected to exceed dividends, and excess income would be used to liquidate participations over its projected 24-year life. By 1875, 18 trusts had been formed in London.[15] It was during this period that the Scotsman Robert Fleming started his famous first trust investing in US railroad bonds. This trust was later named the First Scottish American Investment Trust. During the 1890s, investment trusts were introduced into the United States. Most of the early US investment trusts were closed-end funds, like *Eendragt Maakt Magt,* that issued a fixed number of shares. New shares, or repurchases, were not precluded but were infrequent. Moreover, the repurchase or issue price was not necessarily proportional to the intrinsic value of the underlying portfolio.

This changed in 1924, when the Massachusetts Investors Trust became the first US mutual fund with an open-end capitalization. This allowed for the continuous issue and redemption of shares by the investment company at a price that is proportional to the value of the underlying investment portfolio. Open-end capitalization has become the dominant model for mutual fund organization, suggesting that it has been an important innovation contributing to its modern success. One cannot fail to be surprised, however, by how many features of 18th-century investment funds survive today.

---

[15]See Bullock (1959).

Concluding Remarks

Financiers in 18th-century Netherlands produced a remarkable set of innovations that form the foundation of modern-day markets for mortgage-backed securities, pension funds, mutual funds, and depository receipts. Merchant bankers constructed new claims and securities that repackaged existing financial instruments. As such, these innovations mark the origins of structured finance.

In designing these new financial instruments, it appears that many concepts of modern finance were well understood, including the notion of diversification, value investing, the importance of collateral, investor preference for positive skewness, and agency conflicts associated with delegated money management.

The puzzle that emerges from this episode of history is why the ultimate adoption of these financial innovations has been relatively slow.[16] The solution to this puzzle is relevant for modern-day practitioners that seek to introduce new financial innovations. All too often new financial products are introduced at great cost but fail to attract interest from investors. Understanding the factors that drive failure and success in financial innovation is a necessary first step. The study of financial history can likely provide us with important clues.

---

[16]See Lerner and Tufano (2011) for a recent review of the literature on financial innovation.

References

Barberis, N., and M. Huang. 2008. "Stocks as Lotteries: The Implications of Probability Weighting for Security Prices." *American Economic Review*, vol. 98, no. 5: 2066–2100.

Berghuis, W.H. 1967. *Onstaan en Ontwikkeling van de Nederlandse Beleggingsfondsen tot 1914*. Assen: Van Gorcum & Company.

Bosch, K.D. 1948. *Nederlandse Beleggingen in de Verenigde Staten*. Amsterdam: Elsevier.

Bullock, H. 1959. *The Story of Investment Companies*. New York: Columbia University Press.

Chambers, D., and R. Esteves. 2014. "The First Global Emerging Markets Investor: Foreign & Colonial Investment Trust 1880–1913." *Explorations in Economic History*, vol. 52 (April): 1–21.

Investment Company Institute. 2016. *Investment Company Fact Book*. 56th ed. Washington, DC: Investment Company Institute.

Lerner, J., and P. Tufano. 2011. "The Consequences of Financial Innovation: A Counterfactual Research Agenda." *Annual Review of Financial Economics*, vol. 3 (December): 41–85.

Neal, L. 1990. *The Rise of Financial Capitalism: International Capital Markets in the Age of Reason*. Cambridge, UK: Cambridge University Press.

Riley, J. 1980. *International Government Finance and the Amsterdam Capital Market, 1740–1815*. Cambridge, UK: Cambridge University Press.

Rouwenhorst, K.G. 2005. "The Origins of Mutual Funds." In *The Origins of Value: The Financial Innovations That Created Modern Capital Markets*. Edited by W.N. Goetzmann and K.G. Rouwenhorst. Oxford, UK: Oxford University Press: 249–270.

Van Winter, P.J. 1933. *Amsterdam en de Opbouw van Amerika*. Gravenhage, Netherlands: Martinus Nijhoff.

13. The Origins of High-Tech Venture Investing in America

Tom Nicholas
William J. Abernathy Professor of Business Administration, Harvard Business School

The United States has developed an unparalleled environment for the provision of high-tech investment finance. Today it is reflected in the strength of agglomeration economies in Silicon Valley, but historically its origins lay in the East Coast. Notably, immediate post-WWII efforts to establish the American Research and Development Corporation created a precedent for "long-tail" high-tech investing. This approach became institutionalized in the United States over subsequent decades in a way that has been difficult to replicate in other countries. The role of history helps to explain why.

Introduction

The development of high-tech investment finance is intertwined with the history of the venture capital (VC) industry in the United States. America has created what amounts to an almost unassailable advantage in the deployment and management of risk capital. VC investment increased to $49.3 billion in 2014, the third highest amount in history (after 1999 and 2000), with around 90% of this total being deployed in high-tech sectors. Within the United States, Silicon Valley stands out with the state of California accounting for 57% of total investments (National Venture Capital Association 2015). Moreover, the United States dominates in a global context. According to one estimate, it accounts for more than double the level of venture investment in Europe, China, India, and Israel *combined* (EY 2014). Given that innovation is a key driver of economic growth (e.g., Romer 1990), it is reasonable to assume that this long-standing leadership position in the provision of high-tech finance has had a profound effect on aggregate economic activity.

From very early on in its history, the United States has been characterized by an auspicious link between finance and innovation. Venture-style investing can be seen in the way that the early whaling industry was structured in the 18th century—with its emphasis on capital pooling, partnerships, principal–agent relationships, and long-tail investments (Nicholas and Akins 2012). The birth of the US industrial revolution in New England textiles owed much to a group of investors known as the Boston Associates, who were willing to finance risky technological development (Dalzell 1987). The rise of midwestern cities like Cleveland as entrepreneurial hotspots in the 19th century depended on such financiers as Andrew Mellon (1855–1937), who selected entrepreneurs and actively participated in governing his investments (Lamoreaux, Levenstein, and Sokoloff 2006). For all its relevance today, US exceptionalism in the high-tech venture area should be placed in a deeper historical context.

The relevance of a historical perspective can be vividly illustrated through an important post-World War II breakthrough. A group of local elites, who were members of The New England Council (NEC), which had been formed in 1925 to promote regional economic activity, decided in 1946 to incorporate in Massachusetts what was ostensibly a venture capital firm, American Research and Development Corporation (ARD). A French émigré, Georges Doriot, a well-known Harvard Business School professor, became president. With an ultimate focus on high-tech ventures and "creative capital," ARD marked a turning point in the institutionalization of US VC (Ante 2008). ARD's 1957 investment in a risky nascent computer start-up, Digital Equipment Corporation (DEC), returned a sizeable multiple, verifying that this type of payoff strategy could work. ARD's DEC investment was one of the most important in VC history and set a precedent for what would follow. The remainder of this chapter draws on Nicholas and Chen (2012) to provide a summary of how ARD and the DEC investment came about and then elaborates on the significance more generally.

The Pathway to ARD: Formation and Structure

As a consequence of military expenditure, World War II was a catalyst to technological advancements in such areas as radar detection and microelectronics. On the demand side, however, it was not the best time to be seeking investment capital for start-up innovation. For example, during testimony to a subcommittee of the Committee on Banking and Currency in 1939, Edward E. Brown, a well-known banker from Chicago, stated: "In my opinion it has always been difficult for small business to get risk capital. I think the difficulties today, for a variety of causes, are greater in getting proprietary risk capital for small- and moderate-size businesses, than was the case in former years" (Stoddard 1940). Although large corporations could finance innovation through retained earnings, entrepreneurial firms were more likely to be starved of capital.

Against this backdrop and a general malaise in the regional economy, a group of prominent New Englanders including Ralph Flanders, who would become a Senator for Vermont, and Karl Compton, then-president of MIT, responded by engaging in discussions at the NEC in an effort to support existing industries in the region and promote new directions. Because around three-quarters of the immediate post-war growth in New England derived from metal working, much of the NEC's efforts went into promoting the region as a steel-making cluster (Warren 1987, p. 324). However, on 6 June 1946, a key step toward facilitating high-tech investing was made when ARD was incorporated in Massachusetts.

ARD was not intended to be a substitute for bank financing; instead, it represented a new approach to the provision of entrepreneurial finance. Doriot, who was named president in December 1946, stated: "ARD does not invest in the ordinary sense. Rather, it creates by taking calculated risks in selected companies in whose growth it believes" (Ante 2008, p. 112). Governance was a primary objective of the new investment entity. ARD's first report states: "research and development, new technical ideas, and young small businesses are not in themselves the certain keys to great success. They must be supplemented by sound management, adequate financing, competent production methods, and aggressive merchandising" (Doriot 1971).

ARD had a number of important organizational characteristics. Unlike modern VC firms, which are mostly organized as limited partnerships with fund lives of approximately seven to twelve years, ARD was formed as a closed-end fund. That is, it raised permanent capital by selling a limited number of public shares. This structure was aligned with Doriot's objectives to select investments and govern them effectively over the long run. Writing several years after ARD's initial founding, Doriot explained, "It should again be emphasized that American Research is a 'venture' or 'risk capital' enterprise. The Corporation does not invest in the ordinary sense. It creates. It risks. Results take more time and the expenses of its operation must be higher, but the potential for ultimate profits is much greater" (Doriot 1951).

Given the risk profile of its potential investments and the desire for long-term stakeholders, ARD's founders aimed to secure at least half of the initial capital from institutions. However, legal constraints militated against this objective and, in principle, also constrained ARD's ability to function as an investment entity. Specifically, the Investment Company Act of 1940 restricted investment companies from owning more than 3% of another investment company's voting stock. The Act, however, allowed an exception for companies that were engaged "in the business of underwriting, furnishing capital to industry, financing promotional enterprises, and purchasing securities of issuers for which no ready market is in existence." Through lobbying efforts, ARD was permitted to have institutional investors, who could each acquire up to 9.9% of its stock (Ante 2008, p. 110).

ARD was able to acquire capital from nonfamily sources, which was a source of its distinctiveness. Other private equity firms that formed around this time, including J.H. Whitney & Company and the Rockefeller Brothers Company, mostly relied on individual families for capital. For ARD, casting a wider net for capital was seen to be advantageous. Ralph Flanders stated, "There are in particular two large-scale repositories of wealth [life insurance companies and investment trusts] which have a stake in the Nation's future and who should be concerned with a healthy basis for the prosperity of these postwar years."[1] **Figure 13.1** illustrates the mix of investors in ARD in 1947 and includes such investment companies as Massachusetts Investors Trust, such insurance firms as John Hancock Mutual Life Insurance, and such educational institutions as MIT, Rice Institute, University of Pennsylvania, and the University of Rochester. ARD intermediated because it was difficult for such investors to go to portfolio companies directly. In 1947, over half of the shares were owned by institutional investors broadly defined, although it is

Figure 13.1.   The Composition of ARD Investors, 1947

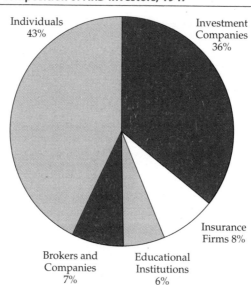

Source: Compiled from data in Hsu and Kenney (2005, p. 591).

[1]Martha L. Reiner, "Innovation and the Creation of Venture Capital Organizations," *Business and Economic History*, Vol. 20, papers presented at the thirty-seventh annual meeting of the Business History Conference (1991), pp. 206–207.

important to note that ARD (unlike most VC firms today) was still heavily reliant on financing provided by individuals.

Finally, ARD established an internal structure to facilitate deal flow and select investments. ARD maintained an eminent technical advisory board populated with MIT talent, including Karl Compton; Edwin R. Gilliland, a professor of chemical engineering; and Jerome Clarke Hunsaker, a professor in aeronautical engineering. Like Doriot, all were well respected as educators and practitioners, and their presence created a strong network at the intersection of MIT and Harvard. ARD's board of directors reflected a blend of legal, financial, and technology expertise, and a small staff undertook due diligence and publicized ARD to potential entrepreneurs. ARD maintained high standards for filtering projects, insisting on pursuing those that were commercially practicable, had patent protection, and had high profit potential (Etzkowitz 2002). In principle, the structure established by ARD was commensurate with both effective *ex ante* investment selection and the effective governance of portfolio companies.

Initial Investments

Yet, this ostensibly favorable strategy and structure did little to attract investors. ARD aimed to raise $5 million in the public markets, and although falling short of its goal, it began immediately deploying the $3.5 million it had raised in the search for new opportunities. ARD made three initial investments. It invested $150,000 in Cleveland-based Circo Products, which made automobile tools; $200,000 in High Voltage Engineering Corporation, which was developing a special, high-powered generator; and $150,000 in Tracerlab, a manufacturer of radiation detectors. The latter two firms had strong links to MIT.

A total of five investments were made in the first year. Although none were spectacular from the standpoint of returns, Tracerlab became a modest success story. In 1948, Tracerlab had sales of $700,000, giving it a profit of $30,000. It then underwent an IPO in March 1948 that raised $1.3 million. In reference to the governance mechanisms associated with ARD, William E. Barbour, Jr., the company's founder and president, commented on how Doriot's guidance had been essential to growth and development: "[Doriot] provides the two things that a young scientific organization most needs: enthusiasm and appreciation. Like all the others, I started out with a hatful of ideas and a lot of long-range plans. In a couple of years, I got bogged down in detail. Doriot stepped in just in time to pull me out of a rut" (Ante 2008, p. 119).

Because the demand for capital at this time was so high, ARD received an abundance of project proposals. In keeping with its restrictive investment criteria, ARD never invested in more than 4% of the project proposals that it received each year; frequently, the percentage was much lower (Hsu and Kenney 2005, p. 593). This selectivity enabled ARD to negotiate favorable terms for its investments. By early 1949, ARD had acquired a controlling interest in 13 companies in a wide variety of industries, including Cleveland Pneumatic Tool Company, Ionics Incorporated, and Snyder Chemical Corporation. At that point, ARD began running low on capital, so it offered another 153,000 shares of stock to raise $4 million. Despite encouraging returns from its portfolio companies, however, ARD could not convince investors to buy. By late 1949, the company had sold only around 44,000 of its shares, raising roughly $1 million. That year, ARD reported an operating loss of $38,000 (Ante 2008, p. 114).

Even with these setbacks, ARD continued taking risks on unproven companies, and sometimes the strategy paid off. One of ARDs first investments, Flexible Tubing, proved to be a lucrative one. In 1948, Doriot had assigned an ARD employee—a former student—to be the struggling tubing manufacturer's director, treasurer, and manager. Within a year, the company began reporting profits thanks to supply contracts with several large organizations. ARD's investment in Baird Associates, a company that specialized in chemical analysis instruments, also bore fruit; its sales grew significantly after 1947. Still, ARD was not immune to losses. Island Packers, a tuna company in which ARD had invested $250,000, went bankrupt after the company determined that it would not be able to catch the amount of fish necessary to sustain itself. This led to a $239,000 write-off by ARD. Nonetheless, by 1951 ARD had invested in 26 companies and employed over 3,000 people. Twenty-one of these companies were profitable (Ante 2008, p. 114). ARD had also begun charging consulting fees to portfolio companies in an attempt to raise revenues and further reinforce its business model.

During the 1950s, ARD continued to have difficulty attracting investors, even after issuing its first dividend of $0.25 per share in 1954. Deal flow slowed down from an average of 382 proposals per year between 1947 and 1951 to just 127 projects in 1954. Partially as a result of this and partially due to several key members of the firm going on leave, ARD did not invest in a single new project in 1954. Notably, that year ARD's shares fell to $16 from a high of $29, even as its net asset value (NAV) remained at $28 per share (Ante 2008, p. 138). Although it is not unusual for closed-end funds to be marked down relative to NAV, this amounted to a steep discount. **Figure 13.2** shows that ARD's stock price did rebound during the late 1950s and into the early 1960s; however, it had not systematically proven out its new investment model.

Figure 13.2. Net Asset Value and Net Asset Value per Share of ARD, 1946–1971

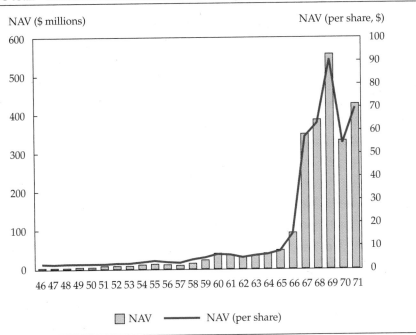

Note: All dollar values are given in nominal amounts.
Source: Compiled from data in Doriot (1971).

Digital Equipment Corporation

ARD was revitalized by a single investment, which also helped to spur the development of US VC in general. In 1957, Kenneth Olsen, a US Navy veteran and MIT engineer, co-founded with his colleague Harlan Anderson a new start-up—Digital Equipment Corporation (DEC)—to develop circuit board modules and then later, fast and efficient computers.

Prior to the PC revolution of the late 1970s and early 1980s, computers were bulky and expensive. Olsen started to work with transistors, a relatively new technology that yielded faster and more efficient processing. He helped to design and build the TX-0, a room-sized computer that was much smaller than other similarly capable computers at the time. The TX-0 was popular with MIT students, and Olsen became convinced that he could build a business around such computers. Olsen and Anderson planned to make circuit boards for use by research institutions and small businesses that needed high-powered but cost-effective solutions. ARD founders struggled to access funding because of the risks associated with the new technology, the failure of a number of similar companies, and an economic recession.

Olsen and Anderson sent a proposal to ARD that outlined their need for a $100,000 investment, and they were invited to pitch it. Impressed by the founders and their idea, ARD offered $70,000 for a 78% equity stake and promised additional loans. Olsen and Anderson accepted, knowing they were operating in a risky high technology area where further funding would be needed for R&D and commercialization. DEC was soon incorporated and began shipping its first products, which were instantly popular. By the end of 1958, DEC sold $94,000 worth of modules and was already profitable. ARD provided additional financing as DEC met milestones. That year, the rest of ARD's portfolio companies also performed well, and its stock price reached a high of $38. As **Figure 13.3** illustrates, ARD's portfolio shifted away from such traditional areas as chemicals and industrial equipment and toward such high-tech sectors as electronics.

In 1960, DEC started to sell its first computer, the PDP-1 (Programmed Data Processor-1). It was approximately the size of a refrigerator and

Figure 13.3. ARD's Portfolio Investments: Comparing 1946–50 with 1966–73

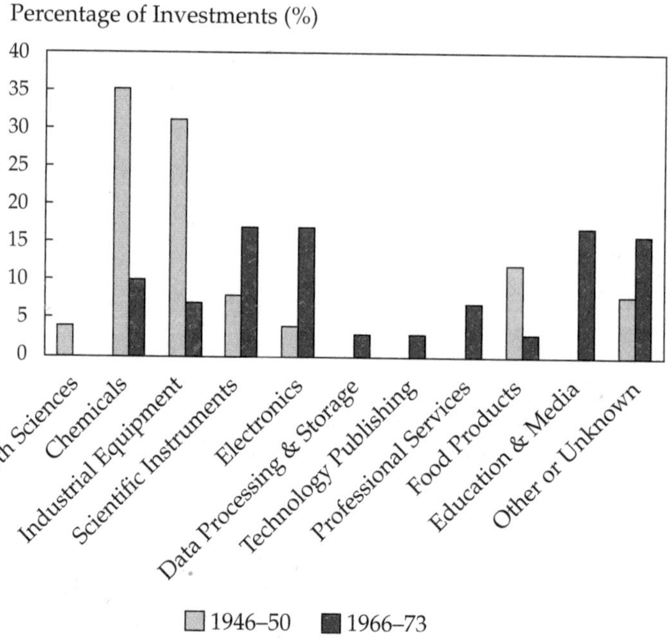

Source: Compiled from data in Hsu and Kenney (2005, p. 593).

revolutionary in terms of functionality. Although it cost $120,000, IBM's mainframes frequently cost in excess of $1 million. Users could observe graphical displays, input commands, and receive results interactively rather than having to wait for processing to be completed in the customary batch queue environment. The PDP-1 could also be configured for specialized applications, including basic word processing. In 1962, DEC earned $6.5 million in sales and continued to be profitable.

The PDP-1 spawned subsequent generations, each with slightly different configurations and prices. In 1963, the PDP-5 was introduced at a price of $27,000. Introduced in 1965, the PDP-8 became the first mass production minicomputer at an $18,000 price point. DEC sold 50,000 PDP-8s over the device's lifespan. As Chandler, Hikino, and Von Nordenflycht (2005, p. 104) point out, "the strategy of low price/high performance succeeded brilliantly. In the single year, 1966, DEC's revenues ascended from $15 million to $23 million, and from 1965 to 1967 its profits rose sixfold." DEC underwent an IPO in August of 1966, selling 375,000 shares at a price of $22, and it subsequently experienced strong growth in market capitalization (see **Figure 13.4**). DEC became ARD's most significant asset. By the time the value of

Figure 13.4. DEC Market Capitalization, 1966 to 1971

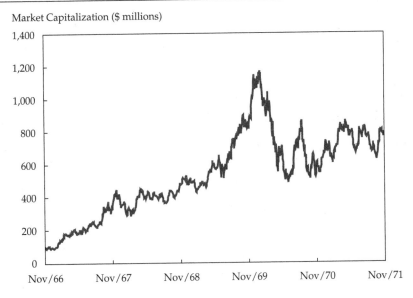

Market Capitalization ($ millions)

Source: Compiled from data provided by CRSP (Center for Research in Security Prices).

the DEC stock was fully distributed to ARD's investors in 1971, it was worth $355 million (Liles 1977, p. 83; Hsu and Kenney 2005, p. 599).

Venture Capital Supply and Entrepreneurial Demand Implications

To understand the significance of ARD's investment in DEC for the development of the VC industry and high-tech investing, it is helpful to think of the main implications of supply and demand factors. First, the DEC investment showed that one could systematically build a portfolio of long-tailed investments; the return of the few that hit the long tail would offset the losses and mediocre gains of the others. Although the precise figures are open to some debate, Liles (1977) estimated that from 1946 to 1971, ARD achieved a compound annual return of 7.4% without DEC and 14.7% with DEC included. By comparison, the DJIA (Dow Jones Industrial Average) returned 12.8% over the same period (Hsu and Kenney 2005, p. 599). Such was the impact of DEC on ARD's portfolio that it provided a spur to the supply of new venture firms seeking to also generate outsized returns from high-tech investments. Ironically, as new entities started to compete with ARD, it became increasingly difficult for the firm to retain its best employees. With its closed-end fund structure, ARD was essentially displaced around 1970 as a new era of VC limited partnerships began to operate. By the late 1970s, at least 250 venture capital firms were operating in the United States; two decades later, that number had risen to over 1,000 (Etzkowitz 2002, p. 99).

Second, ARD supplied both capital and governance. That is, it was not only selective about the initial investments it chose to make, but it also actively participated in the management of those investments. A long-standing question in the VC literature revolves around the extent to which venture capitalists add value simply by screening effectively *ex ante* for investments versus professionalizing entrepreneurial firms *ex post* (Hellman and Puri 2002). ARD identified and deployed professional managers, and it utilized its technical advisory group and staff to help monitor the performance of portfolio companies. ARD placed five trusted and dependable advisers on the DEC board (Ante 2008, p. 151). Doriot was the archetypal networker.

Third, ARD specifically and Doriot more generally shaped a pool of talent that entered the industry over subsequent decades. In 1965, William Elfers, a senior vice president at ARD, left the firm to found Greylock in Massachusetts, which then became a top-tier venture capital firm. Unlike ARD, which operated as a closed-end investment fund, Elfers organized Greylock as a series of limited partnerships, each of which pooled the investment capital that its general partners and limited partners committed for finite lifetimes. Furthermore, as a professor at Harvard Business School, Doriot instructed, mentored, and/or influenced a generation of future venture capitalists. These included Arthur Rock, who started his first investment partnership in 1961 with Thomas Davis in San Francisco; Tom Perkins, who helped establish Kleiner Perkins Caufield & Byers in 1972 in San Francisco; and Charles Newhall and Richard Kramlich, who co-founded (with a Princeton graduate, Frank Bonsal, Jr.) the bi-coastal VC firm New Enterprise Associates in 1977.

Finally, although it is difficult to establish causality, by creating opportunities for wealth accumulation, ARD probably created an entrepreneurial demand-side spur to venture capital. When DEC underwent its IPO, Ken Olsen's ownership of the company translated into a $7 million valuation (Ante 2008, p. 196). This would have provided powerful incentives from the standpoint of occupational choice. Around the time of the DEC IPO, the number of business plans evaluated by ARD doubled when comparing the period 1961–1965 to 1966–1973 (Hsu and Kenney 2005, p. 593). Although demand conditions may also have played a role (the stock market boomed during the late 1960s), the fact that there was an environment in which high-tech ventures could be financed and governed to generate long-tail payoffs must have positively affected the number of entrepreneurs who decided to start new firms.

Regional Advantage, Investment Cycles, and Bubbles

Beyond the specifics of the relationship between ARD and DEC, this episode in history has a broader significance for understanding the conditions under which high-tech investment finance can flourish. DEC was an East Coast firm, yet, over time, regional comparative advantage became firmly established in Silicon Valley. At least one explanation for the shift was cultural. The Route 128 agglomeration in the Boston area reflected conservative East Coast values, while Silicon Valley prospered on the basis of what might be described as an open collaboration-mixed-with-competition culture that was symbiotic to the development of high-tech entrepreneurship. According to Saxenian (1994), electronics entrepreneurs ventured west because of "a distrust [of] established East Coast institutions and attitudes" and a related desire to be out in the more culturally and physically open West. Route 128 had ephemeral computer manufacturers like DEC and Wang, whereas Silicon Valley produced enduring firms like Hewlett Packard and Intel. Cultural characteristics tend to be persistent over time, and high-tech is a fundamentally important sector in terms of its contribution to long-run economic growth. Thus, it is hard to imagine a world in which Silicon Valley's superiority in tech-based VC finance will not be maintained.

It could be argued that VC investing in high-tech firms in the United States evolved to be complementary to public markets. DEC was financed through ARD specifically because it was a high-risk, nascent start-up; its founders were unable to raise capital through alternative bank-based channels. By adopting a portfolio approach, selecting entrepreneurs on expected success, and governing investments to fruition, ARD assumed that it would be able to capture future outsized returns. More generally, empirical evidence reveals that from the 1970s to the early 1990s, VC-backed IPOs performed better over the long run than non-VC-backed IPOs (Brav and Gompers 1997). Although this finding is sensitive to time period specification and even tends to be reversed for the modern era (Ritter 2015), one implication is that VC firms can relax credit constraints for firms that ultimately drive the performance of the high-tech sector. As Brown (2005) put it, "the true legacy of venture capital finance extends well beyond the IPO."

At the same time, VC activity may lead to the creation, or amplification, of productive or destructive investment cycles. Venture capital firms exit their positions through a sale or an IPO in order to return capital to their limited partners over the duration of a fund. Experience in the timing of exits tends to matter. Gompers (1996) finds that inexperienced VCs take their firms public earlier, their IPOs are more underpriced, and the VC equity stake they hold is significantly smaller relative to their more experienced VC counterparts. Doriot's experience was instrumental to the favorable pricing of ARD's IPO from DEC's perspective. While the underwriter Lehman Brothers aimed to price the shares at $17, DEC held out for $22 (Ante 2008, p. 195). DECs stock price accelerated during the stock market run-up of 1969 (see Figure 13.4). Other run-ups, such as 1998–2000, were inextricably linked to investments in high-tech firms.

Although run-ups can lead to bubbles and the destruction of capital (the stock market lost $5 trillion in market value between 2000 and 2002), they can also create the type of financing environment that leads to the production of especially valuable innovations. Nanda and Rhodes-Kropf (forthcoming) argue that during "hot" markets, more experimental and ultimately innovative projects receive funding because capital freely flows to these ideas. In "cold" markets, by contrast, capital dries up because there are (in expectation) insufficient funds to carry these types of projects to full fruition. In other words, the type of technologies being developed at certain junctures depends on financing risk.

These types of financing dynamics and complexities underscore why the US model of VC financing in high-tech industries is difficult to imitate. For example, in European capital markets in which VC is not institutionalized to the same degree, alternative risk-sharing channels have become prominent. These include angel investing, crowdfunding, and the use of public funds to support entrepreneurship. These channels, however, tend to be weak substitutes because they do not always lead to the supply of capital being optimally matched to the distribution of new ideas (Lerner 2009). Better start-ups may self-select into the VC channel, or effective selection and governance of investments by VCs may lead to superior start-up performance. Either way, the US financing environment has evolved to establish a strong advantage in the intermediation of risk capital.

Conclusion

The preeminence of US VC in high-tech investment finance is a reflection of a long-standing historical process. The basic logic behind ARD's DEC investment—to screen multiple investments and govern the best ones with the expectation of a large payoff through a liquidity event—is something that all venture firms today aim to imitate. Of course, the pathway from the past to the present is not always seamless. Notably, ARD got the organizational model wrong as venture firms quickly gravitated away from the closed-end form to the limited partnership, which had tax advantages and was more suited to the creation of high-powered compensation incentives (Sahlman 1990).

Furthermore, such related developments as the rise of Silicon Valley, cultural predispositions toward entrepreneurship and risk taking, and the liberalization of investment rules permitting pension funds to increase the flow of funds to venture capital—all helped to create an environment in which VC investing could flourish. Yet, the significance of history and ARD's place in it is nonetheless profound. Other countries have attempted to develop ecosystems for high-tech venture finance or alternative financing with limited success. Given the importance of stage-setting by ARD and the breakthroughs made by the venture capital firms that followed in the 1970s and 1980s, it is perhaps no accident that the US model has been so hard to replicate.

I am very grateful to Robert Shulman, David Chambers, and Elroy Dimson for comments and to the Division of Research and Faculty Development at Harvard Business School for funding.

References

Ante, Spencer E. 2008. *Creative Capital: Georges Doriot and the Birth of Venture Capital*. Boston: Harvard Business Press.

Brav, Alon, and Paul A. Gompers. 1997. "Myth or Reality? The Long-Run Underperformance of Initial Public Offerings: Evidence from Venture and Nonventure Capital-Backed Companies." *Journal of Finance*, vol. 52, no. 5 (December): 1791–1821.

Brown, James R. 2005. "Venture Capital and Firm Performance over the Long-Run: Evidence from High-Tech IPOs in the United States." *Journal of Entrepreneurial Finance*, vol. 10, no. 3: 1–33.

Chandler, Alfred D., Takashi Hikino, and Andrew Von Nordenflycht. 2005. *Inventing the Electronic Century: The Epic Story of the Consumer Electronics and Computer Industries*. Cambridge, MA: Harvard University Press.

Dalzell, Robert F. 1987. *Enterprising Elite: The Boston Associates and the World They Made*. Cambridge, MA: Harvard University Press.

Doriot, Georges F. 1951. "American Research and Development Papers." Boston: Baker Library Historical Collections, Baker Library|Bloomberg Center, Harvard Business School.

———. 1971. "ARD Annual Report." Boston: Baker Library Historical Collections, Baker Library|Bloomberg Center, Harvard Business School.

EY. 2014. *Adapting and Evolving: Global Venture Capital Insights and Trends, 2014*. EYGM Limited.

Etzkowitz, Henry. 2002. *MIT and the Rise of Entrepreneurial Science*. London: Routledge.

Gompers, Paul. 1996. "Grandstanding in the Venture Capital Industry." *Journal of Financial Economics*, vol. 42, no. 1: 133–156.

Hellman, Thomas. and Manju Puri. 2002. "Venture Capital and the Professionalization of Start-Up Firms: Empirical Evidence." *Journal of Finance* vol. 57, no. 1 (February).

Hsu, David H., and Martin Kenney. 2005. "Organizing Venture Capital: The Rise and Demise of American Research & Development Corporation, 1946-1973." *Industrial and Corporate Change*, vol. 14, no. 4: 579–616.

Lamoreaux, Naomi R., Margaret C. Levenstein, and Kenneth L. Sokoloff. 2006. "Mobilizing Venture Capital during the Second Industrial Revolution: Cleveland, Ohio, 1870–1920." *Capitalism and Society*, vol. 1.

Lerner, Josh. 2009. *Boulevard of Broken Dreams: Why Public Efforts to Boost Entrepreneurship and Venture Capital Have Failed—and What to Do About It* Princeton, NJ: Princeton University Press.

Liles, Patrick R. 1977. *Sustaining the Venture Capital Firm*. Boston: Management Analysis Center.

Nanda, Ramana, and Matthew Rhodes-Kropf. Forthcoming. "Financing Risk and Innovation." *Management Science*.

National Venture Capital Association. 2015. *2015 National Venture Capital Association Yearbook*. Thomson Reuters.

Nicholas, Tom, and Jonas Peter Akins. 2012. "Whaling Ventures." Harvard Business School Case 813-086 (October).

Nicholas, Tom, and David Chen. 2012. "Georges Doriot and American Venture Capital." Harvard Business School Case 812-110 (January).

Ritter, Jay R. 2015. "Growth Capital-Backed IPOs." *Financial Review*, vol. 50, no. 4 (November): 481–515.

Romer, Paul. 1990. "Endogenous Technological Change." *Journal of Political Economy*, vol. 98, no. 5.

Sahlman, William A. 1990. "The Structure and Governance of Venture-Capital Organizations." *Journal of Financial Economics*, vol. 27, no. 2 (October): 473–521.

Saxenian, AnnaLee. 1994. *Regional Advantage: Culture and Competition in Silicon Valley and Route 128*. Cambridge, MA: Harvard University Press.

Stoddard, William. 1940. "Small Business Wants Capital." *Harvard Business Review*, vol. 1, no. 8.

Warren, Kenneth. 1987. *The American Steel Industry, 1850-1970: A Geographical Interpretation*. Pittsburgh: University of Pittsburgh Press.

14. The Rise of Institutional Investors

Janette Rutterford
Professor of Financial Management, Open University Business School

Leslie Hannah
Visiting Professor of Economic History, London School of Economics

Since the beginning of the 20th century, institutional investors have gained prominence in UK and US financial markets not only because of changes in economic access but also because of changes in the way governments protect investors. In this chapter, we discuss how markets have evolved in response to these changes by focusing on four types of investment management institutions: insurance companies, pension funds, investment trusts, and unit trusts. We conclude that intermediaries and policymakers need to balance market competition and regulation to insure a system capable of delivering adequate pensions and other services in the future.

Introduction

We document the rise of institutional investors during the 20th century in the United Kingdom and the United States by looking at the four main types of investment management institutions: insurance companies, pension funds, investment trusts (closed-end funds), and unit trusts (open-end funds). At their peak in 1992, UK institutional investors held over 50% of all UK government bonds and over 60% of UK-listed equities. By 2010, their share had fallen to 23% of UK-listed equities. Because of increasing globalization, half of that 23% was held by overseas investors (mainly similar institutions) as well as by newer institutions, such as hedge funds.

London was the center of global investment in the early 20th century and is still an important financial center, but we also discuss developments in other markets, particularly the United States, in which the NYSE became the largest stock market in the world in the 1920s and still holds that position. Institutional investors' rise to dominance in the US equity market took longer than in the United Kingdom but has since surpassed it: 6% in 1950, 37% in 1980, and 67% in 2010 (Traflet 2013, p. 174; Blume and Keim, forthcoming 2017). Moreover, growth in the value of listed securities has been phenomenal: The capitalization of the US equity market grew by a factor of more than 200 between 1950 and 2010 (Aguilar 2013). Institutional investors also dominate in the corporate bond market, the capitalization of which represents 130% of GDP in the United States (compared to less than 20% in the United Kingdom).

This chapter also shows that stock markets have tended to be less important for institutional investors in other countries, such as Germany and France. In these countries, (universal) banks and insurance companies have larger shares of the institutional investment market than do pension and mutual funds.

Origins

It is generally recognized that, in the early 20th century, the world's many stock exchanges were already large relative to the size of their economies.[1] Most investors in both equity and bond markets were individuals, either investing on their own behalf or acting as trustees for others (such as the proverbial widows and orphans) who were thought to need guidance. At the time, London hosted the world's largest stock market and served overseas issuers—and, to a lesser extent, overseas investors—as well as its home economy. The London Stock Exchange (LSE) was as big as the exchanges of New York and Berlin combined, despite the fact that the UK economy represented only one quarter of the combined GDP of the United States and Germany. The LSE's total market capitalization, including overseas and domestic government and corporate bonds as well as equity, was well over 400% of UK GDP (high, even by today's standards). There were also well-developed London, provincial, and overseas markets in other asset classes such as commodities, rented housing, other property, and mortgages.

London's institutional investment landscape in 1900 was representative of the advanced industrial world at the time, although on a larger scale and with more diversification than its peers. For example, investment trusts, invented by the Dutch in the 18th century, were fully developed in London by the early 1900s; however, investment trusts were not significantly promoted to US investors until the 1920s. Railway securities in the United Kingdom, especially bonds, were more attractive to individuals and institutions than low-yielding government securities, but industrial equities played a larger and earlier role on the LSE than on the New York Stock Exchange (NYSE). A large share of the NYSE's listed corporate securities were railways until its 1920s stock exchange boom. In terms of diversification, UK investors in the 1900s held internationally diversified portfolios while US investors typically bought US securities. A sample of 508 UK investor portfolios during

---

[1]It is interesting to note that, in real terms, even advanced industrial countries in the early 20th century had living standards not much higher than China's today.

the period 1870 to 1902 included, on average, more than 20% in foreign and colonial securities by value (Rutterford 2013).

The rise of institutional investment in both countries was likely driven by the extension of shareholding to less-wealthy people—those with limited experience in managing investments and thus in need of more assistance in the management of their assets. It is certainly the case that individual investors, along with endowed charities, now use professional managers more than their predecessors did. Thus, the rise of institutional investors could be a result of an increasing division of labor as the market expanded and professional specializations emerged—all reinforced by technologies that facilitated cheaper data processing of client accounts and lower dealing costs. As this chapter outlines, however, there were other key factors in the development of investment institutions. These included government intervention in the form of tax advantages and regulation as well as developments in diversification and risk management.

Why They Grew

Of the four main types of investment institutions, insurance companies have the longest history; many insurance companies started offering life policies as early as the 18th century. As well as offering protection, some insurance companies evolved as investment institutions, offering payouts on expiry of the policy or on the death of the policyholder. Since the first declarations of bonuses by the Equitable Life Assurance Company in the 18th century, it had become common for both mutual and proprietary insurers to offer "with profits" (i.e., "participating") endowment policies.[2] After covering the costs of administration and death benefits, these were, in effect, long-term savings products based on a broad investment portfolio.

Payouts were originally in the form of annuities or lump sums with payments guaranteed in nominal terms. More recently, since the 1960s and 1970s when inflation began to erode fixed returns, payouts became more commonly linked to stock market performance. If we exclude banks, building societies (UK), and savings and loan companies (US),[3] the largest institutional investment managers globally were insurance companies, particularly those primarily involved in longer-term life and annuity business.

Pension funds were not significant institutional investors before World War II, but from the 1950s onward, the rise in value of pension fund assets was meteoric. Valued at only £2 billion in 1957 and approximately £820

---

[2]In the United Kingdom, life insurance and life assurance are interchangeable terms.
[3]These were excluded because, especially in the Anglosphere, they were focused on managing portfolios of loan, discount, and mortgage contracts rather than tradable securities and property.

billion by the year 2000, UK pension fund assets grew at an annual rate of 16% in nominal terms and 8% in real terms over the period. UK insurance companies had assets of £4.9 billion in 1957, twice that of pension funds, but by 2000 they only matched the pension funds in size. Direct comparisons are now hampered by the fact that insurance companies offer pension products and pension funds invest in insurance company-managed funds. By 2009, UK insurance companies held assets worth 100% of GDP compared to 80% for pension funds. In the United States, the comparable figures for 2009 were 40% of GDP for insurance company assets and 65% for pension fund assets (Trusted Sources 2011, p. 7).

The increase in the importance of both pension funds and life insurance companies as investment institutions has largely been the result of active government encouragement. William Gladstone, then Chancellor of the Exchequer, introduced tax relief on life assurance premiums in 1853 (Daunton 2002, p. 262). Life assurance companies benefited from major tax advantages attached to life assurance policies until 1984, in the form of full tax deductibility of premiums at the taxpayer's marginal (i.e., highest) income tax rate, as well as exemption from capital gains tax when this tax was introduced in 1965. These tax advantages were significant when compared with the punitively high taxes on individually held stocks and shares. The highest tax rate on dividends peaked at 98% between 1974 and 1979 in the United Kingdom, and capital gains tax was set at 30% in 1965. Even since 1984, certain advantages remain for some types of life assurance savings schemes, particularly those for the higher rate taxpayer.

UK life assurance companies also benefited from less stringent constraints on marketing, allowing them to employ salesmen who could "cold call" potential policyholders at home until the passage of the Financial Services Act 1986. These advantages dated from the days when pension schemes were not widespread and pension benefits, such as they were, did not provide an adequate retirement income. Thus, individuals catered for their own retirement through savings schemes linked to life insurance. To encourage this, the government accorded tax relief and marketing advantages for such investments. This pattern was similar in the United States, with the government promoting long-term investment in life insurance products in an environment of high personal taxation. In the United States, the highest income tax rate on unearned income peaked at 91% in the 1950s and early 1960s, with the rate on capital gains tax—introduced much earlier in the United States—ranging between 25% and 40%. Tax rates did not decline significantly until the 1980s (Rutterford 2010). The rationale for US government encouragement was given in 1990:

The principal justifications for the current tax treatment of life insurance and annuity products are to encourage the provision of financial support of dependents after the death of a wage earner, to allow protection against outliving one's assets, and to encourage private long-term savings. (US Department of the Treasury 1990)

Despite the United Kingdom's recent reduction in tax incentives for individuals to save via life assurance policies, life assurance companies have continued to grow, this time helped by government financial incentives to encourage private sector pension schemes. Since 1975, when legislation was introduced in the Social Security Pensions Act, companies have been obliged either to contract into the State Earnings Related Pension Scheme (SERPS) for their employees or provide their own scheme on equivalent or better terms. These privately organized pension plans are either run as pension funds separate from the company or managed by financial intermediaries, such as banks or insurance companies, on behalf of the employer company.

Elsewhere, private pension plans are sometimes smaller and/or differently invested. In Germany, for example, the state earnings-related pensions are more generous. Smaller pension funds are invested in the employing corporations' balance sheets and insured against the resultant double jeopardy to employees of losing their jobs and pensions together.

In 1986, the UK Social Security Act allowed employees (as well as the self-employed) to take out personal pension plans that are tied to the individual rather than to the company for which he or she works. At the same time, they offered financial incentives for employees to switch out of SERPS into private sector plans. Doing so transferred the investment risk from the company—with defined benefit (DB) plans—to the individual—with defined contribution (DC) plans.[4] This gave a boost to life assurance companies, the main providers of personal pension (i.e., DC) plans.

Thus, in the United Kingdom as pension plans have spread and as benefits and hence contributions have increased, the assets of the pension funds (and insurance companies) have grown. However, pension plan membership has been declining for several decades, even though sums invested have been rising. This is because of increased restrictions on tax advantages, the legal freedom of employees to opt out, and also, in some well-publicized cases, financial mismanagement of DB schemes. Such factors have reduced employers' attraction to DB schemes. More recently, the number of individual

---

[4]In DB plans, the employer guarantees a certain amount of income to the employee in retirement, the amount usually expressed as a percentage of final or average salary. In DC plans, however, employees choose their own retirement investments—thus assuming the risk that their value on retirement will not be enough to pay the desired pension.

members in DC pension schemes has begun to increase again with the use of 'nudge economics,' in which individuals join a pension scheme automatically unless they (annually) opt out. The current split between DB and DC schemes in the United Kingdom is 71% DB, 29% DC.

Retirement plans in the United States also evolved over time. The most notable developments were as follows. Tax-deferred pension plans for the self-employed and small businesses, known as Keogh plans, were introduced in 1962. The Employee Retirement Income Security Act of 1974 (ERISA) was designed to regulate employee retirement investment accounts to protect participants and their beneficiaries. Individual Retirement Accounts (IRAs) were authorized as a part of ERISA. The Revenue Act of 1978 included a provision for 401(k) pension plans so that employees would not be taxed on deferred compensation. Finally, the Roth IRA (with tax relief on pension payouts, not contributions) was established by the Taxpayer Relief Act of 1997. Between 1950 and 1990, US pension fund assets grew six times faster than the US economy. The number of investment advisers tripled in the 1980s alone (Allen 2015, p. 219). For the 2011 tax year, an estimated 43 million taxpayers had IRAs with a total balance of approximately $5.2 trillion (US Government Accountability Office 2014). DC plans represent 58% of the total, compared with 42% for DB plans.

Unit trusts and investment trusts were not originally conceived as tax-efficient forms of saving for retirement.[5] Both types of investments were set up to offer small investors a way of holding a stake in a diversified portfolio of securities, an opportunity that was otherwise unavailable to them because of high transaction costs. Foreign & Colonial Government Trust (F&C), founded in 1868, was the first UK investment trust. It was explicitly designed to provide small investors with the opportunity to invest in a carefully selected variety of investments. The aim of the trust was to 'give the investor of moderate means the same advantages as the large capitalists in diminishing the risk of investing in foreign and colonial government stocks by spreading the investment over a number of different stocks' (Rutterford 2009, p. 158). By the end of the 1870s, 70 so-called average investment trusts had been launched. After two more 'waves' before WWI, a further 103 investment trusts were launched between 1924 and 1929 (Rutterford 2009, p. 163).

The US investment trust industry did not take off until the 1920s. By the end of the boom, however, more than $7 billion (compared with UK trusts' total investment assets of $1 billion) was invested in 675 investment

---

[5]Unit trusts are open-end funds that vary in size according to supply and demand; closed-end funds are issued much like corporate stocks and are closed to new money but can use leverage to expand.

companies of all types, including 19 open-end funds. The dramatic fall in this sector in the 1929 Wall Street Crash—so severe that investment trusts were blamed for the crash itself—did not affect UK investment trusts in the same way. US investment trusts had higher leverage, had invested mostly in US equities and in other investment trusts, charged high fees, had numerous highly-paid managers and directors, and marked their securities to market. In the United Kingdom, however, investment trusts had avoided equities, diversified internationally, adopted conservative leverage and accounting strategies, and were cheaper to run because directors served on a number of boards and charged lower fees per trust.

In reaction to the poor performance of investment trusts during the crash, a number of so-called open-end trusts were launched in the 1930s, first in the United States and then in the United Kingdom. The open-end structure proved popular because it allowed investors to sell their units back to the trust at asset value. By the late 1930s, open-end mutual funds (called unit trusts in the United Kingdom), invested primarily in equities, were popular on both sides of the Atlantic. Investment trusts offered the advantages of a long history (F&C is still in business today), a wide spread of international investments (though curtailed by post-World War I capital controls), a cautious approach to reserves, and lower fees and costs. Unit trusts offered the advantages of a concentration in equities, liquidity through daily pricing, and no discount to asset value.

UK investment trusts continued to dominate unit trusts by asset size until well after World War II; as late as 1962, investment trusts were valued at £2.4 billion, 10 times the value of unit trusts. However, more-aggressive marketing and the rise of such unit-linked products as mortgages in the 1960s and 1970s meant that, by 2000, unit trusts (and EU-registered open-end investment companies or OEICs) were valued at £221.9 billion, with investment trusts at £57.3 billion. In the United States, investment trusts were hampered by US legislation—in particular, the Investment Company Act of 1940, which removed many of the benefits of closed-end funds. They were overtaken by open-end funds as early as 1944; by 1962, open-end funds were 10 times as large as closed-end funds (Rutterford 2009).

In the United States, several factors accounted for meteoric growth in mutual funds. These factors include the following: aggressive marketing (with no restrictions on content and media from 1979); the rise in the value of the stock market in the 1950s and 1960s; poor investment performance from competing traditional life insurance and pension products that were invested primarily in bonds; the creation of index funds in the 1970s; the creation of tax-exempt funds from the late 1980s; and the creation of exchange-traded funds (ETFs) in the 1990s. Perhaps most important, mutual funds were allowed as part of pension plans from 1979 onwards. By 1999, 40% of a total of 7,791 mutual funds were linked to pension plans in some way (Allen 2015, p. 271). Also, the 1981 Tax Act reduction in capital gains tax made riskier investments relatively more attractive.

What They Invested In

Judging from the evidence of share registers,[6] institutional ownership of UK corporate securities before World War I was probably no greater than 10% of the total by value. However, for other asset classes, such as bonds and property, the share owned by institutions was probably already larger. A sample of 33,078 shareholders in 261 company share registers relating to 47 UK-registered companies, spread across all sectors for the period 1870 to 1935, reveals that only 505 of the shareholders were institutional investors. They held 4.2% of the value of these securities in the decade of the 1900s, 7.7% in the 1910s, 6.0% in the 1920s, and 23.8% by the 1930s. The remaining securities were held by individual investors either directly or through personal trusts (Rutterford, Green, Maltby, and Owens 2010).

In 1906, for example, the United Kingdom's 95 life assurance offices invested the £384 million of funds they managed (which then amounted to 19% of GDP) as follows: 25% in mortgages, 17% in other loans, 11% in government bonds, 10% each in property and corporate bonds, and 9% in corporate equities (Anon 1907, p. 458). Other insurers in the Anglosphere had similar portfolios but to some extent reflected local balances of demand and supply. For example, those in the United States had more in corporate bonds, less in government bonds, and less in corporate equity; the Australians had more in loans and mortgages. In Germany, where the mortgage market was already highly securitized using *Pfandbriefe*, life insurers had as much as 78% in mortgages. In France (where, until recently, the government barred investments in mortgages while guaranteeing railway bonds), insurers unsurprisingly invested more in corporate bonds and less in mortgages.

Two general characteristics may be noted about such institutional portfolios. First, with the exception of the relatively undiversified German insurers, they showed a shift from greater earlier reliance on mortgages and government bonds toward corporate securities. They thus achieved greater diversification than was typically available to private investors. Still, none of these portfolios could really be characterized as having used their scale and diversification adventurously. UK insurance companies invested the highest

---

[6]Unusually, share registers were public documents in the United Kingdom. Many were preserved in the National Archives and have recently been analyzed.

portion in equities, but this was less than 10% of their portfolio and skewed toward relatively safe UK and overseas railways. Although few individual investors had the scale and diversification of insurers, they actually had a far higher proportion of their portfolios in equities, especially industrials, and would accordingly have achieved higher, though more volatile, returns. Institutions, such as UK insurers, had more discretion to invest where they wished than did their overseas counterparts, but they simply seem to have viewed bonds as best matching their liabilities in a period of relatively stable prices (Newman 1908).

The sharp rise in holdings of corporate securities by UK institutional investors during the 1920s can be explained by a number of factors: the relatively poor investment performance of war loans in the interwar years; the sale of US securities, especially during World War I; and the gradual understanding, crystallized by Edgar Smith's 1924 US text, *Common Stock as Long Term Investments*, of the compounding effect of retained earnings as well as the benefits of dividends, all of which made corporate security returns relatively more attractive (particularly equities). Harold Raynes, a UK actuary, confirmed in papers published in 1928 and 1937 that the same compounding effect applied in the United Kingdom (Avrahampour 2015, p. 287). John Maynard Keynes was influenced by Smith's text, and he was one of the first institutional fund managers to allocate the majority of the portfolio (where he had full discretion) to UK and US equities—75% during the 1920s and 57% during the 1930s (Chambers and Dimson 2013, pp. 221–222). UK insurance companies bought equities directly but also via investment trusts, which by the mid-1930s held, on average, 42% of their portfolios in equities. By 1999, UK insurers' long-term funds showed the following asset allocation: a mere 1% in loans and mortgages, 8% in short-term assets, 13% in UK government bonds, 12% in UK corporate and foreign bonds, 9% in unit trusts, 6% in property and other assets, and 51% in equities (Trusted Sources 2011).

In the United States, however, state legislation restricted the asset allocation choices of insurance companies. Influential New York investment legislation, for example, prevented insurance companies in its jurisdiction from holding equities at all in their general accounts until 1951, with limits of 10% in 1969 and 20% in 1990. This encouraged insurance companies to seek higher returns in corporate bonds, real estate, and other fixed-interest securities. By 1990, US insurance companies held 38% of their assets in corporate bonds, 22% in real estate loans and real estate, 9% in equities, and the remainder in other fixed-interest securities (Wright 1992, p. 15). After deregulation in the late 1990s, the equity percentage rose to 30% by 1999 (Trusted Sources 2011, p. 9).

The push toward equities was intensified by pension funds, which were required to match assets with pension liabilities. These liabilities were long term and subject to such risks as longevity risk. To meet promises to link pensions to final salaries (a practice that became normal after World War II), they were expected to grow in real terms. These requirements encouraged pension fund trustees to 'match' known liabilities with fixed-interest securities and unknown future liabilities with equities.

The increased emphasis on equities continued after World War II when the stock market performed well. George Ross Goobey, in charge of Imperial Tobacco's pension fund, recommended a 100% equity allocation for new monies. The equity allocation of the Imperial Tobacco fund rose from 28% in 1953, to 68% in 1957, and 96% in 1961 (Avrahampour 2015, pp. 295–6, 299). By 1963, UK pension funds as a whole held 6.4% of UK-listed equities; this peaked at 32.4% in 1992. By 1999, pension fund assets were allocated 4% to short-term assets, 12% to UK government bonds, 4% to UK corporate and foreign bonds, 4% to property and other assets, 10% to unit trusts (investment trusts and insurance managed funds), and a hefty 61.6% to equities. The target asset allocation strategy then typically used was 60/40. In both the United States and the United Kingdom, this was interpreted as 60% equities, 40% bonds, which matched the relative importance of these two asset classes at the time.

The prudent man rule, which allowed delegation of investment decisions to trustees provided 'prudent' decisions were made, applied to both UK and US pension funds. In the United Kingdom, some funds, such as Imperial Tobacco's pension fund, gave the fund trustee wide-ranging investment powers. In the United States, the equivalent pension fund was General Motors, which in 1950 saw the advantages of equity investment and gave its seven fund managers authority to invest up to 50% in equities. During that decade, as the equity markets boomed 'a considerable change in attitude toward common stocks took place' (Allen 2015, p. 218).

Those UK pension funds that did not have the wide-ranging investment policies of Imperial Tobacco, for example, were limited by trustee legislation that allowed stock selection from a pre-determined 'legal list' of low-risk, low-yield securities. This changed in the United Kingdom after the Trustee Investments Act of 1961, at which point up to 50% could be invested in equities and mutual funds. Full deregulation came in the late 1980s. In the United States, such deregulation took place in 1974, when ERISA provided a regulatory framework for pension plans and specifically required pension portfolios to be diversified but allowed more discretion on asset class choice.

In 1979, for example, pension funds were allowed to invest in mutual funds and private equity (Allen 2015, pp. 269, 282).

One self-imposed constraint remained: US and UK investment institutions were slow to invest internationally.[7] As late as 1970, US pension funds had essentially no money invested in overseas equities, and UK pension funds a mere 2% (Davis 2005). This so-called 'home bias' still remains today, to a greater extent in the United States. Between 1998 and 2010, holdings of domestic equities as a percentage of the total fell from 85% to 65% for US pension funds and from 75% to 40% for UK pension funds. A larger domestic bias remained for government and corporate bonds, with around 90% of US pension fund bond investment remaining domestic (Willis, Towers, Watson 2015).

How They Managed Their Investments

As we have seen, individual investors were by far the most important investors in the early 1900s. Most securities were in the hands of individual investors, who either made their own investment decisions based solely on their own expertise or who relied on the expertise of friends and relatives or of a limited number of intermediaries. Both the United States and the United Kingdom probably had no more than a million investors (i.e., 1% or 2% or so of their populations), and this élite would perhaps not be short of family wealth-holding experience or friends with appropriate knowledge. Bankers, US trust banks, the executor and trustee departments of UK retail banks, solicitors, and stockbrokers were all involved in advisory work for such retail clients; and some held securities and collected dividends on their clients' behalf.

However, most of these intermediaries acted merely as advisers on commission (usually transaction-based), only occasionally working in a fee-based discretionary portfolio management capacity. Such boutiques as the Investment Registry in the United Kingdom or *Finance Univers* in France (which advocated portfolio diversification on recognizably modern lines) would manage whole portfolios, but they seem to have pitched their business model more at reviewing existing individual portfolios and advising on rebalancing. Merchant bankers (like J.P. Morgan in New York or Rothschild in London) managed a few favored client portfolios as well as their own, but they lacked the scale to go much beyond that. Even those with more research capability—probably the largest group of investment analysts globally were the several hundred employed by Crédit Lyonnais in Paris—also mainly acted in an advisory (and order execution) capacity. German banks, however, more frequently held stocks and exercised voting rights on behalf of investors.

---

[7]Pre-World War I UK institutions had pursued a global approach to investment until forced to sell their overseas securities during the war.

© 2016 CFA Institute Research Foundation. All Rights Reserved.

Insurance companies and investment trusts, the main institutional investors of the time, followed so-called 'extension of securities.' This practice was essentially a buy-and-hold strategy that involved the addition of individual securities to the portfolio, each assessed as to capital safety and yield with little consideration of the impact of the new security on the portfolio's existing characteristics (May 1912). This extension policy is evident in the case of the F&C, which in 1879 consolidated five individual trusts into one investment company with a portfolio of around £2.5 million invested in fewer than 90 securities. By 1905, F&C had more than tripled the number of securities to 280, with a portfolio worth only 20% more. The more securities held, the merrier: 'The bigger the company, the more the investments can be spread and the more can any particular risk be minimized' (Rutterford 2009, p. 171).

In the United Kingdom, investment management as a profession was slow to develop. Although insurance companies might employ investment managers or actuaries to manage portfolios, directors were loath to give up their investment decision-making authority. US authors Chamberlain and Hay (1931) commented admiringly that ordinary shareholders in UK investment trusts elected their directors, who 'assume a much greater moral responsibility and are called on for more realistic services than here.' Moreover, they said that investment decisions in UK investment trusts relied on 'the personal judgements of the managers and directors, who ... depend to a considerable extent on personal contacts and the advice of brokers ... The operation of the law of averages is relied on to minimize the effect of mistaken judgments.'

US investment trusts were, in contrast, 'expertly staffed organizations, often of considerable size, to analyze and select securities for investment' (Chamberlain and Hay 1931). Instead of investing in a large number of fixed-interest securities around the globe, as did those in the United Kingdom, US investment trust managers preferred to invest in a small number of equities and were credited with both stock selection and market-timing skills. The United Kingdom concept of just buying a large number of stocks as they were issued and holding them to maturity was considered 'plodding.' Commentators in the United States argued that superior management was a desirable substitute for diversification, with the author of a key text on how to run US investment trusts recommending a field staff of experts throughout the world (Rutterford 2009, p. 176). US investment managers were expected to buy and sell rather than just buy and hold: 'The investment trust manager who devotes his time to whether oils or motors are the more attractive group ... is certainly performing one of the essential functions of management' (Rutterford 2009, p. 176). In practice, in the face of the bull market of the late 1920s, the professional approach to investment and the search for undervalued securities took second place to the purchase of shares that were going up in price. As Graham and Dodd commented after the Wall Street Crash of 1929:

> Most paradoxical was the early abandonment of research and analysis in guiding investment trust policies. Investment had now become so beautifully simple that research was unnecessary and statistical analysis a mere encumbrance. Hence the sound policy was to buy what everyone else was buying ... The man in the street, having been urged to entrust his funds to the superior skill of investment experts—for substantial compensation—was soon reassuringly told that the trusts would be careful to buy nothing except what the man in the street was buying himself. (Graham and Dodd 1934, p. 311)

Performance Measurement

There are essentially two forms of performance measurement: against a peer group and against a passive benchmark. Measuring against a peer group is appropriate if the peer group has essentially the same investment objectives and risks as the portfolio being measured. In the 19th century, for example, insurance companies were judged according to the bonuses they declared on their life funds or on their annuity rates. Also, actively managed closed-end and open-end funds have long been judged according to their position within a group of funds with similar investment objectives. Pension fund asset performance is more difficult to measure because an investment objective usually acts as a proxy for the underlying requirement to be able to meet liabilities when they fall due. However, pension funds can also use peer group performance for each asset class as a measuring stick for their own performance by asset class.

The alternative is to find a rules-based or "passive" portfolio strategy to which an actively managed fund can be compared. Typically, this is taken to be a strategy of mirroring an index or a combination of indices. Although early US investors used the Dow Jones Industrial Average (DJIA) index as a measure of performance, for example, it was a price-weighted capital appreciation index and not a total return index; as a result, it was not comparable with an investment portfolio's returns. In the 1920s, Irving Fisher worked hard to make indices more usable by taking account of the numerous stock splits and other corporate actions that took place in that decade. However, the main impetus for measuring pension fund performance in the United States was the enactment of ERISA in 1974. ERISA required a fiduciary's conduct to be compared to that which a "prudent man acting in a like capacity and familiar with such matters would use in the conduct of an enterprise of like character and with like aims.'[8]

In other words, instead of merely being prudent, fiduciaries were required to be familiar with investment matters. This provision encouraged trustees to delegate investment to professional fund managers (providing an estimated additional $200 billion to be managed by investment institutions), and it encouraged benchmarking of performance against a peer group of fund managers. But it also led to the use of risk-adjusted benchmarks, as advocated by modern portfolio theory. By switching from a requirement for prudence to a requirement for expertise, ERISA encouraged fund managers to use such investment theories as a framework for their investment decision making, making them less liable to be sued for poor performance if they could show they had adhered to well-respected theories (Hutchinson 1976, pp. 42, 48).

It was not until the development of modern portfolio theory in the 1960s and 1970s that investors began consistently to measure investment performance relative to a passive benchmark, which could be adjusted to reflect the relative risk of the investment fund and the index. Outperformance on a risk-adjusted basis has come to be called 'alpha,'—that is, the difference between what the capital asset pricing model (CAPM) predicts the risk-adjusted return will be and what is actually achieved.

For example, as late as 1997, the large Unilever pension fund went from requiring its UK equity portfolio managers to come in the top quartile of their peer group in terms of performance to judging performance against a benchmark UK equity index. When Unilever failed to meet the new requirement, the trustees of the pension fund sued the fund manager for not performing well relative to the benchmark. In fact, the case identified a common problem with performance measurement. The time period over which performance is measured is often shorter than the time horizon of the investor. Underperformance in this case was 10.6% relative to a benchmark over 15 months. If the trustees had waited another two years, the same strategy would have generated no underperformance. The case was settled out of court, but the payments made by the fund manager were significant because other investment clients who had had similar contracts and performance were also able to obtain out-of-court settlements.

Performance measurement for judging the investment managers employed by institutional investors is now relatively sophisticated. There is still room for improvement, however, with respect to performance measurement and

---

[8]See the US Department of Labor's information on ERISA at www.dol.gov/general/topic/retirement/erisa.

performance reporting to retail investors. Exchange-traded funds (ETFs)[9] allow individual investors to compare the performance of their actively managed open-end or closed-end investment funds to that of a portfolio made up of different ETFs with the same asset allocation as that of the actively managed fund. This will be practicable when full and timely disclosure of investments in ETFs becomes available.

The Changed Situation Today

Since the 1920s, US markets have been the world's largest and most developed. Because China's and Japan's equity markets are now larger than the LSE, it is appropriate to base our analysis of modern trends on the United States rather than the United Kingdom. In 2010, domestic holdings of US equities were divided accordingly: 42% in "households" (mainly individual investors), 32% in insurance and pension funds, and 28% in mutual and exchange-traded funds. If we added foreign holdings (mainly by institutions), the institutional share would be considerably higher. It is clear that most of this rise has occurred since 1952, when only 7% of shares were held by institutions and individual holdings still dominated. For US and foreign bonds, in 2010 the proportion held by US "households" was even smaller at 20%. In the United Kingdom, institutions have become even more dominant: Equity ownership by individuals has declined from 54% in 1963 to 11% today. Changes in other categories in official UK statistics are difficult to interpret. The largest rise is in ownership by the "rest of the world," but this includes holdings by asset managers based in London whose parent companies are based overseas. For example, US asset management firms such as Capital, Fidelity, and Blackrock have substantial London offices managing their holdings in UK companies often on behalf of UK clients, and major sovereign wealth funds also have London offices. London is the world's largest center for asset management and invests a good deal beyond the United Kingdom. Still, John Kay's 2012 *Review*, commissioned by the UK government to assess the market, suggested that if funds managed from Boston and San Francisco were added to those of New York, the total of funds under management in the United States would be greater than in the United Kingdom.

Insurers now own more equities than they did in the early 20th century, but they are now less dominant among asset managers. In the United States, they own only 18% of bonds and 6% of equities; in the United Kingdom, they own only 9% of equities. It is now the norm for endowed institutions (such as universities) to outsource investment management, although some run

[9]ETFs are a form of low-cost index fund available in a wide range of markets, securities, and sectors.

their own (now more professionalized) investment offices. Exchange-traded funds offer relatively cheap access to diversification for individuals, and some large investors, like the Norwegian sovereign wealth fund, successfully follow similar strategies of long-term "beta" returns. This style of investment management has greater economies of scale than the more traditional form, and it accounts for much of the increased concentration in the industry globally; however, many boutiques and smaller scale operations remain in the industry. Some investors prefer the endowment model, or "Yale" approach, of pursuing alpha in less conventional investment classes. Large numbers of hedge funds, venture capitalists, and private equity firms cater to such tastes. With larger scale and greater professionalization has also come specialization of function. Such ancillary services as custody, registry, nominees, and investment consultancy are also now separate from investment management. The academic consensus that there is little serial correlation in investment management returns has not kept large numbers of investment managers from attempting to achieve it and large numbers of investors from attempting to identify winning managers.

Some question whether there is now too much financial intermediation by those who have lost sight of their investors' objectives. As Kay (2012, p. 11) put it:

> [. . . C]ompetition between asset managers on the basis of relative performance is inherently a zero sum game. The asset management industry can benefit its customers—savers—taken as a whole, only to the extent that its activities improve the performance of investee companies. This conflict between the imperatives of the business model of asset managers, and the interests of UK business and those who invest in it, is at the heart of our analysis of the problem of short-termism.

Corporate Governance, Agency Costs, and Institutional Investors

The rise of intermediaries in principle offered several improvements. One was the hope of cost reductions through economies of scale and enhanced competition as well as tax advantages. Another was improvement in monitoring of investments and the efficient allocation of capital relative to the inefficiently dispersed and less professional efforts of individual investors who earlier dominated shareholding. A third was increased concern for governance standards and externalities deriving from their perspective as owners (albeit mainly as agents) of most quoted assets (Dimson, Karakaş, and Li 2015).

The extra layers between investors and multiple intermediaries have introduced further problems of agency and added costs to the investment chain. In addition, according to some accounts, they have exacerbated short-termism—a problem that one might have thought long-term institutional commitment would alleviate. The net effects of these cross-cutting forces on investor returns are not easy to untangle, not least because the counterfactual (what the world would now be like if intermediaries did not exist) is inherently difficult to establish. The growing control of investment banks over the initial public offering (IPO) process and greater regulation have led not to a reduction of but to an exacerbation of underpricing. This has disadvantaged those raising capital through public offers (Chambers and Dimson 2009), but it may also have provided windfalls for institutions with preferential allocations.

Nonetheless, history suggests some skepticism about any alleged tendency toward long-run improvements in investment performance after intermediation costs. It has, for example, been argued that corporate governance mechanisms were better aligned with investor interests on the pre-1914 LSE than on the 1990s NYSE (Foreman-Peck and Hannah 2013) and that early intermediaries offered effective diversification and high returns (Chambers and Esteves 2014). Yet, investment trust management fees in that period were below those charged by modern intermediaries (Chambers and Esteves 2014, p. 5). If this is true, it is surprising given both the substantial reduction in transaction and record keeping costs added by modern technology and, in some areas, the lower marketing costs in principle facilitated by state compulsion (pensions) or tax incentives (various investments). One clear difference between the early and late 20th century is that the proportion of the population with a beneficial interest in securities is now much larger; as a result, the administrative costs of servicing many small investors might be expected to be greater than those of serving a small elite. In the late 1960s, for example, the NYSE curbed its wider share ownership campaign because its brokers were unable to handle the paperwork for millions of investors (Traflet 2013, p. 159).

In most of the economy, competition stimulates cost minimization and many intermediaries are in workably competitive sectors. Thus, in the late 20th century investors sometimes gravitated to lower-cost options (notably the recent move to exchange-traded funds). In other cases, they did not; for example, some were encouraged to invest in unit trusts with higher commissions and larger bid–ask spreads rather than in less expensive investment trusts (Rutterford 2009). Problems of agency and information especially frustrate the efficient operation of the competitive process in finance, and developments in behavioral finance are identifying other barriers to optimality. Divisions of labor and specialization generally also reduce costs. Specialization is rampant in the investment field: Asset managers are now complemented by registrars, custodians, trustees, investment consultants, rating agencies, funds of funds, retail and wholesale distributors, independent financial advisers (IFAs), and others. All of them employ lawyers and auditors. Kay (2012) suggested that this specialization indicates declining trust within and of the sector, a problem that actually increases transaction and management costs. His is only one among many voices arguing that securities churning and competition to improve performance among asset managers is inherently a zero-sum game (for any skilled buyer, there is a dud seller). In this view, the best way for institutional investors to improve investor returns is to invest in fewer companies, engage with them, and improve their performance. Others argue that this kind of active management is not achievable, preferring to concentrate on index funds, such as ETFs, and efficient diversification.

Early investment institutions sometimes insisted on good corporate governance in cases where they occupied board positions; in fact, private bankers were sometimes active managers and monitors of their own and clients' investments. Sometimes, however, investment trusts, insurers, and bankers were accused of being the problem rather than the solution. Thus, many important steps toward improving governance and transparency rules—such as the formation of the US Securities and Exchange Commission in 1934 or the UK Companies Act in 1948—derived from politicians' views that legal enforcements (i.e., reducing the role and discretion of some intermediaries or gatekeepers) were required. Such regulatory forces as well as stronger financial repression were particularly evident between the 1930s and 1960s, although liberalization and globalized markets eventually restored the freer pre-1914 conditions.

Technological changes both improved market integration and lowered costs. Investment intermediaries were instrumental in using the technology to create trading platforms that function as an alternative to stock exchanges and in persuading governments to apply competition laws to exchanges to lower dealing costs. They also sometimes lobbied effectively for improved corporate governance. The stronger promotion of investor interests in takeover bids in the United Kingdom can be seen as the beneficent result of institutions driving the process. This is in contrast to the United States, where state legislators sympathetic to poison pills and other incumbent defenses caused takeovers to be more difficult.

The outlawing of dual-class voting by some exchanges also resulted from actions by institutional investors, although they have tolerated backsliding by internet firms.[10] Some pension funds, such as CalPERS and Hermes, have taken the lead in initiatives to improve corporate governance by direct intervention (a strategy taken further by some interventionist hedge funds and corporate raiders). Others maintain that their most effective weapon against poorly performing management is the sale of shares.

It is difficult to conclude that investment institutions have unequivocally improved governance and returns, although clearly they have sometimes done so. The lesson of history is that both policymakers and intermediaries need to engage seriously in creating rules of the game—a balance of market competition with better but perhaps less complex and intrusive regulation—if confidence is to be maintained in a system capable of delivering adequate pensions and other services to investors by intermediating investment flows to businesses. The failure to address such issues in the 1930s was a major cause of the decades of financial repression by (often damaging) regulation that followed. The chairman of the NYSE who insisted changes were unnecessary after the 1929 crash was soon serving time in jail (albeit for his actions, not his opinions). Likewise, the investment management industry would be unwise to assume that the fallout from the Global Financial Crisis of 2008 will remain largely confined to the banking sector if customers' and politicians' concerns about costs and investment performance are not creatively addressed in the longer term.

---

[10]Hong Kong did not introduce restrictions on dual voting until 1987, but today it is the only major exchange to maintain them.

Bibliography

Aguilar, Luis. 2013. "Institutional Investors: Power and Responsibility." Speech (19 April): www.sec.gov/News/Speech/Detail/Speech/1365171515808.

Allen, David Grayson. 2015. *Investment Management in Boston: A History.* Amherst and Boston: University of Massachusetts Press.

Anon. 1907. "The Life Assurance Companies of the United Kingdom" (extracted from the Parliamentary Returns for 1906, published in 1907)." *Journal of the Institute of Actuaries*, vol. 41, July: 457–460.

Avrahampour, Yally. 2015. "Cult of the Equity: Actuaries and the Transformation of Pension Fund Investing, 1948–1960." *Business History Review*, vol. 89, Summer: 281–304.

Blume, Marshall E., and Donald B. Keim. Forthcoming 2017. "The Changing Nature of Institutional Investors." *Critical Finance Review*, vol. 6, no. 1.

Chamberlain, L., and W.W. Hay. 1931. *Investment and Speculation.* New York: Henry Holt and Company.

Chambers, David, and Elroy Dimson. 2009. "IPO Underpricing over the Very Long Run." *Journal of Finance*, vol. 64, no. 3 (June): 1407–1443.

———. 2013. "Retrospectives: John Maynard Keynes, Investment Innovator." *Journal of Economic Perspectives*, vol. 27, Summer: 213–228.

Chambers, David, and Rui Esteves. 2014. "The First Global Emerging Markets Investor: Foreign and Colonial Investment Trust 1880–1913." *Explorations in Economic History*, vol. 52: 1–21.

Daunton, Martin. 2002. *Just Taxes: The Politics of Taxation in Britain, 1914–1979.* Cambridge, UK: Cambridge University Press.

Davis, E. Philip. 2005. "Pension Fund Management and International Investment—A Global Perspective." *Pensions, an International Journal*, vol. 10: 236–261.

Dimson, Elroy, Oguzhan Karakaş, and Xi Li. 2015. "Active Ownership." *Review of Financial Studies*, vol. 28, no. 12 (December): 3225–3268.

Foreman-Peck, James, and Leslie Hannah. 2013. "Some Consequences of the Early Twentieth-Century British Divorce of Ownership from Control." *Business History*, vol. 55: 543–564.

Graham, Benjamin, and David Dodd. 1934. *Security Analysis*. New York: McGraw-Hill.

Hutchinson, James D. 1976. "The Federal Prudent Man Rule under ERISA." *Villanova Law Review*, vol. 22, no. 1: 15–59.

Kay, John. 2012. *The Kay Review of UK Equity Markets and Long-Term Decision Making: Final Report*. Ref: BIS/12/917 (July): www.gov.uk/government/consultations/the-kay-review-of-uk-equity-markets-and-long-term-decision-making.

May, George. 1912. "The Investment of Life Assurance Funds." *Journal of the Institute of Actuaries*, vol. 46: 134–168.

Newman, Philip. 1908. "A Review of the Investments of Offices in Recent Years, with Notes on Stock Exchange Fluctuations and the Future Rate of Interest." *Journal of the Institute of Actuaries*, vol. 3, July: 294–336.

Rutterford, Janette. 2009. "Learning from One Another's Mistakes: Investment Trusts in the UK and the US, 1868 to 1940." *Financial History Review*, vol. 16, no. 2: 157–181.

———. 2010. "Gross or Net: The Impact of Taxation on the History of Equity Valuation." *Accounting History*, vol. 15, no. 1: 41–64.

———. 2013. "A Preliminary Study of Investor Portfolios 1870 to 1902." Conference paper, AHIC, Seville (September).

Rutterford, Janette, David R. Green, Josephine Maltby, and Alastair Owens. 2010. "Who Comprised the Nation of Shareholders? Gender and Investment in Great Britain, c. 1870–1935." *Economic History Review*, vol. 64, no. 1 (February): 157–187.

Smith, Edgar. 1924. *Common Stocks as Long Term Investments*. New York: Ferris Printing Company.

Traflet, Janice. 2013. *A Nation of Small Shareholders: Marketing Wall Street after World War II*. Baltimore: John Hopkins University Press.

Trusted Sources. 2011. "Insurance Companies and Pension Funds as Institutional Investors: Global Investment Patterns." Report prepared for the City of London Corporation (November): www.cityoflondon.gov.uk/

business/economic-research-and-information/research-publications/Pages/
Insurance-companies-and-pension-funds.aspx.

US Department of the Treasury. 1990. "Report to the Congress on the Taxation of Life Insurance Company Products" (March).

US Government Accountability Office. 2014. "Individual Retirement Accounts." Report to the chairman, Committee of Finance, US Senate (October): www.gao.gov/assets/670/666595.pdf.

Willis Towers Watson. 2015. "Global Pensions Assets Study—2015" (www.towerswatson.com/en-GB/Insights/IC-Types/Survey-Research-Results/2015/02/Global-Pensions-Asset-Study-2015).

Wright, Kenneth M. 1992. "The Life Insurance Industry in the United States: An Analysis of Economic and Regulatory Issues." Working Paper 857, World Bank (February).

5. New Frontiers in Financial History

15. Financial History in the Wake of the Global Financial Crisis

Barry Eichengreen

George C. Pardee and Helen N. Pardee Professor of Economics and Political Science at the University of California, Berkeley

Easier access to data and recent concerns highlighted by the 2008–2009 global financial crisis are changing the direction of research in financial history. The lower cost of assembling and digitizing historical datasets on individual securities and firm, bank, and household balance sheets enables researchers to pursue microeconomic analyses that were previously infeasible. The financial crisis has brought concerns about financial innovation, risk taking, bank operations, and government regulation to the fore—concerns that can best be understood by delving further back into financial history. But researchers must be mindful to not become data driven in their analyses and to focus as much on the differences as the similarities with past financial crises.

Introduction

The frontier of research in financial history will look different to different researchers depending on their perspective. One is reminded of the *New Yorker* cover by Saul Steinberg, "View of the World from 9th Avenue," or of post-modern treatments of Frederick Jackson Turner's "Frontier Thesis," which argue that the frontier is as much a conceptual or narrative construct as it is a matter of physical or economic geography.[1]

My own perspective is that the research frontier in financial history will now be shaped by two sets of considerations. First, the greater ease of digitizing archival data will allow financial historians to pursue microeconomic analyses of a sort that were prohibitively costly before. They will be able to construct representative samples of individual households, firms, and banks that can be used to study how financial behavior depends on time, place, and historical circumstance. This is not to deny the value of macroeconomic analysis, which is useful for drawing out the implications of financial relationships

---

[1]The Steinberg cartoon was on the 29 March 1976 cover of the *New Yorker* and has its own Wikipedia page: https://en.wikipedia.org/wiki/View_of_the_World_from_9th_Avenue. Turner's "Frontier Thesis," which he proposed in 1893, states that westward expansion is the most important factor in American history. For post-modern treatments of his thesis, see Klein (1997) and Slatta (2001).

for the economy as a whole and which filters out, by averaging, idiosyncratic behavior that can prevent individual data points from being generalizable. Nor does it deny the value of detailed case studies, which can shed light on nuances of financial behavior in controversial episodes as well as those that tend to be submerged in panel data and aggregate time series.

Still, it is at the level of individual banks, firms, and households that consequential financial decisions are made. It is here that new techniques and improved existing ones are changing research practice. These new and improved techniques are made possible by low cost digital photography, scanning technology, and the globalization of data entry. They permit financial historians to more easily assemble and analyze large amounts of bank, firm, and household data. Where once upon a time researchers were required to painfully transcribe archival data, a picture of bank balance sheets and ledgers can now be snapped by anyone with a smartphone. These pictures can, in turn, be digitized in the comfort of the researcher's home (or by the data entry company). Easier access to large amounts of data on individual banks, firms, households, and securities will consequently shape the research agenda of financial historians.

In addition to being data driven, the research frontier in financial history will be driven by a second consideration: concerns highlighted by the 2008–2009 global financial crisis. There is likely to be more historical work on both the positive and negative manifestations of financial innovation, the determinants of risk taking by institutional and individual investors, the governance problems of bank and nonbank financial firms, and the causes of stock market volatility. Policy makers and financial market participants have long shown interest in the light that research in economic and financial history can shed on concerns. Likewise, financial historians have always responded to questions from the public policy community (and to the research funding they offer). A few years ago, President Barack Obama's chief economic adviser, Lawrence Summers, observed that when seeking guidance in the midst of the 2008–2009 crisis, he found little of value in the writings of theorists but derived considerable insight from the work of financial historians.[2] In the more volatile environment that will prevail in the wake of the so-called Great Moderation,[3] it is probable that this constructive symbiosis between financial

---

[2]Cited in DeLong (2011).

[3]From the mid-1980s to 2007, the United States experienced a period of low and relatively stable inflation and the longest economic expansion since World War II. This time period has been called the "Great Moderation." It was preceded by the "Great Inflation" (1973–1982) and came to an end in December 2007 when the "Great Recession" began.

historians, policy makers, and market participants will grow even closer, shaping the agenda for research.

Effects of Technology on Research

The lower cost of assembling and analyzing large datasets will incline research in financial history in directions that capitalize on their availability. I illustrate this point with examples of recent historical work on corporate governance, external finance, financial development and growth, financial institutions and financial stability, and emergency assistance in crises—all of which take advantage of large datasets.[4]

The studies discussed in this chapter are heavily focused on the United States and often are products of National Bureau of Economic Research affiliates. This may reflect the nature of the research landscape—that US researchers and NBER affiliates have been pioneers in this process. It may reflect the prominence given to the US experience in the 1930s and, more generally, in such classic financial histories as those by Galbraith (1955) and Friedman and Schwartz (1963). Or, it may simply reflect my own intellectual biases. Nonetheless, these studies support my broader point that research in financial research is adapting to technological advances.

Given the recent availability of data on the finances of individual banks and firms and the composition of their boards, corporate governance is the first obvious theme for financial historians to pursue. An example is Bodenhorn and White (2014), who consider developments in corporate governance through the lens of banks chartered in New York State between the mid-19th and mid-20th centuries. Insiders dominated boards of directors at the start of this period, which weakened governance protections for outsiders. Over time, however, a variety of legal and regulatory rules progressively limited the ability of bank presidents to also serve as board chairmen, better aligning the interests of management and individual shareholders. After the implementation of these rules, only rarely did a board member own a majority or even a large minority of shares that could enable him to impose his will on the board. Boards also grew smaller, which incentivized directors to advocate their own interests and those of associated stakeholders. Bodenhorn and White establish these points using a century of data on bank balance sheets that were gathered from annual reports of the New York Bank superintendent. They also use data on bank directors that were gathered from city directories and the records of the New York State Banking Department.

---

[4]My survey is necessarily selective given the format.

Calomiris and Carlson (2014) similarly consider the scope for bank managers to use their control rights to grant themselves high salaries and favored access to credit as well as to take risks at the expense of depositors and outside shareholders. The authors employ national bank balance sheets for the United States in the 1890s derived from call reports and bank examination reports from the Office of the Comptroller of the Currency for banks in 37 cities. These provide not only balance sheet information but also the names of directors and officers, their salaries, and commentary on whether the board exercised oversight of the officers, and, if so, what kind. The results confirm that salaries and insider lending were greater when managerial ownership was higher, except when high managerial ownership was neutralized by effective corporate governance controls. Banks with relatively strong managerial control and few formal corporate governance restraints also tended to hold less capital as a cushion against risk, consistent with the insider-control and moral-hazard hypotheses.

A second theme of recent research concerns the determinants of access to external finance. Frydman and Hilt (2014) use the Clayton Antitrust Act of 1914[5] as an experiment for studying the role of bankers on corporate boards in facilitating access to external finance. The authors gather accounting information for all railroads listed on the NYSE (New York Stock Exchange) between 1905 and 1929. They match the names of railroad directors to the names of partners and directors of securities underwriting financial firms using *Moody's Manuals*. Rather than simply constructing a binary indicator of whether there was a railroad–underwriter connection on the board, Frydman and Hilt are able to develop a measure of the intensity and scope of underwriting services on the basis of statistical and qualitative sources. They find that railroads that had previously maintained strong affiliations with their underwriters indeed saw declines in their market valuations, investment rates, and leverage ratios, along with increases in the cost of borrowed funds, as a result of Clayton Act restrictions.

A third theme of recent research is the classic issue of finance and growth—that is, whether, and to what extent and when, increases in the size of the finance sector stimulate general economic growth. The many macroeconomic studies of this question have been less than definitive in their conclusions. This uncertainty is partly caused by the difficulty of disentangling cause from effect and the prevalence of omitted variables that affect both financial development and economic development. As an alternative, Tang (2013) uses an extensive dataset of individual Japanese firms from the

---

[5]Section 10 of the Clayton Act prohibited investment bankers from serving on boards of railroads for which their firms underwrote securities.

269

Meiji period[6] to analyze how development of the financial sector affected firm activity across industries and locations. Comparing prefectures, which differed in terms of bank presence, he is able to demonstrate that financial intermediation had a positive effect on new firm establishment—especially in light manufacturing, including textiles, which was the key sector for a newly industrializing country.

Similarly, Atack, Jaremski, and Rousseau (2014) use data for more than 240 counties in the American Midwest between 1840 and 1860 to explore the connections between bank presence as a measure of financial development and the subsequent evolution of transportation links. They find that counties inheriting a bank from earlier periods were more likely to acquire a railroad connection, something that was key to economic development in this period. Disaggregating and pairing adjoining or otherwise comparable prefectures or counties may not be a perfect way of controlling for omitted variables correlated with financial development, but it is a step in the right direction.

A fourth focus of recent research involves the institutional determinants of financial stability. Bernstein, Hughson, and Weidenmier (2014), for example, use the establishment of a clearinghouse on the NYSE in 1892 as an experiment to analyze the impact of centralized clearing on counterparty risk. Their methodology capitalizes on the fact that the largest stocks listed on the NYSE were also listed on the Consolidated Stock Exchange (CSE, or "Little Board," as opposed to the "Big Board"), which already had a clearinghouse. The authors collect end-of-month data on transaction prices (high, low, open, and closing), bid and ask closing prices, and trading volume for all stocks included in the Dow Jones Industrial Average. Compared to identical securities listed on the CSE, securities traded on the NYSE showed significantly reduced volatility and increased prices immediately after the introduction of the NYSE clearinghouse. These effects suggest that centralized clearing reduced counterparty risk. The authors also find that securities prices become less sensitive to call loan rates following the introduction of centralized clearing, reflecting reductions in the cost of financing overnight positions as a result of multilateral netting.

Flandreau, Gaillard, and Panizza (2010) study investment bank underwriters and connect them to financial stability concerns. The authors assemble data on the universe of foreign government bonds—those of sovereign, sub-sovereign, sovereign-owned, and sub-sovereign-owned entities—issued in the 1920s in New York City, which was the leading financial center of the time. They then use these data to analyze the underwriting choices of

---

[6]Known as the "Meiji Restoration" (1868–1912), this period of Japan's history is credited with bringing about the modernization of Japan.

intermediaries, again using manuals published by Moody's. They show that reputation played an important role in the decision of intermediaries to underwrite riskier issues and that newer houses with less reputation were more likely to take a flyer on riskier issues that ultimately lapsed into default. Their findings substantiate a point developed earlier, although less formally, by Mintz (1951). These conclusions have obvious implications for the originate-and-distribute model of securitization. They point to the existence of pervasive agency problems and support the case for arms-length regulation (or at least self-regulation).

A fifth topic—featured prominently in 2008–2009 and which is certain to spark additional historical research—involves cross-border spillovers and the contagious spread of crises. Richardson and Van Horn (2011), for example, study contagion in the trans-Atlantic crisis of 1931. That crisis started in Austria, Hungary, and Germany but quickly migrated across the Atlantic. Richardson and Van Horn describe how banks in New York City were affected by events in Europe. They gather data for all New York City Federal Reserve member banks (state as well as federally chartered) from unpublished call reports of the Comptroller of the Currency and from weekly reports on the condition of banks assembled by the Federal Reserve. These quantitative sources are supplemented by memos that summarize conversations between leading bankers and officials of the Federal Reserve Bank of New York. Using these balance sheet data, the authors establish that the effects of events in Central Europe were muted by the fact that the spread of the crisis was not entirely unanticipated. US commercial banks accumulated additional reserves in advance of the crisis, protecting them against the increase in volatility and allowing them to continue business as usual.

Finally, there will surely be more historical research on a sixth topic: the general management of financial crises. For example, Calomiris, Mason, Weidenmier, and Bobroff (2012) examine the crisis management efforts of the US Reconstruction Finance Corporation (RFC) in the 1930s. The RFC followed two approaches: it extended emergency assistance to troubled banks in the form of loans, and it purchased preferred stock in troubled financial institutions. The question is, which approach was more effective? To answer this question, the authors study the universe of US Federal Reserve member banks (both federally and state chartered) in the State of Michigan, because the Michigan banking crisis of 1932–1933 was a turning point in the Great Depression. Calomiris et al. (2012) trace these banks over time using reports from the Comptroller of the Currency and *Rand McNally Bankers' Directory*. They find that RFC loans had no statistically significant effect on bank failure rates in the 1930s. This finding is consistent with the idea that debt assistance simply increased the indebtedness of financial institutions and, by subordinating depositors, undermined confidence at the retail level. In contrast, issues of preferred shares—capital injections that did not increase indebtedness or subordinate depositors—raised the odds of bank survival. The authors also find that surviving banks that received RFC assistance increased their lending relative to other banks as US recovery from the Great Depression proceeded. These results shed light on the likely effects of official intervention in banking systems in the global crisis of 2008–2009 and provide a guide for policy makers looking to the future.

Disaggregated data from security markets and bank balance sheets will not solve all problems. Still, these studies show that new technologies that facilitate the assembly of large historical databases based on such sources will continue to shape the financial research agenda going forward.

Effects of the Global Financial Crisis on Research

The research agenda in financial history also will be shaped by the 2008–2009 financial crisis. To be sure, previous crises have similarly worked to shape the intellectual agendas of financial historians. But 2008–2009 was the first true global financial crisis in nearly 80 years. No region and no segment of financial markets were untouched. The only comparable 20th-century event, the Great Depression, spawned an immense literature. Investigators tried to understand it not only as a specific historical episode but also as a way to highlight issues that might similarly arise in other historical times and places. The recent crisis will do likewise.

A first obvious issue that flows from the crisis is the problem of banks that are too important for systemic stability to be allowed to fail. As the case of Lehman Brothers highlights, this is not just a matter of bank size ("too big to fail") but also bank "connectedness" (how much an individual bank can impact stability through its connections with other banks and with the system as a whole). An older literature on correspondent banking in the United States—in which country banks held balances with reserve city banks, which held balances with central reserve city banks—considers similar questions. James and Weiman (2010) have made a start by revisiting these issues during the National Banking era prior to 1913. Richardson (2007) extends the literature on the United States under the National Banking Acts of 1863 and 1864 with a study of the impact of the Federal Reserve Act of 1913 and the role of correspondent banking in the Great Depression. Mitchener and Richardson (2016) study correspondent banking relationships in the United States in the 1930s, showing how withdrawals by banks in the interior of the country led reserve city banks to curtail their lending; this reduced lending to the economy as a whole by as much as 15%. In an analysis of loans by London merchant banks to German counterparties on the eve of the 1931 financial crisis, Accominotti (2012) similarly opens up a number of issues about correspondent relationships that will be pursued further by future financial historians.

Recent experience has highlighted the prevalence of agency problems in securitization markets; as a result, there will surely be more research on security underwriting, on the role of such so-called independent monitors as rating agencies, and on the early history of mortgage-backed securities. Flandreau and Slawatyniec (2013) and Flandreau and Mesevage (2014) have considered the historical role of rating agencies in signaling asset quality, while Snowden (2010) has analyzed the early history of mortgage securitization. The evidence from the 19th and early 20th centuries presented by Flandreau and his coauthors raises doubts about the effectiveness of rating agencies as a mechanism for overcoming the information asymmetries that give rise to problems of adverse selection and moral hazard in securities markets. Snowden's analysis of late-19th-century mortgage securitization reminds us that there is nothing new about the fact that the incentives of loan originators, who work on a fee-for-service basis, and investors, who are more concerned with the long-term performance of the loan portfolio, may not be well aligned.

We are similarly apt to see more work on the connections between banks and sovereign debt problems—what is known in the context of the euro crisis as the "bank–sovereign doom" loop. To be sure, banking crises and sovereign debt crises in history have been extensively studied using both macroeconomic and disaggregated data. But the connections between the two—the linkages between sovereign debt and banking problems running in both directions—have yet to be fully explored. Jordà, Schularick, and Taylor (2016) provide an overview of these issues using a large panel of aggregate cross-country data extending from the late-19th century to the present, but here, as in many contexts, aggregate data only scratch the surface. The alternative is a case study approach, such as the famous case of the German debt and currency crisis of 1931. Ferguson and Temin (2003) have considered this case study in detail, and Schnabel (2004) and Adalet (2009) unpack it further by bringing to bear data on individual banks. But this particular episode is special because of its prominent political dimension relating to reparations. As a result, there remains room for work to explore this nexus in other crises.

The role of public policy in the market for housing finance is especially controversial in the wake of the recent global financial crisis. Jordà, Schularick, and Taylor (2014) consider the macroeconomic determinants and consequences of fluctuations in house prices using long historical time series for industrial countries, but they do not focus on the effects of public housing policy per se. Fishback, Rose, and Snowden (2013) describe the role of the Home Owners Loan Corporation, created during the Great Depression in the United States, not just in stabilizing a distressed housing market but also in setting the stage for the creation of long-term, federally guaranteed mortgages. But work on the role of public policy in the development of housing finance in other countries has only barely begun.

Similarly, there is sure to be more research on household finance in the aftermath of a global financial crisis in which high levels of household debt played a prominent role. Some time ago Mishkin (1978), working with aggregate data, considered the role of household balance sheets in the Great Depression in the United States. Although disaggregated data on household finances in the 1930s exists (for the US case, see Jacobs and Shipp 1993), they have yet to be applied to such questions.

The recent crisis also directs attention to the role of regulation and regulatory structure, competition, and capture in the maintenance of financial stability. History is a rich potential source of information on how the structure of regulation shapes its effects and effectiveness and on the political determinants of that structure. US states have long differed in how they organize supervision and regulation, a variation that has been explored by Mitchener and Jaremski (2014), among others. Cross-country comparisons are another obvious source of variation and information on the effectiveness of regulation that financial historians can be expected to mine.

Finally and perhaps most fundamentally, the crisis and its aftermath have spawned intense debate about whether the 21st-century financial system is in some sense too big—whether the advanced countries suffer from "excessive financialization." Using data for a panel of countries and recent years, Cecchetti and Kharroubi (2012) and Arcand, Berkes, and Panizza (2012) find evidence of diminishing and even negative effects on growth as financial systems grow very large relative to GDP. In contrast, Cline (2015) argues strongly that this finding of negative effects is an artifact of the macroeconomic data and empirical methods used by the authors.

This dispute will not be resolved by more intensive crunching of numbers generated by recent experience alone. Financial historians have already done considerable work on earlier periods, exploring connections between the size and structure of the financial system on the one hand and economic growth on the other. An example is Ventura and Voth (2015), who explore the role of the rapidly growing market in public debt in 18th-century Britain. They find that extensive issuance of highly liquid government bonds allowed landowners to diversify out of low-return agricultural investments, leading to the change in relative factor prices that ignited modern economic growth. Fohlin (2011) studies the impact of the different structures of financial systems in European countries on the pace and contours of 19th-century economic growth. Recent work by these and other scholars has sought to further unpack these finance–growth connections by comparing the historical performance of firms with differential access to finance (see, for example, Fohlin 2002 and Tang 2013). With the stakes so high today, we are sure to see more work in this area going forward.

Conclusion

Research in financial history has enjoyed a renaissance in recent years, and this chapter has explored two of the reasons why. One is the lower cost and greater efficiency with which it is now possible to assemble and digitize historical datasets on individual securities and firm, bank, and household balance sheets. Another is the 2008–2009 financial crisis, which trained attention on the limitations of abstract theorizing and empirical analysis based entirely on data generated in the course of only recent events. These two developments are allowing scholars to offer more-detailed answers to the questions asked by practitioners, and they also are directing more attention and interest toward the work of financial historians.

But these trends are not danger-free. The ability of researchers to harness Big Data runs the risk that research in financial history will become increasingly data driven, losing sight of fundamental questions and neglecting the historical context in which those data were generated. If financial historians are expected to base their research on large, newly digitized historical datasets, there will be the temptation to look for data first and to adapt the questions asked to the material available. Economists are prone to "look for the $20 bill under the lamp-post because that's where the light is"—that is, to concentrate on questions that are readily answered given their methods. Financial historians attracted by Big Data should be mindful of this risk.

The experience of the 2008–2009 crisis also creates dangers for the financial historian who draws parallels with the crisis of the 1930s. Parallels can definitely be drawn—from the credit booms that preceded the two crises to the roles of housing and real estate finance and the contagious spread of banking and financial panic. But there were also differences between the two episodes. For example, "shadow banking" (derivative securities, money market mutual funds, and repo) has had greater importance in recent events as compared to the plain-vanilla commercial banking that lay at the center of the 1930s financial crisis. Indeed, it can be argued that the very influence of the dominant historical narrative about the 1930s crisis—that it resulted from the failure of authorities to prevent the contagious failure of commercial

References

Accominotti, Olivier. 2012. "London Merchant Banks, the Central European Panic, and the Sterling Crisis of 1931." *Journal of Economic History*, vol. 72 (March): 1–43.

Adalet, Muge. 2009. "Were Universal Banks More Vulnerable to Banking Failures? Evidence from the 1931 German Banking Crisis." Koc University Research Forum Working Paper 0911.

Arcand, Jean-Louis, Enrico Berkes, and Ugo Panizza. 2012. "Too Much Finance?" IMF Working Paper 12/161 (June).

Atack, Jeremy, Matthew Jaremski, and Peter Rousseau. 2014. "American Banking and the Transportation Revolution before the Civil War." NBER Working Paper 20198 (June).

Bernstein, Asaf, Eric Hughson, and Marc Weidenmier. 2014. "Counterparty Risk and the Establishment of the New York Stock Exchange Clearinghouse." NBER Working Paper 20459 (September).

Bodenhorn, Howard, and Eugene White. 2014. "The Evolution of Bank Boards of Directors in New York, 1840–1950." NBER Working Paper 20078 (April).

Calomiris, Charles, and Mark Carlson. 2014. "Corporate Governance and Risk Management at Unprotected Banks: National Banks in the 1890s." NBER Working Paper 19806 (January).

Calomiris, Charles, Joseph Mason, Marc Weidenmier, and Katherine Bobroff. 2012. "The Effects of Reconstruction Finance Corporation Assistance on Michigan's Banks' Survival in the 1930s." NBER Working Paper 18427 (September).

Cecchetti, Stephen, and Enisse Kharroubi. 2012. "Reassessing the Impact of Finance on Growth." BIS Working Paper 381 (July).

Cline, William. 2015. "Too Much Finance, or Statistical Illusion?" Policy Brief 15-9, Peterson Institute for International Economics, Washington, DC (June).

DeLong, J. Bradford. 2011. "Economics in Crisis." *Project Syndicate* (29 April): www.project-syndicate.org/commentary/economics-in-crisis?barrier=true.

Ferguson, Thomas, and Peter Temin. 2003. "Made in Germany: The Germany Currency Crisis of July 1931." *Research in Economic History*, vol. 21: 1–53.

Fishback, Price, Jonathan Rose, and Kenneth Snowden. 2013. *Well Worth Saving: How the New Deal Safeguarded Home Ownership*. Chicago: University of Chicago Press.

Flandreau, Marc, and Gabriel Geisler Mesevage. 2014. "The Separation of Information and Lending and the Rise of Rating Agencies in the USA (1841–1907)." *Scandinavian Economic History Review*, vol. 62, no. 3.

Flandreau, Marc, and Joanna Kinga Slawatyniec. 2013. "Understanding Rating Addiction: US Courts and the Origins of Rating Agencies' Regulatory License (1900–1940)." IHEID Working Paper 11/2013.

Flandreau, Marc, Norbert Gaillard, and Ugo Panizza. 2010. "Conflicts of Interest, Reputation, and the Interwar Debt Crisis: Banksters or Bad Luck?" IHEID Working Paper 02-2010 (February).

Fohlin, Caroline. 2002. "Corporate Capital Structure and the Influence of Universal Banks in Pre-World War I Germany." *Jahrbuch für Wirtschaftsgeschichte*, vol. 43, no. 2: 113–134.

———. 2011. *Mobilizing Money: How the World's Richest Nations Financed Industrial Growth*. Cambridge, UK: Cambridge University Press.

Friedman, Milton, and Anna Schwartz. 1963. *A Monetary History of the United States, 1867–1960*. Princeton, NJ: Princeton University Press for the National Bureau of Economic Research.

Frydman, Carola, and Eric Hilt. 2014. "Investment Banks as Corporate Monitors in the Early 20th Century United States." NBER Working Paper 20544 (October).

Galbraith, John Kenneth. 1955. *The Great Crash, 1929*. Boston: Houghton Mifflin.

Jacobs, Eva, and Stephanie Shipp. 1993. "A History of the U.S. Consumer Expenditure Survey 1935–36 to 1988–89." *Journal of Economic and Social Measurement*, vol. 19: 59–96.

James, John, and David Weiman. 2010. "From Drafts to Checks: The Evolution of Correspondent Banking Networks and the Formation of the Modern U.S. Payments System, 1850–1914." *Journal of Money, Credit and Banking*, vol. 42: 237–265.

Jordà, Òscar, Moritz Schularick, and Alan Taylor. 2014. "Betting the House." NBER Working Paper 20771 (December).

————. 2016. "Sovereigns versus Banks: Credit, Crises and Consequences." *Journal of the European Economic Association*, vol. 14, no. 1 (February): 45–79.

Klein, Kerwin. 1992. *Frontiers of Historical Imagination: Narrating the European Conquest of Native America, 1890–1990*. Berkeley, CA: University of California Press.

Mintz, Ilse. 1951. *Deterioration in the Quality of Foreign Bonds Issued in the United States, 1920–1930*. New York: National Bureau of Economic Research.

Mishkin, Frederic. 1978. "The Household Balance Sheet and the Great Depression." *Journal of Economic History*, vol. 38: 918–937.

Mitchener, Kris, and Matthew Jaremski. 2014. "The Evolution of Bank Supervision: Evidence from U.S. States." NBER Working Paper 20603 (October).

Mitchener, Kris, and Gary Richardson. 2016. "Network Contagion and Interbank Amplification during the Great Depression." NBER Working Paper 22074 (March).

Richardson, Gary. 2007. "The Check Is in the Mail: Correspondent Clearing and the Collapse of the Banking System, 1930 to 1933." *Journal of Economic History*, vol. 67: 643–671.

Richardson, Gary, and Patrick Van Horn. 2011. "When the Music Stopped: Transatlantic Contagion during the Financial Crisis of 1931." NBER Working Paper 17437 (September).

Schnabel, Isabel. 2004. "The German Twin Crisis of 1931." *Journal of Economic History*, vol. 64: 822–870.

Slatta, Richard. 2001. "Taking Our Myths Seriously." *Journal of the West*, vol. 40: 31–39.

Snowden, Kenneth. 2010. "Covered Farm Mortgage Bonds in the Late 19th Century U.S." NBER Working Paper 16242 (July).

Tang, John. 2013. "Financial Intermediation and Late Development in Meiji Japan, 1868 to 1912." *Financial History Review*, vol. 20: 111–135.

Ventura, Jaume, and Hans-Joachim Voth. 2015. "Debt into Growth: How Sovereign Debt Accelerated the First Industrial Revolution." NBER Working Paper 21280 (June).

Named Endowments

The CFA Institute Research Foundation acknowledges with sincere gratitude the generous contributions of the Named Endowment participants listed below.

Gifts of at least US$100,000 qualify donors for membership in the Named Endowment category, which recognizes in perpetuity the commitment toward unbiased, practitioner-oriented, relevant research that these firms and individuals have expressed through their generous support of the CFA Institute Research Foundation.

Ameritech
Anonymous
Robert D. Arnott
Theodore R. Aronson, CFA
Asahi Mutual Life
Batterymarch Financial
   Management
Boston Company
Boston Partners Asset Management,
   L.P.
Gary P. Brinson, CFA
Brinson Partners, Inc.
Capital Group International, Inc.
Concord Capital Management
Dai-Ichi Life Company
Daiwa Securities
Mr. and Mrs. Jeffrey Diermeier
Gifford Fong Associates
Investment Counsel Association
   of America, Inc.
Jacobs Levy Equity Management
John A. Gunn, CFA
John B. Neff
Jon L. Hagler Foundation
Long-Term Credit Bank of Japan, Ltd.
Lynch, Jones & Ryan, LLC

Meiji Mutual Life Insurance
   Company
Miller Anderson & Sherrerd, LLP
Nikko Securities Co., Ltd.
Nippon Life Insurance Company of
   Japan
Nomura Securities Co., Ltd.
Payden & Rygel
Provident National Bank
Frank K. Reilly, CFA
Salomon Brothers
Sassoon Holdings Pte. Ltd.
Scudder Stevens & Clark
Security Analysts Association
   of Japan
Shaw Data Securities, Inc.
Sit Investment Associates, Inc.
Standish, Ayer & Wood, Inc.
State Farm Insurance Company
Sumitomo Life America, Inc.
T. Rowe Price Associates, Inc.
Templeton Investment Counsel Inc.
Frank Trainer, CFA
Travelers Insurance Co.
USF&G Companies
Yamaichi Securities Co., Ltd.

Senior Research Fellows
Financial Services Analyst Association

For more on upcoming Research Foundation
publications and webcasts, please visit
www.cfainstitute.org/learning/foundation.

Research Foundation monographs
are online at www.cfapubs.org.

RESEARCH FOUNDATION
CONTRIBUTION FORM

☑ **Yes**, I want the Research Foundation to continue to fund innovative research that advances the investment management profession. Please accept my tax-deductible contribution at the following level:

Thought Leadership Circle..................... US$1,000,000 or more
Named Endowment .... US$100,000 to US$999,999
Research Fellow .... US$10,000 to US$99,999
Contributing Donor............................US$1,000 to US$9,999
Friend .... Up to US$999

I would like to donate US$ _____.

☐ My check is enclosed (payable to the CFA Institute Research Foundation).
☐ I would like to donate appreciated securities (send me information).
☐ Please charge my donation to my credit card.
        ☐ VISA ☐ MC ☐ Amex ☐ Diners

Card Number

____ / ____

Expiration Date   Name on card   P L E A S E   P R I N T

☐ Corporate Card
☐ Personal Card

                                   Signature

☐ This is a pledge. Please bill me for my donation of US$_____
☐ I would like recognition of my donation to be:
    ☐ Individual donation ☐ Corporate donation ☐ Different individual

_____
PLEASE PRINT NAME OR COMPANY NAME AS YOU WOULD LIKE IT TO APPEAR

PLEASE PRINT   ☐ Mr.☐ Mrs.☐ Ms.   MEMBER NUMBER _____

_____
Last Name (Family Name)   First (Given Name)   Middle Initial

_____
Title

_____
Address

_____
City   State/Province   Country ZIP/Postal Code

Please mail this completed form with your contribution to:
The CFA Institute Research Foundation • P.O. Box 2082
Charlottesville, VA 22902-2082 USA

For more on the CFA Institute Research Foundation, please visit
www.cfainstitute.org/learning/foundation/Pages/index.aspx.

Acknowledgments

We would like to thank Carn Macro Advisors, CFA Society United Kingdom, the Credit Suisse Research Institute, Fidelity Investments, J.P. Morgan Asset Management, Newton, and Sandaire, whose generous support contributed to the convening of the workshop at Cambridge Judge Business School, University of Cambridge where chapters from this monograph were first presented.

Investment Office